Lost-Time Injury Rates

Studies in Critical Social Sciences Book Series

Haymarket Books is proud to be working with Brill Academic Publishers (www.brill.nl) to republish the *Studies in Critical Social Sciences* book series in paperback editions. This peer-reviewed book series offers insights into our current reality by exploring the content and consequences of power relationships under capitalism, and by considering the spaces of opposition and resistance to these changes that have been defining our new age. Our full catalog of *SCSS* volumes can be viewed at https://www.haymarketbooks.org/series_collections/4-studies-in-critical-social-sciences.

LOST-TIME INJURY RATES

A Marxist Critique of
Workers' Compensation Systems

RODRIGO FINKELSTEIN

Haymarket Books
Chicago, IL

First published in 2022 by Brill Academic Publishers, The Netherlands
© 2022 Koninklijke Brill NV, Leiden, The Netherlands

Published in paperback in 2023 by
Haymarket Books
P.O. Box 180165
Chicago, IL 60618
773-583-7884
www.haymarketbooks.org

ISBN: 978-1-64259-817-9

Distributed to the trade in the US through Consortium Book Sales and
Distribution (www.cbsd.com) and internationally through Ingram Publisher
Services International (www.ingramcontent.com).

This book was published with the generous support of Lannan Foundation and
Wallace Action Fund.

Special discounts are available for bulk purchases by organizations and
institutions. Please call 773-583-7884 or email info@haymarketbooks.org for more
information.

Cover design by Jamie Kerry and Ragina Johnson.

Printed in the United States.

10 9 8 7 6 5 4 3 2 1

Library of Congress Cataloging-in-Publication data is available.

Contents

Acknowledgements

This book is a revised version of my doctoral dissertation. It is the product of my six-year Ph.D. research at the School of Communication, Simon Fraser University. However, the topic of this book germinated a bit earlier. It came about in 2011 after my forced resignation from a workers' compensation board due to my zeal in ensuring prevention and compensation benefits to my fellow workers as the president of the Joint Health and Safety Committee. This book is thus the amalgamation of my righteous indignation and my intellectual inquisitiveness. It aims to advance social justice as well as to lay bare the information-intensive operations of Workers' Compensation Systems in their capacity to underallocate compensation benefits and underrepresent work injuries.

I owe my most intellectual debt to the work of Karl Marx. This book is firmly grounded in Marx's historical materialism, materialist dialectics and socio-economic theoretical framework. I argue that only Marxian political economy offers an adequate theoretical foundation for the understanding of Workers' Compensation Systems in capitalist societies. Also, I am intellectually indebted to the work of critical political economists of information/communication who have applied Marxist theory to the information sector. Among them, I owe much to Dallas Smythe and Vincent Mosco.

Aside from acknowledging my intellectual debts, I must express my gratitude to my Ph.D. supervisor Enda Brophy. I am also very grateful to Katherine Reilly for her criticism of and suggestions for many sections of my work. My thanks to John Calvert for introducing me to the Centre for Research on Work Disability Policy and serving on my doctoral committee. I am also very thankful to Robert Cahill for his careful copy editing.

I wish to thank the Centre for Research on Work Disability Policy for their financial support and their many activities that were paramount to my research. The provincial forums, cluster working meetings and partner/stakeholder meetings were priceless experiences. I am grateful to the student fellows and all the people at the Centre for Research on Work Disability Policy for accompanying me during this academic journey and the many ways they provided help. Thank you Andrea Jones, Piotr Majkowski, Mary Catharine Breadner, Kathy Padkapayeva, Sabrina Imam, Dan Samosh, Steve Mantis, Mieke Koehoorn, Emile Tompa, Ellen MacEachen, and John Calvert.

Finally, many thanks to the people involved at Brill. This book would not be in its current form were it not for the editors of this series: David Fasenfest and Alfredo Saad-Filho.

Figures and Tables

Figures

Tables

CHAPTER 1

Overview

1   Introduction

This book is about the information-producing operations of recording and processing work-related accidents, diseases and fatalities carried out by Workers' Compensation Systems (WCS s). By interrogating these information processes, this book contributes to the understanding of how injury information services a specific sector of the economy by constructing lost labour power for sale. As part of the information sector, WCS s cannot be divorced from the information-intensive operations that go with them. Injury information, or more specifically, injury rates, are essential to WCS s' process of exchanging lost labour power in the form of compensation payments and benefits. Situated within the field of political economy of information/communication (see Garnham, 2014; Mosco, 2009; Murdock and Golding, 1973), this book attempts to uncover the social relations that condition the production and functioning of injury rates. It follows the longstanding tradition among political economists that explore how information resources are produced, exchanged and distributed in information industries (see Bolaño, 2015; Garnham, 1990; Guback, 1969; Herman and Chomsky, 2002; Mosco, 2005, 2009, 2014; Pendakur, 1990, 2003; Schiller, 1973, 1976, 1989; Smythe 1957, 1977).

In addition, this book is also about capitalism – not capitalism as a background or economic context but rather as a series of specific relations that are inextricably woven into injury rates. It identifies and analyzes the capitalist relations that condition the existence and functioning of injury rates, in other words, the social structures, mechanisms and power relations of a capitalist mode of production in their capacity to shape injury rates. Drawing from historical materialism and dialectics, injury rates are examined as the sum of social relations in which they stand in capitalist societies. By historically investigating WCS s' information-intensive operations to allocate compensation payments and benefits and how it fits into the capitalist mode of production, this critique exposes the economic role of injury rates in distributing material and symbolic resources in class societies. WCS s' information operations are disclosed in their capacity to support capital at the expense of wage labour. The capitalist class is favoured by a system that exchanges lost labour power below the real lost value produced by a work injury thus resulting in lower premiums, the underallocation of compensation benefits and the underrepresentation of occupational risks. On the one hand, full compensation and the satisfaction of wage labourers' necessary needs are halted. On the other, the underrepresentation of work injuries in the form of distorted injury rates is circulated, thus producing the fiction that the capitalist labouring process is safer than it actually is. I argue that WCSs' information operations occupy a central place in understanding the systematic robbery of wage labourers in the form of unpaid lost labour or the underpayment of medical and wage-replacement benefits. Like the capitalist extraction of surplus value or unpaid labour, WCSs produce a specific mode of exploitation that extracts surplus lost value or unpaid lost labour in support of the capitalist class.

Overall, this book is a Marxist critique of injury rates as the cornerstone of WCSs and the capitalist relations that correspond to it. It examines how injury rates, as a group of signs that embody the substance of lost labour power, arose and developed and how it fits into the capitalist mode of production. This critique historicizes, re-abstracts and reconstructs injury rates as a social relation based on (a) its ties to its origins and development in the nineteenth century, (b) its ties to the particular moments of its process, and (c) its ties with the present capitalist mode of production. The central argument of this critique can be stated as follows: grounded in the capitalist mode of production, injury rates constitute an historical social relation that, by taking the semblance of inductive indicators, conceal specific capitalist relations that bring about the exchange and distribution of lost labour power among capitalists and wage labourers.

2   My Encounter with Injury Rates

Back in 2010, I was elected as the workers' representative and president of the Joint Health and Safety Committee at the biggest workers' compensation board in Chile. Under my leadership, the committee focused on facilitating the reporting of work-related accidents and diseases, implementing an anti-harassment program and promoting the social dimensions of health. Every time a worker experienced a work-related accident or disease, I personally took care of the paperwork to ensure my co-workers would receive the full medical and wage-replacement benefits prescribed by the laws related to WCSs. After the committee had been operating for a couple of months, the chief executive officer (CEO) took extremely aggressive measures against it. In an attempt to curb the autonomy of the committee, the CEO fired my colleague workers' representatives, removed the totality of the companies' representatives and appointed upper management, including the top lawyer of the company. The CEO aimed to re-establish corporate-friendly management and suppress what he framed as a radical pro-worker governance. Due to the CEO's unlawful maneuver, I suspended the committee and called for government mediation. After months of struggle to defend the committee's autonomy and following the refusal of the government regulatory body to intervene and the lack of resources to pursue a long legal fight, I dropped the case and was forced to resign. The reasoning for my discharge was presented as empirico-practical rather than political. The argument was that I had failed to decrease the number of injuries, the number of working days lost, and other injury-related indicators. In terms of inductive indicators, my tenure was undoubtedly a failure. Due to my zeal for facilitating the reporting of work injuries to disburse medical and wage-replacement benefits, the majority of the injury rates increased dramatically. This experience made me aware of the relevance of injury indicators. In an interesting inversion of reality, I learned that signs that represent the existence and degree of health take primacy over real and concrete human suffering. Disciplined by a violent movement of injury representations, I was forced back into the job market. The topic of this critique ensues directly from this episode of my professional career.

3   Injury Rates as a Collection of Inductive Indicators

Injury rates in capitalist societies, where WCS s prevail, appear as a collection of inductive indicators that measure the existence and degree of occupational health and safety. Presenting itself as a proxy for work-related accidents, diseases and fatalities, injury rates appear at first sight as a group of signs used to make sense of workplace hazards and enable preventive measures. Conventional literature on occupational health has historically treated injury rates as a group of signs that point to the existence and degree of workplace health. Narrowly abstracted as inductive indicators, the category of injury rates has predominantly been regarded as a means to reach conclusions on the riskiness of workplaces. Since the twentieth century, scholars from various disciplines have correlated injury claims, working days lost, and fatality rates, among other measures, to multiple factors to provide a better understanding of health at work (see the early works of Greenwood and Woods, 1919; Heinrich, 1950; Hill and Trist, 1953; Bird and Loftus, 1976). Regarded as a proxy that advises on risk levels, props up awareness among workers, and facilitates the identification of labour hazards, injury rates have been used as fact-finding input for the improvement of health and safety at the worksite (see Balka and Freilich, 2008; Balka et al., 2006; Campioleti et al., 2006; Koning, 2009;

Mansfield et al., 2012; Moore and Tompa, 2011; Tompa, 2012; Tompa et al., 2012a, 2012b, 2013, 2016; Ussif, 2004).

Now, why is this problematic? What exactly is the issue with of abstracting injury rates as inductive indicators and using them as fact-finding input? I argue that this is problematic because it establishes the category of injury rates as an indisputable fact rather than a social construct conditioned by a myriad of background factors. Born from an empiricist and ahistorical process of abstraction, injury rates as inductive indicators obscure boundaries and connections, causing the historical, political and economic features of injury rates to disappear. As statistical proxies of work-related accidents, diseases and fatalities, injury rates appear exclusively as an injury-driven measurement of the existence and degree of occupational health and safety. Working days lost, fatality rates, the number of injuries and the permanent impairment rate, assert themselves as statistical facts expressing workplace hazards and risk levels. Confined in terms of statistical facts, inductive indicators strip away the historical, systemic and deep structure of relations that imposes pressures on the category.

Statistico-empirical approaches ignore the historic and economic environment in which injury rates are recorded, processed, commodified and exchanged. Their conclusions stem from analyses that treat injury rates as facts in disregard of procedures, exchange mechanics, class dimensions, institutional context, and a series of other structural factors thus producing dubious results. This happens because empiricists have accepted as given the structure of the capitalist system where WCS s' operate. By dismissing WCS s' information-intensive operations to exchange lost labour power and its articulated combination within the capitalist mode of production, statistico-empirical analyses are oblivious to the complex set of social relations that move injury rates up and down. In addition, they have taken at face value the abstractions and terms of WCS s and operated with them. By doing so, occupational health scholars have mostly confined themselves within the narrow circle of ideas expressed by those terms. Caught in a WCS s' empiricist epistemology, one that regards injury rates as independent objects that can be objectively measured in terms of their quantitative relationship with other factors, mainstream scholars disregard the inner structure of the category and its connections with the capitalist mode of production of which it is part. These scholars can scrutinize injury rates and their correlation to observed phenomena as much as they want, but they will never grasp any of the background conditions we have been discussing if inquiries are pursued at an empiricist level. No matter how much mainstream scholars scrutinize measurable signals – e.g., the number of injuries, fatality rates, working days lost, rates of compensation – they will never tease out the deeper reality at their empiricist level. Their greatest error is to sacrifice the analysis of injury rates to a consideration of the measurement of the existence and degree of workplace health only. But the point that injury rates are not a measurable reality arises from the fact that they are not a thing but the concept of a relationship, the concept of an existing social structure of compensation.

Now, I should specify that I am not critiquing positivism as such, but rather crude deterministic positivism or the reliance on empirical analysis which disregards social theory. As statistical representations or factual observations, injury rates and their correlation to assorted factors cannot reveal the conditioning historical, political and systemic relations upon which they are based. Without an adequate repertoire of conceptual categories to make sense of social realities such as labour power, the commodity form, wage labour, class, exchange value, and use value, among many others, the background forces that shape injury rates will not make themselves visible to statistico-empirical analyses. These abovementioned conceptual categories are essential to make sense of injury rates not as a proxy for work-related accidents, diseases and fatalities, but rather as a social relation of an existing social structure of compensation in capitalist societies. Thus, the social reality of injury rates and their background conditioning, I argue, can only be attained with the aid of social theory. Only by deploying theory it is possible to penetrate the limitations inherent in injury rates as a group of observable signs.

4　How to Approach Injury Rates

The starting point of this critique is therefore a rejection of the idea that injury rates are accessible through direct observation without their theoretical construction. Since injury rates are a social reality, it is necessary to abstract and construct it as a concept in order to grasp it. This critique formulates the concept of injury rates, which, like every concept is never legible in visible reality and thus must be constructed. In addition, this critique rejects injury rates as an indeterminate ahistorical abstraction which is absolute, universal, and free from the development of history and the influence of other factors. Following Marx's historical materialism (1978a, 1978b, 1993), I argue that to understand and conceptualize any social phenomenon it is necessary to explore how it arose and developed and how it fits into the larger economic system of which it is a part. Without an understanding of the historical process within which injury rates were produced, it is impossible to understand it adequately. Such a perspective leaves us in the last instance to the role played by the forces and relations of production of material life in their movement through history. Based on this standpoint, I approach the category of injury rates from Marx's subject/predicate inversion: rather than divorcing the category from capitalist societies and making it an idea or an autonomous being, the category is brought under the authority of specific capitalist relations (see Marx, 1978d; Ranciere, 2015). The subject is the historical capitalist mode of production and the predicate is injury rates, which, like every predicate is the result of a subject.

This critique proposes an interpretation of injury rates as conditioned by an already-established capitalist mode of production. Drawing from historical materialism, the focus is thus on those necessary material conditions that are peculiar to capitalist societies that enable injury rates to historically arise and function in a certain manner. Why historical materialism? Following Marx (1978a, 1978b, 1993), Engels (1845) and contemporary critical scholars (see Althusser, 2015; Bhaskar, 1979, 1986; Bukharin, 1971; Burkett, 1999; Foster, 2000; York and Clark, 2006; Mills, 1961; Ollman, 2003; Sweezy, 2004) I argue that knowledge of the social world cannot be obtained by relying on value-free empirical research. Social reality is shaped by economic, political and technological factors and contingent historical events. Dynamic and perennially-evolving material forces transform and govern social phenomena which never operate in isolation. As a result, empirical observations cannot lead to an accurate understanding of the social world unless a myriad of social relations and their historical situatedness are taken into account. The consideration of the organization and structure of capitalist societies – e.g., ownership of the means of production, the buying and selling of labour power, class division, profit orientation – is essential for understanding causation of social phenomena. As York and Clark (2006) claim, there exist historical background conditions that generate a kind of 'social gravity' that influences social life: "[...] emergent structural forces stemming from historical background conditions [...] have ubiquitous and pervasive effects across a broad spectrum of social conditions [...]" (p. 432).

In regard to the aforementioned background conditions, the inception of injury rates was particularly affected by these structural forces. Injury rates emerged under relations and forces of production that were part of the second industrial phase of the capitalist mode of production (1870–1914). The colossal deterioration and deaths of wage labourers – i.e., the crucial component of the relations of production – caused by equipment, machinery, technology and industrial power – i.e., the forces of production – resulted in an avalanche of injury lawsuits and social upheaval. The build-up in the number of fatalities and social unrest led to the passage of liability acts. Capitalists were alarmed by the high number of cases brought forward under the passage of liability acts that made firms liable for their own negligence. The liability acts were, simply put, not good for businesses: (a) lawsuits were costly, (b) workers were winning, and (c) there was pressure to establish strict liability into every industry. Governments adopted WCS s, that is, no-fault information-intensive systems as a substitute for the liability system that fostered litigation. This historical departure is grounded in the material preconditions that enabled the category to appear and function in capitalist societies as part of WCS s' information-producing operations. It dates back to the German Act of 1884, which established the first WCS to compensate lost labour power in replacement of a juridical order based on the common law defense. Rather than compensating lost labour power via the courts, capitalists were historically compelled by the state to compensate lost labour power regardless of fault in the form of an insurance guarantee. Injury rates have their roots in the reorganization of legal and institutional arrangements leading to an informational compensation system to award medical and wage-replacement benefits as a way to replace a juridical order.

This investigation periodizes and locates the origins of injury rates in the midst of an historical rupture, one that took place across almost the entire globe: the discontinuous transition of a litigation-based mode of compensation to an information-intensive mode of compensation – i.e., a WCS. Rather than emerging from an intervention governed by the limits of the litigation-based mode of compensation, injury rates emerges from an intervention of political practice, one which bears the mark of state power, whose result led to an information-intensive mode of compensation. The transition from one mode of compensation to another resulted in the replacement of the social relations that together articulate the quantification and distribution of compensation payments and benefits. Removed from the plain, direct and concrete relations of a court appeal, which revealed the horrors of workers' labouring conditions, compensation payments began to be allocated among the capitalist class collectively based on the information operations of recording and processing work-related accidents, diseases and fatalities. By setting lost labour power apart from juridical principles of justice and translating it into the principles of exchange value, the Act of 1884 inaugurated the process of commodifying lost labour power to exchange compensation payments and benefits. I call this historical transition the replacement of the severity of justice with the ruthlessness of the commodity.

It is important to point out that the chronicled focus is not the historic position of injury rates but rather its articulated combination within the historical capitalist mode of production. What matters is not the historical sequence of the development of injury rates through time, but its examination as part of the development of those social and economic formations set free by the dissolution of a litigation-based mode of compensation, which coalesced into the novel information-intensive mode of compensation. The focus in this critique is placed on the synchronic analysis – i.e., vertical analysis – of the structure of the information-intensive mode of compensation rather than the diachronic analysis – i.e., horizontal analysis – of its formation. Thus, far from being a theory of the origin of injury rates, this critique is a theory of its inner connections, interactions and mechanics, not as something isolated but as an articulated social relation grounded in the historical capitalist mode of production. As the co-existence of all the elements with one another and their articulation with the capitalist mode of production, injury rates are primarily examined as a medium of exchange and distribution monopolized by a particular activity in society: WCS s' commodification of lost labour power.

Fundamentally, what I investigate is injury rates as the essence of an information-intensive mode of compensation and the specific capitalist relations and forms of intercourse that correspond to it. If I use the information-intensive mode of compensation established by WCS s as the institutional context for my analysis, it is not only because of its determinate historical relevance but because in its very exposition I am able to designate, reconstruct and expound injury rates in their pivotal role of exchanging lost labour power. I claim that injury rates, as a class relation of exchange and distribution of lost labour power, constitutes the nucleus of every information-intensive mode of compensation. As Machlup (1962) points out, WCS s' economic process of exchange cannot be divorced from the information operations that go with them. The disbursement of compensation payments and benefits is mediated by the information-producing operations of recording and processing work injuries. Therefore, examining injury rates as part of the standard and prevailing mode of functioning of every WCS – i.e., as an information-intensive mode of compensation – enables a clear understanding of those social relations that condition injury rates to behave the way they do. This vantage point emphasizes information as the core of every WCS and lays bare the myriad relations in which it stands and functions. It establishes injury rates as a priority and brings into focus the exchange value principles and dynamics that condition injury rates in capitalist societies. As I shall demonstrate, the articulation of injury injury rates and lost labour power are immanent to every information-intensive mode of compensation. Summing up, this is a study of the social relations of a model whose social relations are valid for every information-intensive mode of compensation that is a case of the model. It is a study about injury rates within an information-intensive mode of compensation in its ideal average, an examination of a general structure, not its accidental or superficial traits peculiar to any particular time or place.

Notwithstanding this critique's focus on WCS s as information-intensive modes of compensation, it is necessary to acknowledge their diversity. The complexity and variety of these modes of compensation is significant. They differ in terms of ownership, market coverage, market competition, risk pricing, compensable injuries, deeming process, entitlement parameters, rate-setting mechanics and state supervision, among many other structural and procedural factors. Within this diversity, two models have dominated around the globe: the German model and the British model (see Meredith, 1913). This critique focuses on the German model because it is the first information-intensive mode of compensation that historically arose within and ultimately completely replaced the previous court-based system to award compensation. Alternatively, the British model kept the role of courts – i.e., Tort Law – to allocate compensation payments and benefits (see Moses, 2018). The German model comprises an unadulterated and pure information-intensive mode of compensation. In the true sense of the word, the German model, is *per se* the information-intensive mode of compensation. As such, it is appropriate to locate the institutional context for this analysis around the history and functioning of the German model in exclusion of the hybrid British model. In this regard, this is an investigation of injury rates within an information-intensive mode of compensation that is a case of the German model. It is valid for present-day German-based WCS s in place in capitalist countries such as Canada, Chile, Austria, New Zealand and Italy, among many others.

5   Theoretical Contribution

In the first place, this critique fills the aforesaid conceptual vacuum by abstracting and reconstructing injury rates as a determinate historical abstraction, namely, a social relation belonging to a historical economic formation: an information-intensive mode of compensation. It involves a radical break with the whole frame of reference of WCS s' empiricist terminology and the construction of a new problematic and its basic concepts. It proposes an epistemological rupture, a new criterion for the way the problem should be considered, presented and examined. Rather than reducing the category to inductive indicators as the conventional literature does and examining it as a proxy in terms of its quantitative relationship with miscellaneous variables, this critique approaches the category from a structural-explanatory mode of theorisation that penetrates social structures, mechanisms and power relations that condition its production and functioning. This mode of theorisation does not intend to quantitatively predict the movements of injury rates, in other words, how much or little does the injury rate or number of the working days lost move under particular conditions. That is only a surface manifestation. Here, the concern is about providing explanatory power, explaining how injury rates appear and function in terms of its myriad connections within capitalist societies. The questions of when, why, how and with what consequences did injury rates come about in capitalist societies are taken seriously.

This radical break in the theoretical orientation leads to a change in the theoretical problem, a shift from injury rates as a proxy for work injuries to the concept of injury rates and its historical definition. This rupture queries the validity of injury rates as an object of knowledge. It aims to solve the empiricist confusion between the thought and the visible, the concept and its sensory appearance, the object of knowledge and the real object. Drawing from Marxian dialectics (see Ollman, 2003), injury rates are abstracted and examined as a social relation or the sum of connections in which it stands, as the set of connections that condition its existence and functioning. A great emphasis is placed on history and the capitalist mode of production as a way of understanding the interaction of the interdependent parts that compose injury rates. The historical separation of workers from the means of subsistence, the conflict between the forces of production and the relations of production, and the dominance of money as a medium of measurement and exchange for all values in society, all created the conditions for the appearance of injury rates to allocate compensation benefits and payments. Injury rates are firmly rooted in history, it is a concrete historical phenomenon, one that is socially created as part of the development of the second industrial phase of capitalism. By examining the origins and development as well as the particular moments of its general movement, injury rates are presented through its connections to particular historical events. This retrospective analysis is relevant since the origins and development of injury rates constitute an essential part of what they actually are in the present. Also, by examining the manner in which injury rates have been realized within the capitalist economy, the complex interaction encompassing the specific relations of the capitalist mode of production – e.g., wage labour, commodity, use value, exchange value – are disclosed as constitutive parts of injury rates. This allows an understanding of how injury rates mirrors and responds to specific relations of the capitalist mode of production rather than solely being an effect of injury-driven events.

In the second place, this critique contributes to the understanding of how injury rates services a capitalist mode of production by constructing expected lost labour power for sale. The economic role of injury rates as a specific sector of the economy with particular characteristics puts forth a decisive vantage point for grasping WCS s, where information is central. Following the legacy of critical political economists of communication and information (see Bolaño, 2015; Garnham, 1990; Mosco, 2009; Murdock and Golding, 1973; Schiller, 2007; Smythe 1977) this critique focuses on injury rates as a commodity that satisfies needs as a means of production within a specific sector of the economy. It penetrates injury rates in its commodity form as the essence of the informational character of WCS s. In opposition to the behaviourism tradition in communication which analyzes human responses to information and communication (see Bernays, 2005; Cantril, 2005; Katz and Lazarsfeld, 2006; Laswell, 2013; Lippmann, 2020; Rogers, 2003), the emphasis of investigation switches from the domains of the empirical to the causal mechanisms, social structures, powers and relations that govern the production and exchange of injury rates as a commodity. This critical approach opposes behaviourism, information society theory, and modernization theory, in their pluralist assumption that the information and communication field is a neutral space of competing group interests (see Mosco, 2009; Garnham, 1990). It takes into account not only the formation of WCS s' information-intensive operations but who controls them, whose benefit they serve, to whose detriment they function, as well as the series of power relations that condition the commodification of injury rates as an insurance guarantee against expected lost labour power.

Contrary to neoclassical economists who analyze information in terms of prices, I see value as a significant category to analyze and make sense of the commodity form of injury rates. Drawing from Marx (1990, 1991, 1992), this critique contributes to the understanding of injury rates as a use value, an exchange value, and a value. As a use value, injury rates are presented as an insurance guarantee that protects capitalists from: (a) lengthy and expensive disputes in court, (b) the full cost of individually compensating lost labour power, (c) the unpredictability of compensation payments, and (d) the costs of wage labourers' social needs by limiting compensation benefits to necessary needs – i.e., medical and wage-replacement benefits. As an exchange value, injury rates are formulated as the rate of compensation or a wage-relation formula at which expected lost labour power can be effectively exchanged by money. In terms of value or the amount of labour time socially necessary for its production, injury rates as a commodity are disclosed as the embodiment of lost value rather than value, that is, the crystallization of lost labour time due to work-related accidents, diseases and fatalities. In addition, this critique distinguishes the many value forms of lost value. By formulating the model of the circuit of metamorphosis of lost labour power, the value form of injury rates is revealed in its capacity to change into money value, investment value, medical

value and wage-replacement value. WCS s are expounded as information organizations whose main activity is the recording and processing of injury rates to
construct, measure, monetize, exchange and transform lost value into multiple
forms in order to allocate compensation payments and benefits.

Regarding the allocation of medical and wage-replacement resources, the
major contribution of this critique is the theoretical discovery of *surplus lost
value* or the notion that the value quantity of injury rates is set below the real
lost value produced by a work injury. The reporting procedure, the deeming
process, the rate-setting mechanics, the underreporting practices, the appealing of legitimate claims, and the early-return-to-work programs, among other
social relations, restrain the value magnitude of injury rates leading to surplus
lost value or unpaid lost labour. Capitalists are favoured by an information-
intensive system that enables the exchange of lost value below the real lost
value produced by a work injury. Injury rates serve the capitalist mode of production by indirectly appropriating surplus lost value in the form of unpaid
medical and wage-replacement benefits. Overall, the economic role of injury
rates as a specific sector of the economy contributes to the understanding of
how surplus lost value is produced, monetized, transformed, exchanged and
distributed in capitalist societies.

6   Outline of the Successive Chapters

Based on historical materialism, Chapter 2 narrates the preconditions underlying the historical origin of injury rates. Injury rates are addressed in relation to
the necessary material preconditions that enable it to appear and function as
it does in capitalist societies. This chapter goes back to the German Act of 1884,
which introduced WCS s as a response to the social unrest caused by massive
worker deaths and a related tide of injury lawsuits. With the aim of removing
social turmoil and forestalling radicalism, WCS s' information-producing operations of recording and processing work injuries were introduced to assure
compensation benefits to injured workers regardless of the determination of
fault. The main purpose of Chapter 2 is to lay bare the preconditions for the
particular form that injury information takes in present-day WCS s. It discusses
the historical separation of workers from the means of subsistence and the burgeoning of the capitalist class as central preconditions. Only when the worker
is the free proprietor of his own labour power and the owner of the means of
production finds the worker available on the market can work-related injury
information be recorded and processed to allocate compensation benefits and
payments. In addition, the chapter addresses the conflict between the forces

of production and the relations of production, which, manifested in the form of colossal accidents and huge number of injury lawsuits, put at stake the continuity of capitalism. Specifically, it examines the high costs of the previous liability system, the economic burden being placed on industry by pro-worker judges, and the political call to expand strict liability to every enterprise, thus making the liability system a ticking time bomb. The novel science of statistics and probability is also dealt with as the scientific and technical means available to predict the costs of work injuries and collectively spread them as compensation payments among firms. In tandem with these scientific means, money is disclosed as a main precondition to convert expected work injuries into value. Predicted injuries can only be economically exchanged when money – i.e., the universal equivalent – has appeared both as a medium of measurement and exchange for all values in society. Finally, Chapter 2 tackles the capitalist state as a necessary precondition not only to enforce a compulsory compensation system but to legislate around risk classes, risk pricing, compensable injuries, entitlement parameters, methods of rating, adjusting claims and settling disputes, among a bulk of other legislative and bureaucratic compensation issues.

Chapter 3 examines WCS s' main operative unit: insurance boards. Drawing from Mosco's (2009) ontological approach to analyze institutions as social processes, insurance boards are dissected in terms of their informational process of exchange. This vantage point, which establishes information as a priority, emphasizes insurance boards' information-producing operations of recording and processing work injuries to distribute compensation payments and benefits. The chapter explores insurance boards' information-producing operations in their goal to (a) construct risk as a medium of measurement and exchange of expected lost labour power, (b) organize firms in branches of industry according to their mass of expected lost labour power, and (c) set the price of the guarantee against expected lost labour power. One of the main points of Chapter 3 is to reveal how insurance boards' information-intensive processes put compensation payments and benefits in subordination to an information assessment mechanism based on the risk of the type of workplace and every firm's workplace rather than the real value of work injuries. Next, based on dialectics – thereby bringing into focus a set of interdependent capitalist relations – this chapter reconceptualizes insurance boards as the landlords of the circuit of metamorphosis of lost labour power in capitalist societies. This reconceptualization brings to light how lost labour power is converted by insurance boards into money value, investment value, medical value, and wage-replacement value, thus disclosing how different elements become forms of one another. The circuit of metamorphosis brings together a triad that links insurance boards, capitalists and wage labourers in a set of conflicting interests that periodically erupt in the form of class struggle. Chapter 3 ends by presenting insurance boards as the informational landlords of lost labour power, monopolies whose revenue is linked to their exclusive control in the information process of recording and processing work injuries at every type of workplace. Rather than realizing profit through the exploitation of their own workforce, insurance boards are disclosed as agencies that appropriate value in the form of ground-rent from individual firms without directly producing it.

Chapter 4 provides an exhaustive inspection of the lost-labour-power commodity and its commodification process. Following Marx's (1990) analysis of the commodity, this chapter examines insurance boards' act of producing lost labour power as a commodity during the first stage of the circuit of metamorphosis of lost labour power. Through the information-intensive process of recording and processing work injuries to construct risk into its many configurations – e.g., group rate, experience rate, rate of compensation – lost labour power is successfully transformed into a commodity. Based on the provisional theory of the twofold split, the lost-labour-power commodity is theorized as a dual-order commodity, namely, as a representation – i.e., lost-time injury rates – and a reference – i.e., lost labour power. As a representation, it is a material object, a group of signs in the form of numbers that can be written, typed, deleted, and circulated independently. As a reference, it is an immaterial substance: wage labourers' incapacity to work due to a work accident, disease or fatality. Chapter 4 continues by locating the commodity in relation to the satisfaction of needs. Conceptualized as a means of production, the lost-labour-power commodity is described as a cost element, an intermediate commodity required by every firm for the production of anything else. Next, the lost-labour-power commodity is analyzed as a use value, an exchange value and a value, the three basic value forms of any commodity. Based on Marx's (1990, 1991, 1992) value theory, this chapter elucidates the capacity of the insurance boards' commodity to transform lost value into value in order to exchange expected lost labour power for money at equivalent proportions. Chapter 4 concludes with the five information-intensive moments that lost labour power endures in the commodification process. It abstracts, conceptualizes and describes (a) the working-day-lost moment, (b) the reporting moment, (c) the recording moment, (d) the processing moment and (e) the programing moment.

The fetish character of the lost-labour-power commodity is the subject matter of Chapter 5. It addresses the social structures, mechanisms and power relations involved in the value formation of the commodity. As a fetish, the commodity comes across as being the embodiment of the total mass of lost labour power produced in society; it appears as an injury-driven formation whose magnitude is directly proportional to the lost value of work injuries. This appearance is, I argue, an illusion. This chapter confronts and critiques the semblance of the merely injury-driven determination of the magnitude of value of the commodity. It presents both the absolute and relative value of the lost-labour-power commodity as a socially conditioned phenomenon, namely, the outcome of social relations which are procedurally and structurally conditioned, as well as class-concealed. Chapter 5 penetrates these social relations that disguise the mass of lost value which is not objectified in the commodity. It reveals the reasons why the commodity's value fluctuates. The reporting procedure, the deeming process, the rate-setting mechanics, the level of underemployment, the underreporting practices, the appealing of legitimate claims, and the early-return-to-work programs, among other social relations, are singled out as examples of procedurally, structurally and class-related social relations that condition the value magnitude of the commodity. By expounding on the different combinations among these social relations, the pretense of the commodity's value as determined by work injuries is ruled out. Why is this crucial? As the chapter explains, the effective mass of lost value crystallized in the commodity manifests as a tension between the two classes of society in the form of cheaper premiums and unfulfilled medical and wage-replacement benefits. While cheaper premiums are welcomed by the capitalist class, partial medical and wage-replacement benefits are strongly rejected by the working class. Chapter 5 reveals that the fetishism of the commodity, which hides the fact that the total mass of lost value never gets fully reconverted in the form of medical and wage-replacement benefits, comprises the inner mechanics of WCSs that advance the sectional interests of the capitalist class at the expense of wage labourers' health interests.

Chapter 6 brings all the previous chapters together to reconstruct the category of lost-time injury rates as a determinate historical social relation. It presents the category as a cluster of internal ties between specific historical conditions and specific capitalist relations. Following Hegel's (1977) definition of truth as the extent to which something expresses the whole, the purpose of this chapter is to present the truth of lost-time injury rates, namely, to lay out their myriad connections to the social totality. To reveal their truth in opposition to their distorted appearance, Chapter 6 uncovers the many relations through which lost-time injury rates express the whole through an essence/appearance exposition. Each section didactically begins with how lost-time injury rates spuriously come into view – i.e., their appearance – and proceeds by revealing their fundamental quality – i.e., their essence. Partially grasped as a medium of measurement of workplace health, this chapter discloses lost-time injury rates as a class relation of exchange and disproportionate distribution of lost labour power in capitalist societies. The chapter continues by reabstracting lost-time injury rates as pertaining to the capitalist mode of production rather than to WCS s' information-intensive process. Next, it distinguishes the various value forms of lost labour power – i.e., money value, investment value, medical value, and wage-replacement value – in contrast to the single and monolithic value form of the premium or money value. In this vein, the lost-labour-power commodity is disclosed as a value quantity that emerges from a complex web of social relations rather than exclusively from injury-driven incidents. Defying their assumed capacity to deliver accurate information, lost-time injury rates are laid out as work-injury misinformation and conceptualized as an ideology that maintains class relations of domination. The chapter ends with reference to social class. It concludes with a passage that emphasizes the role of an information-intensive mode of compensation in preventing social change via the solidification of the capitalist/wage labourer bond.

CHAPTER 2

Preconditions

1   Introduction

In this chapter I examine the preconditions, namely, the social and economic formations underlying the appearance and functioning of injury rates in capitalist societies today. As a product of human history conditioned by a set of already established material relations, I discuss injury rates in relation to what I argue are the necessary material preconditions that enable injury rates to appear and function as they do in capitalist societies. This chapter goes back to the Act of 1884, through which the first WCS was introduced in Germany, thus inaugurating the information-producing operations of recording and processing work-related injuries, disabilities and fatalities. Injury rates have historically been produced under the monopoly of WCS s. Their introduction and functioning are inextricably linked to these systems, which serve the task of gathering, recording and processing widely dispersed injury information at work to allocate among corporations the costs of compensating injured workers.

Chapter 2 deals specifically with the first WCS that, historically, arose in capitalist societies: the German system. The British system, partially copied from the Germans by Joseph Chamberlain in 1897 (Kleeberg, 2003; Moses, 2018), will not be part of this analysis. Although both systems have dominated workers' compensation laws around the globe (Meredith, 1913) I have chosen to ground this historical analysis exclusively in the German model because it set the blueprint for replacing the court-based system that depended on litigation to award compensation. As Eghigian (2000) points out, modern WCS s began with Bismarck's introduction of a state-sponsored WCS in Germany. Also, I have chosen the German model because it constitutes an absolute information-intensive mode of compensation – the hybrid British model maintained the role of courts (see Moses, 2018). Thus, this chapter centers on the German model in place in capitalist countries such as Canada, The United States (some territories), Austria, Norway, New Zealand, Italy, Chile, and many others. Its purpose is to lay bare the preconditions for the particular form that injury rates take in present-day German-based WCS s; that is, information-intensive compensation systems based on (a) no-fault compensation, (b) collective liability (c) employer funding, (d) compulsory insurance and (e) medical and wage-replacement benefits.

The focus of this analysis is not the history of the German WCS but its examination as part of the development of social and economic formations that enable it to record and process work injuries to allocate compensation payments and benefits. I will not be historicizing the German WCS but examining it as part of the historical and material conditions that led to the information-producing operations of recording and processing work-related injuries, disabilities and fatalities. Chapter 2 is therefore, strictly speaking, the genealogy of the preconditions or historical elements which constitute the structure of an information-intensive mode of compensation, a fragmentary analysis that traces element by element. It is not a true history in a theoretical sense but a historical exposition of the individual preconditions that together made possible the German-based WCS. As part of this task, this chapter contemplates separately the formation of six main preconditions which enter into the structure of an information-intensive mode of compensation: (a) wage labour, (b) the conflict between the forces and relations of production, (c) a thriving capitalist class, (d) the science of statistics and probability, (e) money, and (f) a capitalist state. In the lines that follow I will contextualize, abstract, conceptualize and describe the six aforementioned preconditions for the emergence of the German WCS which are valid for every WCS that is a case of the German model.

2   First Precondition: Wage Labour

In 1884, under the conservative direction of Otto von Bismarck, Germany introduced a state-sponsored compulsory insurance system to deliver financial and medical compensation to workers injured during employment. Germany was the first country to enact a nationwide compulsory insurance system to compensate workplace accidents in replacement of a litigation-based system. Conceptually, the Act of 1884 designated workplace accidents as 'the consequences of accidents happening in the operation of work' (Moses, 2018). Therefore, only accidents proven to be work related would be awarded medical and economic compensation. This insurance mechanism inaugurated the information-intensive operations of recording and processing work-related injuries, disabilities and fatalities to assess workplace hazards to allocate compensation payments and compensation benefits among employers and injured workers, respectively. As an alternative to the litigation-based mode of compensation, the German insurance model established the template for an information-intensive mode of compensating injured workers.

The Act of 1884 was developed to address many interrelated political problems that at the time were broadly summed up by German officials, politicians and the industrialist elite as the "Worker Question" (Eghigian, 2000). However, the "Worker Question" was not related to work or labour *per se*, that is, the concrete human activity aimed at producing articles to satisfy human needs. It was related to wage labour, a historically-specific form of labour that became prominent in Germany in the 1850s. It is precisely wage labour, the type of work that came to dominate production in capitalist societies, that is one of the main preconditions underlying the inception of WCS s. Therefore, WCS s and their injury information-intensive operations are, first and foremost, grounded in the specific wage labour relation and its series of historical, economic, social and legal connections.

The difference between work and wage labour is essential to understanding the emergence and functioning of WCS s and their injury information-producing operations. While 'work' refers to an activity common to people in any human society, 'wage labour' refers to an activity peculiar to people in capitalist societies and their division into classes – i.e., those who own and control the means of production and those who only own their labour power. In addition to their difference at the level of generality – e.g., relating to human society or specifically to capitalist societies –, work and wage labour concretely differ in terms of their outcome and purpose. Work can be defined as an activity aimed at the production of use values – i.e., useful objects that satisfy human needs (Marx, 1990). The outcome of work is a product, "[...] a use value, a piece of natural material adapted to human needs by means of a change in its form" (Marx, 1990, p. 287). Its main purpose is production for direct consumption. Work is not under the compulsion to produce for a market; it is not market-dependent (McNally, 1993). In contrast, wage labour is not an activity aimed at the production of products but rather of commodities destined to be sold in the market (Marx, 1990). As Marx (1990) explains, to become a commodity, the product must cease to be produced only to satisfy a human need, as it also must be exchanged in the market, based on the magnitude of labour embodied in it. Since exchange value dominates in commodity production, wage labour can simply be considered an activity aimed at the production of exchange values. Its main purpose is production for market exchange; thus, it is a market-dependent activity.

What specific elements of the labour process create the conditions necessary for the existence of wage labour? There are no elements in particular that can be exclusively attributed to wage labour. It is only the distribution of the elements of the labour process that distinguish wage labour from work. Both work and wage labour include in their process what Marx (1990) calls the main elements of labour: (a) purposeful activity, (b) the object on which work is performed – e.g., land, water, timber, and in general the means of subsistence –, and (c) the instruments of that work – e.g., baskets, draft-horses, spinners, steam-engines, etc. However, what changes in the labour process between work and wage labour is the ownership and control of the mentioned basic elements. Under an economy based on wage labour both (b) the object on which work is performed and (c) the instruments of work are under the control of a capitalist. In this regard, what creates wage labourers is the separation of workers from the means of subsistence and production (Marx, 1990; McNally, 1993; Meiksins, 2002).

The peasants who once were able to exploit the common land, give pasture to their animals, gather wood, hunt and fish were driven out from their land onto the labour market as "[...] free, unprotected and rightless proletarians [wage labourers]" (Marx, 1990, p. 876). It is expropriation from the land that forms the basis of the whole process, as peasants become wage labourers only after having been separated from the means of subsistence. At the same time, separation from the soil is the basis for private property and the development of the capitalist class. Marx is clear on the twofold consequences of this split:

> The process [...] which creates the capital-relation [wage labour/capitalist] can be nothing other than the process which divorces the worker from ownership of the conditions of his own labour; it is a process which operates two transformations, whereby the social means of subsistence and production are turned into capital, and the immediate producers are turned into wage-labourers.
>
> MARX, 1990, p. 874

Through the enclosure of the commons, direct producers were torn away from their land and transformed into wage labourers at the disposal of agrarian and industrial capitalists, compelled to obtain their value in the form of wages (Marx, 1990; McNally, 1993; Meiksins, 2002). It was through parliamentary decrees that the capitalists granted themselves the peasants' land as private property (Marx, 1990). "[...] the law itself becomes the instrument by which the people's land is stolen [...]" (Marx, 1990, p. 885). This operation dramatically increased the supply of wage labourers – i.e., peasants driven from their land.

Central to the appearance of a WCS in Germany in 1884 is the separation of a large proportion of workers from the means of subsistence and production. Like other Europeans, German peasants experienced a fundamental economic transformation (see Polanyi, 2001). Around the middle of the 19th century, a large-scale transfer of landownership created a massive exodus of peasants from the countryside, thus increasing the number of wage labourers and its accompanying consequences – e.g., unemployment, poverty, hunger (Eghigian, 2000). Freedom of movement was granted in 1867 in all German states, thus increasing the mobility of property-less peasants (Gerstenberger, 1985). Peasants were liberated from their feudal masters through a series of political reforms (1808–25) aimed at freeing the productive forces in line with free trade (Eghigian, 2000). It was the development of industrial capitalism that exerted the pressure needed to completely expropriate the common land or its access. The enclosure of the commons took place in every country that embraced the capitalist mode of production and Germany was no exception. A mass of newly propertyless wage-dependent labourers inundated towns seeking jobs. Those who could no longer be a peasant or an artisan had no other option but to become a wage labourer (Gerstenberger, 1985).

The so-called "Worker Question" in Germany was about the challenges to society that arose from wage labourers and their working and living conditions. Disabled and invalid wage labourers, the chronically ill, the elderly, widows, and unemployed wage labourers became the new faces of poverty (Eghigian, 2000). The streets were increasingly filled with beggars, paupers and prostitutes. The growth of an impoverished and propertyless working class came to be perceived as a threat to the social order (Eghigian, 2000). In 1870, poor relief boards were established in German municipalities according to the newly promulgated National Poor Law (Gerstenberger, 1985). Injured workers who could not find jobs began to rely on these boards for subsistence. Observers complained that the cost of industrial accidents was being absorbed by these poor relief boards and thus by taxpayers (Guinnane and Streb, 2015).

This social malaise resulted in the first WCS being introduced in 1884 as a part of a broader social insurance scheme to deal with the "Worker Question". The WCS's Accident Insurance fund was part of two complementary interrelated insurance funds: the Sickness Insurance fund in 1883 and the Invalid and Old-age Insurance fund in 1891. All three of these institutions were implemented to find a way to create a viable social order (Eghigian, 2000). These branches of social insurance covered millions of wage labourers, reducing in part the economic burden of poor boards (Gerstenberger, 1985). Initially, the WCS covered only wage labourers employed in dangerous trades such as mining, manufacturing and transportation (Hobbs, 1939). During the first year, 194,601 companies and a total of 2,986,248 wage labourers were brought under coverage (Eghigian, 2000). In 1886, wage labourers engaged in agriculture, forestry and public services were added; in 1887, those from building trades and navigation; and by 1911, almost every industry was covered (Hobbs, 1939). By 1914, around 27,965,000 wage labourers (mostly men) were covered by the WCS's accident insurance fund (Eghigian, 2000).

The establishment of the first WCS in a capitalist society was part of a major defensive strategy to integrate wage labourers into society, manage social conflict, bring social peace, and secure the loyalty of the emerging working class (Eghigian, 2000; Hobbs, 1939; Moses 2018). The Paris Commune, a radical government that ruled Paris in 1871, was a vivid example of the shape working-class radicalism could take as a result of unaddressed grievances. It was thought that an inadequate response could lead to social evils. In tandem with a wide antisocialist sentiment, Bismarck's government, conservative groups and industrialists supported the introduction of a WCS not only to bring social peace but also to undermine socialism and the trade unions (Eghigian, 2000). As Hobbs (1939) puts it, Bismarck's purpose "[...] was to remove a perennial source of social unrest by establishing a paternalistic scheme through which the worker would be assured of assistance [...]" (p. 71). Harbutt Dawson's (The Athenaeum, 1912) cold-hearted quotation of Otto von Bismarck regarding the purpose of the insurance system clarifies its purpose: "to bribe the working classes, or, if you like, to win them over to regard the State as a social institution existing for their sake and interested in their welfare" (p. 702). Did Bismarck's insurance system accomplish its goal of reducing social conflict and making wage labourers loyal to the state? Although the answer to this question is not clear, the end of mass migration from Germany is a positive indication of the effects of Bismarck's social policy (Kleeberg, 2003).

Wage labour, as a relation that encompasses the historical separation of workers from the means of subsistence, the establishment of private property and the development of a market exchange economy based on commodities, constitutes a central precondition for the rise of WCSs and their injury information-intensive operations. Historically, the capitalist mode of production and its specific relation of production – i.e., wage labour – are conditions required for both the emergence and functioning of WCSs. First, WCSs arise with the historical expansion of wage labourers and the social instability they caused. These systems were part of what Eghigian (2000) describes as the administrative reorganization of "a society stripped of its traditional, feudal bonds" (p. 25); that is, the dissolution of the landlord/serf dyad and the appearance of the capitalist/wage-labourer dyad. Perceiving the formation of wage labourers as a threat to the social order is central to the development of WCSs. This perception is not only present in the genealogy of Germany's WCS but also in the accounts of Austria's WCS (see Jenks, 1965), Canada's WCS (see Meredith, 1913), Italy's WCS (see Moses, 2018), and the United States' WCS (see Holdren, 2020).

Second, WCS s' function as a mechanism to compensate workers injured during employment is particularly targeted toward wage labourers. This insurance mechanism was developed to tame wage labourers' discontent because of their inability to earn a living due to an industrial accident. Capitalists were not inclined to hire injured wage labourers, leaving them to rely on poor relief boards and charity. Rather than delivering medical and financial benefits to the whole working class – e.g., independent peasants and artisans –, a WCS would award benefits only to wage labourers. WCS s not only distinguish poverty from wage labour, as Gerstenberger (1985) correctly points out, but establish a distinction between wage labourers and independent workers.

WCS s are not only conditioned by the capitalist wage labour relation, but they, in turn, condition the capitalist mode of production by reinforcing the wage labour relation through the delivery of medical and wage-replacement benefits. Wage labour and the sum of all its historical connections – i.e., enclosure of the commons, private property, production for market exchange, production of commodities – are essential attributes of WCS s and their information-intensive operations. Only when an economy based on wage labour is established can WCS s' information-intensive operations come into existence. Now, due to wage labour being a constitutive attribute, WCS s' information-intensive operations will be henceforth conceptualized in this critique as the recording and processing of wage-labour-related injuries and fatalities rather than simply work-related injuries and fatalities. This distinction is important because the quality and quantity of information on reported, recognized and processed accidents, disabilities and fatalities tend to reflect the employment conditions of wage labourers rather than the working conditions of self-employed workers, precarious workers, under-the-table workers, and immigrant workers. For example, the total number of reported injuries tends to decrease during economic crises due to the rise in unemployment and underemployment rather than improvements in working conditions (see Azaroff et al., 2004; Cox and Lippel, 2008; Fortin et al., 1996; Hartwig et al.,1997; Tompa, 2012c). When the total number of employed wage labourers decreases, the total number of reported injuries, disabilities and fatalities tends to decrease as well. The total expenditure of benefits – e.g., medical, pensions, wage-replacement – is strongly correlated to the number of wage labourers covered (see Eghigian, 2000, Table 1, p. 27). Demographic changes in society do have important impacts on WCS s, including the solvency of the system itself (Guinnane and Streb, 2015). Grounded in the wage labour relation, injury rates are reflective of the employment and underemployment conditions of society.

3   Second Precondition: The Conflict between the Forces of
       Production and the Relations of Production

The introduction of a WCS in Germany in conjunction with two complementary interrelated insurance funds – i.e., the Sickness Insurance fund and the
Invalid and Old-age Insurance fund – to deal with the "Worker Question" has as
its base the wage labour relation as a main precondition. However, wage labour
as a precondition does not account for the specificities of the establishment of
an accident fund to compensate injured wage labourers. Why was an accident
fund instituted to compensate the injured? What was taking place in Germany
in the 1860s–1880s? As historians point out, the German WCS was a response to
the high number of injuries and fatalities of wage labourers during the second
industrial phase of the capitalist mode of production. More precisely, it was a
response to the significant social unrest caused by these injuries and deaths
which were also generating a tide of injury lawsuits (Eghigian, 2000; Hobbs,
1939; Kleeberg, 2003; Moses, 2018). The problem was not just the adverse
impact on wage labourers but the high cost of a liability system that fostered
litigation and caused serious problems to the capitalist mode of production.

In general, the adoption of WCSs by other capitalist societies follows the
same German pattern: (a) a series of horrible and widespread work accidents, (b) the passage of liability acts, and (c) the establishment of WCSs (see
Dümmer, 1997; Holdren, 2020; Jenks, 1965; Meredith, 1913; Moses, 2018). In this
regard, the prediction of the head of the new Imperial Insurance Office in
Germany proved to be right: "[...] workers' insurance will take its successful
course around the world, just like steam power and electricity" (Moses, 2018,
p. 71). The precondition for this pattern in capitalist economies can be traced
back to the conflict between the forces of production and the relations of production. The search for profit during the second industrial phase set the forces
of production – e.g., widespread use of machinery, new technologies, petro-
leum, electricity and industrial power – on a collision course with one of the
main relations of production: wage labourers. Let us consider the matter more
closely.

A mode of production is the sum of the economic forces and human relations upon which a society's social, cultural, and political dimensions rest. It is
formed by the skills, machinery and the means of production deployed by people to produce life – i.e., the forces of production – and the bonds between people to organise and carry out production – i.e., relations of production (Marx,
1978a). Wage labour is a critical part of the relations of production of the capitalist mode of production. It is the essential mechanism through which surplus
value – i.e., unpaid labour – is extracted in a capitalist economy (Marx, 1990).

As already explained, wage labour is a product of the historical separation of the peasants from the means of subsistence and its appropriation by a dominant group – i.e., the capitalists – in order to develop an economy based on production for exchange rather than direct consumption. A capitalist economy can be synthesized in the relationship between the group who appropriated the means of subsistence and production – i.e., the capitalists – and the group robbed of those means and forced to work for the capitalists in return for a wage to keep themselves alive – i.e., wage labourers.

The capitalist/wage-labourer dyad is the historical bond of the capitalist mode of production. What makes this dyad so peculiar is that it is not formed based on coercion but necessity (Marx, 1990). While the previous master/slave and landlord/serf dyads are the consequence of direct force, the capitalist/wage-labourer dyad appears to be voluntary. The capitalist never forces a wage labourer to produce for a market in return for a wage; the wage labourer does it to keep himself alive. It is necessity that drives wage labourers to enroll themselves under the direction of a capitalist who made them wage labourers in the first place by appropriating the means of subsistence and production. In addition, what makes this bond unique is that the pressures are set outside of the relationship itself. Wage labourers are forced to work under the conditions established by the market. It is not the individual capitalist who sets the conditions but rather the market where the products will be exchanged. As McNally (1993) explains, wage labourers are forced to produce at the average level of intensity and productivity determined by the market. They are subjected to the pressures of an abstract system of exchange whose purpose is the accumulation of profit.

This takes us to the dangers to wage labourers posed by the capitalist mode of production. In terms of health at work, the capitalist mode of production has as its core an inherent contradiction between its aim – i.e., production for profit – and its critical part of the relations of production – i.e., wage labour (Allende, 1939; Engels, 1845; Marx, 1990; Navarro, 1980, 1982; Waitzkin, 1981). Marx (1990) noted that this mode of production not only produces a deterioration of the health of wage labourers but also their early exhaustion and death. As he puts it, "It [capital] attains its objective by shortening the life of labour-power [...]" (Marx, 1990, p. 376). However, rather than blaming individual capitalists for their lack of will, humanity and compassion, Marx explained this phenomenon as the result of capital personified, where the immanent laws of capitalist production – i.e., competition and profit maximization – confronted individual capitalists as a force external to them. Marx went beyond those characteristics that are general to a group of people – i.e., the capitalists – and identified the problem at a higher level of generality as one that is peculiar to a group of people due to their functioning in a capitalist society. Injuries, diseases and deaths take place during the working day due to how production is organized under capitalism. It is not the capitalist himself but the capitalist mode of production that exploits workers without regard for their health and well-being in order to produce surplus value.

Specifically, it is the conditions of the labour process that surround the production of surplus value that are pernicious to wage labourers. By extending the working day and increasing the intensity of labour, capitalist production – the production of surplus value – produces injury or death to wage labourers (Marx, 1990). Marx explores, in detail, how the extension of the working day and working conditions injure and kill wage labourers. His portrayal of the matches industry describes this process: "With a working day ranging from 12 to 14 to 15 hours, night-labour, irregular meal-times, and meals mostly taken in the workrooms themselves, pestilent with phosphorus, Dante would have found the worst horrors in his Inferno surpassed in this industry" (Marx, 1990, p. 356). Marx's descriptions of the labour of blacksmiths, dressmakers and silk mill workers show how the length and intensity of the working day undermines the health of wage labourers, thus leading to premature death. Overwork, overcrowded workplaces, speed-ups and increasing intensity have a detrimental impact on wage labourers. As Marx (1990) puts it, "It is not only in dressmakers' room that working to death is the order of the day, but in thousand other places; in every place I had almost said, where 'a thriving business' has to be done [...]" (p. 366).

It is important to note that while the capitalist mode of production is not liable for work-related accidents it is historically liable for wage-labour-related accidents. Work accidents can happen due to other causes rather than a particular mode of production. For example, a peasant working for himself can have a fall on the same level or been struck by an object while taking out his animals for pasture. In this case, the work accident is not a consequence of a mode of production but of the working activity as a general activity. However, wage-labour-related accidents can happen only in capitalist economies where the capitalist/wage-labourer dyad is dominant. They occur in a system that indirectly forces wage labourers to produce at the average level of intensity determined by the market in return for a wage. The point is that the capitalist system itself, as a system that produces for profit on the basis of human exploitation, inherently tends to bring about work injuries and diseases (Allende, 1939; Engels, 1845; Marx, 1990; Navarro, 1982; Waitzkin, 1981). Wage labour accidents and diseases in capitalist economies are the consequence of the "voracious appetite for profit" (Marx, 1990). These evils are ingrained in a system where surplus value comes from excess labour produced and appropriated from wage labourers by means such as increasing the length and intensity of labour. In this regard, the struggle over the length of a working day, the outcome of which was laws limiting the working day, was due to the abovementioned contradiction between profit and wage labour. For example, in the UK, the factory legislation from 1833 to 1864 on the compulsory limitation of the working day (the Ten Hours Bill) was a direct response to the detrimental effects of an unlimited working day.

The precondition for the passage of liability acts that finally led to the Act of 1884 is found in the third mechanism enforced to produce surplus value, one that Marx's death did not allow him to analyze during his lifetime: productivity. Productivity is a revolution of the technical and social process of labour prompted by the quest for surplus value (Marx, 1990). Capitalists can extract surplus value not just by lengthening and intensifying the labour process but by revolutionizing the technical and social conditions of the labour process. The Industrial Revolution, properly called by Hobsbawm (1994) 'the Capitalist Industrial Revolution', is a revolution of productivity, a revolution based on the transformation of the forces of production. What the Capitalist Industrial Revolution did was to substitute machines for muscle power to increase the production of surplus value. "The machine, [...] the starting-point of the industrial revolution, replaces the worker, who handles [a] single tool, by a mechanism operating with a number of similar tools and set in motion by a simple motive power [...]" (Marx, 1990, p. 497). When it was impossible to increase the accumulation of capital by prolonging the working day, capitalists threw themselves into the development of machines. "The machine is a means for producing surplus-value" (Marx, 1990, p. 492).

The development of machines and industrial technology not only increased the overall risk at the worksite, thus increasing the deterioration of labour power, but created a new phenomenon called mass accidents (see Kleeberg, 2003; Holdren 2020; Moses, 2018). Hundreds of wage labourers would perish at the same time during employment in a unique event, leaving hundreds of widows and children behind. In this regard, the capitalist mode of production is not only responsible for wage-labour-related accidents but for the massive build-up – i.e., a quantitative change – in the number of wage-labour-related accidents and deaths. "Capitalist production [...] only develops the techniques and the degree of combination of the social process of production by simultaneously undermining the original sources of wealth – the soil and the worker" (Marx, 1990, p. 638). In terms of workers' health, the capitalist industrial revolution presents itself as the clash between the revolutionized forces of production – i.e., machinery, equipment, technology – and the relations of production – i.e., in this case, wage labourers (see Navarro, 1982). This conflict is a second precondition for the appearance of a WCS in Germany and its expansion to other countries.

What was taking place in Germany in the last half of the 19th century was precisely a conflict between the forces of production and the relations of production that manifested in the form of mass accidents. In fact, the German government was aware of the relationship between accidents on a grand scale and industrial technologies (Moses, 2018). Historical accounts describe horrendous coal mine accidents, steam-boiler explosions, boat fires and railroad crashes. The fatalities in the mining sector were particularly horrifying due to their gross numbers. In Germany, in 1867, the collapse of a coal mine shaft in Lugau entombed 101 miners; in 1868, in South Wales, two methane explosions killed 231 miners; in 1869, another methane explosion near Dresden killed 340 miners (Kleeberg, 2003). The historic records of that period hold that the overall accident rate increased enormously (Hobbs, 1939; Kleeberg, 2003; Moses, 2018). In Germany, from 1978 to 1980, accidents involving machinery rose from 39,040 to 43,754 (Moses, 2018). It was the build-up in the number of fatalities and resulting social unrest that impelled the German state to establish liability acts to hold capitalists liable for damages. As Marx (1990) notes, "Capital […] takes no account of the health and the length of life of the worker, unless society forces it to do so" (p. 381).

In 1871, the German Liability Act made every firm liable for its own negligence, especially the railroads, which were subjected to strict liability (Kleeberg, 2003). This Act introduced a litigation-based mode for compensating injured workers. Under strict liability, the railroad capitalist bore the compensation cost of accidents unless he could prove the accident was due to the fault of wage labourers. For all other industries, the burden of proof was placed on the injured wage labourer. In other words, the capitalist had to compensate the victim only if the wage labourer could prove that the accident was caused by the capitalist's negligence.

The problem with the 1871 law was that it did not abrogate the common law regarding the contract of service (Murray and Nilsson, 2007). According to the common law, the wage labourer assumed the risk of employment and those risks in hand of fellow servants when the foreman or supervisor is found liable. First, under the rule of assumption of risk wage labourers were deemed liable because it implied that they could choose jobs that were known to be dangerous. Second, under the fellow servant rule the employer was not held liable if the accident was the fault of another worker. And third, if the capitalist was found guilty of negligence and at the same time the wage labourer was found guilty of contributory negligence, the employer would not be held liable.

Regardless of the barriers imposed by the common law, the German Liability Act of 1871 created an avalanche of litigation. As Murray and Nilsson (2007) point out, the 1871 Act enabled wage labourers to sue their employers more easily. Wage labourers were no longer willing to bear the costs of workplace accidents. "The ideology of liberal risk, in which workers and employers operated freely in a fair market of labour relations, had lost credibility" (Moses, 2018, p. 63). Capitalists were alarmed by the rapid increase in the number of cases brought forward under the Act (Kleeberg, 2003). However, the real fear was the economic impact, since the law was simply too expensive for the industry. Businesses felt threatened due to the frequency and high cost of compensation. There were three pressing issues: (a) lawsuits were costly, (b) workers were winning, and (c) there was pressure to expand strict liability to every industry. The uncertainty of the Act, which held the capitalist liable only if their managers were at fault, resulted in long, complex and costly litigations (Kleeberg, 2003). In addition, the courts were interpreting the Act in favour of wage labourers – they were reluctant to find contributory negligence – thus placing the burden of accident costs on the industry (Kleeberg 2003). Capitalists were losing more and more often. Also, liberals were calling to expand strict liability to all enterprises, including mines and factories. The German government and conservatives opposed the expansion of strict liability to mining (Kleeberg, 2003). To make things worse, the economic crash of 1873 and subsequent depression made industries even more concerned about the costs of the liability system (Kleeberg, 2003). In sum, the Act of 1871 transformed a social problem – i.e., mass accidents – into an economic one that threatened the capitalist mode of production. The problem was not the phenomenon of mass accidents but rather their cost and distribution among the two classes.

wcss arise when the conflict between the revolutionized forces of production and the relations of production put the expansion of profit and the survival of capitalism at risk. This conflict is a precondition for the replacement of a litigation-based mode of compensation by an information-intensive mode of compensation to indemnify wage labourers' damages and their loss of wages. In fact, the establishment of wcss correlates with the number of injury lawsuits (Holdren, 2020). Only when wage-labour-related accidents due to productivity have risen to a point where the costs of a liability system put at risk the capitalist mode of production is an information-intensive system ready to emerge. This development took an historically indirect route. Instead of a struggle over the limits of productivity, as in the case of the compulsory limitation of the working day, the conflict between the revolutionized forces of production and the relations of production manifested as a struggle over damage compensation. Neither the Act of 1871 nor the Act of 1884 included provisions to halt, contain, limit or inspect the revolutionized forces of production. From the beginning, the struggle was confined to damage compensation. However, this compensation system was never designed to provide full compensation. The 1884 Act was not generous. For example, the calculation of premiums assumed that at least 20% of the insured would die prematurely (Gerstenberger, 1985). Disability payments were normally not enough to keep wage labourers alive for more than a few years. The WCS shielded capitalists from the financial and political consequences of rising wage-labour-related accidents.

The Act of 1884 was not a piece of pro-worker legislation but the opposite. WCS s were introduced in the face of opposition by German workers and labour organisations (Eghigian, 2000; Gerstenberger, 1985; Moses, 2018). Labour leaders went around the country criticizing the system for its "class bias", undue restrictions and unnecessary complexity, among other things (Eghigian, 2000; Moses, 2018). Labour groups pointed their finger at the capitalist mode of production. They argued that industrial accidents reflected the abuse of wage labourers by the capitalist system (Guinnane and Streb, 2015). Surprisingly, it was not just labour groups who correctly identified the problem as a structural one. There was general agreement across every sector – i.e., conservatives, government, industrialists – that capitalism itself was the chief cause of the social crisis, including industrial accidents (Eghigian, 2000). However, the solution gravitated toward a compensation system based on an information-intensive process to allocate compensation payments and benefits. In fact, Bismarck himself was against the passage of safety legislation – e.g., forbidding Sunday work and child labour – and factory inspectors that would hinder industry (Kleeberg, 2003; Moses, 2018). Based on the success of the mining mutual funds already in place in Germany since 1854, Bismarck tilted towards a compensatory model (Moses, 2018). Rather than the safety laws, tax reform, collective bargaining, prevention or fostering of an ethos of mutual responsibility between wage labourers and capitalists proposed by socialists and other progressive bureaucrats, the solution imposed was no-fault damage compensation (Eghigian, 2000; Moses, 2018).

What made the Act of 1884 unique was that in granting compensation, the question of fault was completely removed. Medical and wage-replacement compensation to injured wage labourers would be awarded without regard to who was at fault. WCS s do not determine compensation on the basis of fault but by establishing whether an injury meets the conditions required in order to be insured (Eghigian, 2000; Moses, 2018). This contractual solution ended the costs of lengthy and complex litigation to prove whose negligence caused an accident. Also, the common law defense – i.e., contributory negligence, assumption of risk, and fellow servant – was also abrogated in order to assure compensation to every injured wage labourer. In this regard, WCSS removed the adversarial nature of a litigation-based mode of compensation thus easing social tensions. Class antagonism and radicalism was mitigated by an information-intensive mode of compensating injured workers regardless of fault.

In sum, from a historical materialist perspective, the rise of WCSS was made possible due to the transformation of the superstructure (particularly the legal sphere) caused by the class struggle due to the contradiction between the forces and the relations of production. The transition from a litigation-based mode of compensation to an information-intensive mode of compensation was a result of this structural antagonism. While wage labourers pressed the capitalists due to changes in the standard of physiological needs – i.e., the needs required to maintain and reproduce the worker – produced by an increase of the wear and tear of labour power during the second industrial revolution, capitalists were primarily concerned with the cost and distribution of the change in the standard of needs and its impact on industry. Now, it is relevant to note that the superstructural change leading to WCSS and their information-intensive process did not erode the economic base. Quite the opposite, it added support to the economic base, leading to the reinforcement of the existing relations of production and the forces of production. WCSS were established to shield and reinforce the capitalist mode of production. As Gerstenberger (1985) points out, the establishment of social insurance in Germany has been interpreted as a success for the labour movement rather than what it actually was, a historical defeat.

4   Third Precondition: A Burgeoning Capitalist Class

As seen in the previous section, wage-labour-related injuries and fatalities began to be recorded and processed by WCSS to allocate compensation payments and benefits when the past liability system could not solve the conflict between the forces of production and the relations of production. Only when this historical boiling point is reached is an information-intensive mode of compensation ready to appear in capitalist societies. Of course, the establishment of an information-intensive mode of compensation rather than safety laws, tax reform, risk prevention or collective bargaining constitutes a political decision and is without a doubt a product of human beings. However, it is a product of people conditioned by a set of material relations – e.g., private property, wage labour, economy for exchange, commodities – already in place in a capitalist society.

Under a capitalist mode of production, a collective compensation system seemed better suited than introducing legislation that could set a limit on the revolutionized forces of production and thus the production and expansion of profit. Diminishing profits was one of Bismarck's concerns when deciding on a compensation system (Kleeberg, 2003). In this regard, the creation of an insurance fund to bear the costs of medical and wage-replacement compensations appeared as the most appropriate formula. This was not something novel. As Eghigian (2000) notes, there were already insurance carriers in the sphere of maritime commerce, natural disasters and personal life (widow and orphan funds). However, it was compulsory wage labour protection and the collective mechanism that were the major innovations of the compensation insurance fund. A WCS would distribute the costs of compensations collectively among firms based on loss spreading through insurance (Kleeberg, 2003). Rather than every capitalist being individually liable for the payment of compensation, capitalists would be divided into groups to be held collectively liable for the payment of compensation benefits.

What was already in place in Germany that allowed the establishment of a system to share the costs of compensation? The answer is a large and burgeoning group of capitalists. A collective liability system is not just preceded by (a) the separation of workers from the means of subsistence and production, (b) the conversion of the means of production into private property, (c) the development of an economy for exchange, and (d) the production of commodities as a way of extracting surplus value. A collective system requires that the aforementioned social process, which yields the capitalist/wage-labourer dyad, has resulted in a large number of capitalists to share, collectively, the costs of compensating injured workers. In other words, the largest part of the means of production of a country must be brought under dispersed private ownership and control. A build-up of capitalists, a critical mass, is a precondition for a collective system. Thus, a large market-driven capitalist class must be in place before the emergence and functioning of a collective system to divide the costs of wage-labour-related accidents and deaths. In this regard, the operative model of a WCS based on the organization and grouping of firms in related types of industries confirms that an already large and mature capitalist class was fully functioning in Germany.

The industrialization process created structural changes in the German economy, such as the expansion of the labour market, an increase in the division of labour, and above all the formation of industrial enterprises. During 1850–73, the German economy experienced an intense period of economic growth (Borchardt as cited in Eghigian, 2000). Germany was flourishing under industrial capitalism. During the first years of the establishment of the WCS (1890–1914) unemployment was very low, somewhere around an average of 2.6 percent (Eghigian, 2000). In this economic context, the Act of 1884 set up, as the main operative mechanism, a corporatist scheme under the regulation of the state – i.e., the Imperial Insurance Office (Moses, 2018). These insurance boards were operated by capitalists in branches of industry or in groups of industries. This corporatist model emulated the mining mutual funds already in place in Germany that brought together wage labourers from the same industry (Moses, 2018). This was possible because by 1880 capitalists began to concentrate in large cartels (Böhme as cited in Eghigian, 2000). Each insurance board consisted of a group of firms in a related industry within a particular region or across Germany. For example, the glass industry formed one group, wood processing another, textiles a third, iron and steel a fourth, etc. By 1914, there were 68 insurance boards covering around 835,500 individual plants representing 26 branches of industry (Guinnane and Streb, 2015). On average, each insurance board covered around 12,300 private plants. These numbers are evidence of a burgeoning and strong capitalist class; a group of owners of the means of production producing for market exchange rather than for direct consumption. The Act of 1884 was pro-capitalist, accommodating the interests of businesses rather than workers. It was flexible enough to allow groupings to be regional or nationwide (Guinnane and Streb, 2015). An industry could establish many regional insurance boards within Germany. For example, the construction industry was regionally distributed among 13 insurance boards, covering 195,419 plants, with a total of 1,040,862 workers (Guinnane and Streb, 2015).

Risk classification also operated on the basis of the type of a firm rather than the labour process, type of accident, type of worker, or any distinction related to the labour context. Every firm was classified into different risk groups within each industry by an insurance board (Kleeberg, 2003). Insurance boards assigned firms to risk classes that reflected the costs of medical and wage-replacement benefits in a firm of that type (Guinnane and Streb, 2015). Firms were grouped together based on their risk – i.e., the costs of compensation. As Moses (2018) points out, risk classes co-opted firms into sharing the economic burden of work injuries. Individual firms paid a premium based on their employees' wages that reflected both the risk class assigned and the experience rating. The risk class was a 5-year tariff, whereas the experience rating was a 1-year tariff (Guinnane and Streb, 2015). Each company paid a premium based on its total wage bills and the risk class – i.e., the total expenditure of a class within 5 years – and another portion based on the product of its total wage bills and the experience rating – i.e., its relative share in the total expenditures of the year (Guinnane and Streb, 2015). In sum, every firm's premium was not conditioned by its individual performance but the relative performance of the industry group to which it was assigned. Both the risk class and the experience rating were the average risk level – i.e., average costs of compensation – of all member firms together. This collective system allowed cost-shifting within an insurance board, from large to small firms or from unsafe to safe firms. Capitalists were compelled to share the costs of wage-labour-related accidents. As Guinnane and Streb (2015) point out, given the collective trait of risk calculation, individual firms ignored safety practices and the cost of accidents. In essence, a collective system is designed to shield the whole capitalist class from the financial consequences of wage-labour-related accidents. Let us see how this system functions more closely.

A collective system does not effectively reflect the costs of compensation – i.e., risk level – incurred for each individual firm for the insurance board. This is because losses are spread among firms of the same risk class within a branch of industry. By assigning a large number of firms to a risk class, the impact of each firm's contribution is lessened. A firm's premium contribution is not linked to its own record but to those of all member firms together. The system was not designed to insure individual capitalists on the basis of their own safety performance but the performance of the capitalist class as a whole. This had three economic consequences. As Guinnane and Streb (2015) point out, by creating large and financially solid insurance boards, the system would (a) shield every capitalist from the economic consequences of work accidents by sharing the costs among many capitalists, (b) make costs limited and calculable, and (c) make compensation costs stable.

Insurance boards had to explain the system over and over to firms who saw their insurance costs go up when they had experienced few accidents (Guinnane and Streb, 2015). The insurance costs for a risk class could go up if simply more accidents occurred in member firms of the same risk class. As seen, the purpose and functioning of wcss was not only to compensate injured wage labourers but to spread the costs of accidents across member firms in order to hold capitalists liable collectively. Thus, the information-intensive operations of recording and processing injuries and deaths to come up with risk classes was designed to spread the costs of compensation. This information process distributes the total amount of compensation via (a) grouping firms into a particular branch of industry and risk class, and (b) assessing premiums based on risk class – i.e., the total expenditure of a class within 5 years – and experience rating – i.e., its relative share in the total expenditures of the year.

There is a double tendency towards an equalization of the rate of compensation: between firms of the same industry and between firms of the same risk class. The equalization of the compensation rates presupposes their relative difference. Historical records confirm there was a great deal of variation among compensation levels paid to insurance boards. Although the average rate of compensation was 1.6% of the wage bill, the top 25% of insurance boards paid around 2%, while the bottom 25% paid around 0.1% (Guinnane and Streb, 2015). The information-intensive process is the operating force behind the equalization of the rate of compensation among the flux of accidents between different branches of industry and risk classes. So, independent of the number of accidents produced by every firms' productivity growth, the costs of compensation do not confront the firm as the costs of compensation of their own labour process. To sum up, compensation is a social rather than an individual category, whose social character presupposes the existence of a large capitalist class as a necessary precondition to spread the costs of compensation benefits.

5   Fourth Precondition: Statistics and Probability

Under a collective liability scheme, the costs of compensation produced by the injuries, disabilities and deaths of wage labourers are not directly assigned to each firm based on those it employs. The firm's contribution is proportional to the fraction of wage labourers it employs in relation to those employed by all the capitalists in the same industry and risk class assigned. As we shall see, this results in an average rate of compensation that is more or less applicable to each branch of capital. Now, what scientific and technical means were available at the time in order to establish such a complex system to spread compensation between employers? Among these, the new social science of statistics and probability was one of the most important. Without these scientific methods, a mutualistic form of financing, through which member firms insured one another, would have been very difficult if not impossible to implement. wcs s embraced statistics and probability to rationally spread the costs of compensation and thus effectively shield the capitalist class against wage-labour-related injuries and deaths. Statistics and probability are preconditions for the actual quantitative form and functioning of injury rates under a collective liability scheme. Insurance boards engaged in the recording and processing of wage-labour-related injuries, disabilities, deaths and salaries to construct both the risk class – i.e., the total expenditures of a class within 5 years – and the experience rating – i.e., its relative share in the total expenditures of the year. wcs s and their injury information-intensive operations relied on statistics and probability to spread compensation costs and disburse medical and financial benefits to injured wage labourers. This is the scientific and technical basis of the common interest of all owners of capital in the spread of compensation payments.

In the early 1800s in Germany, insurance schemes were mainly speculative businesses. Insurance carriers in maritime, personal life and natural disasters made their incomes by betting on the future. They were associated with gambling and usury and thus were outlawed for religious reasons in many regions of Germany. However, in the late nineteenth century, insurance practices underwent a profound change by employing rational scientific methods (Eghigian, 2000). Insurance went from something unpredictable, irrational, and immoral, to a rational, predictable and honorable practice. This change was due to the appearance and use of statistics and probability as a method for identifying and evaluating social problems (Eghigian, 2000; Moses, 2018). In 1850–80, German governments came to rely on statistics to prepare legislation and decrees and to quantify the social conditions of contemporary social problems (Moses, 2018). Germany developed a central statistical bureau, the Royal Prussian Statistical Bureau, to empirically collect statistics on social matters ranging from public health to workplace accidents. This new science was seen as a central tool that allowed for the identification and solution of complex social questions. It was well suited to the discovery of regularities in apparent chance events such as industrial accidents and the perfect science to rationally spread the cost of compensation benefits among the capitalist class. As Moses (2018) notes, the collection of accident statistics helped to shift the blame of an accident from workers to the industrialization of labour. Statistics enabled WCS s to recognize and discriminate risks among different economic sectors – e.g., mining, manufacturing, transportation, forestry, shipbuilding.

Under the Act of 1884, insurance boards began to systematically record information about wage-labour-related accidents and subsequently to process it based on the principles of statistics and probability in order to organize firms according to risk classes. By observing the workplace in the aggregate, assigning numerical values to the number of accidents and then determining regularities, insurance boards would construct their risk classes and organize firms. This was a reflection of the instrumental character of accident statistics, which chiefly served the construction of risk classes to set the premiums to be paid by individual firms. Insurance boards would construct risk levels based on the weighted sum of the number of accidents per 1,000 workers: for fatal accidents, the weight was to be 10; for those that caused permanent total disability, 30; for permanent partial disability accidents, 15; and for temporary disability accidents, 1 (Guinnane and Streb, 2015).

Later, in 1896, the German state through the Imperial Insurance Office implemented a new system based on all the expenditures for each type of accident divided by the aggregate wages of the firm concerned (Guinnane and Streb, 2015). This new approach, which set the blueprint for contemporary WCS s, would reflect more neatly the costs incurred by firms for the insurance board. The insurance boards' database of accidents was crucial to constructing risk levels and determining premiums to collectively compensate wage labourers. For a system that relied on information to collect premiums, a lack of injury information was indeed problematic. In some cases, insurance boards did not have the long-term accident statistics to effectively assign individual firms to risk classes; they would provisionally assign them to a similar risk class (Guinnane and Streb, 2015).

It is important to note that under statistics and probability theory, risk is always measured in terms of probability. As Eghigian (2000) explains, "Rooted in statistics and probability, [...], insurance's notion of risk had less to do with the threat of danger than with the hazards of chance and randomness" (p. 56). In fact, the real cost of medical and wage-replacement benefits does not match the premiums collected based on historical accident statistics. For example, in 1923–24, hyperinflation in Germany proved that compensating wage labourers based on statistics and probability rather than real costs could become a significant headache (see Eghigian, 2000). Under the rapidly decreasing value of the currency, the formula based on former wages and premium payments set by risk assessment resulted in financial disaster, since medical and wage-replacement benefits could not keep up with the rate of inflation (An ex-post assessment system based on benefit expenditures would have solved this problem).

WCS s' injury information-intensive processes are an integral part of a statistico-empirical rationality that formed part of economic, political and technological factors and contingent historical events. Based on statistics and probability, the operations of recording and processing wage-labour-related injuries and deaths are a means to situate every firm's risks in relation to the others (see Ewald, 1991). Rather than assessing risks in terms of an absolute standard, injuries and deaths are assessed in relation to each other (Ewald, 1991). The norm, in this case the risk class and the experience rating, made every accident economically comparable. Each injury or death is the mirror and measure of every injury and death. As Eghigian (2000) points out, the logic of risk based on statistical principles of normativity excludes juridical principles of justice – i.e., how culpable one is. Thanks to statistics, compensation is effectively set apart from the juridical order of the Act of 1871. By relying on statistics and probability, injury information-intensive operations thus made compensation a technical issue. What statistics and probability achieved was to depoliticize the problem of industrial accidents by transforming them into a technical issue.

As Starr and Immergut (1987) argue, the passage from the political to the technical is one form of the depoliticization of health care. wcs s' value-free and statistically-based information systems are a main component in the process of depoliticizing work accidents. The use of statistics by the Royal Prussian Statistical Bureau to bring about solutions to social problems was in essence a nonrevolutionary endeavour (Eghigian, 2000). Statistics to predict the probability of explosion in steam engines, the health of disabled war veterans, the living standards of the poor, among others, were used to evaluate social problems in disregard of the organization and structure of capitalist societies – e.g., ownership of the means of production, the buying and selling of labour power, profit orientation, etc. Statistically-based injury information offers a powerful approach to record and process injuries and deaths to compensate workers and appease the masses. It is above all an attempt to rationally and scientifically manage society to make it stable and productive. As an empiricist endeavour, injury information-intensive operations do not penetrate the emergent structural forces stemming from historical background conditions (see York and Clark, 2006) and the production of work accidents but only the determination and measuring of regularities in a quantitative fashion to construct risk classes, predict the cost of compensations and spread them. Injury information processes are not about causes; they cannot respond to why injuries and deaths occur in the first place. As Comte (1999) explains, empirical observations replace the indeterminacy of causes with the determination of constant relations that exist among observed phenomena. Statistico-empirical analysis in exclusion of political and economic background conditions abdicates the goal of discovering the origin of social processes in favour of an attempt to delineate their regularities. Its goal is not an emancipatory one but a practical one that aims at regulating social interaction in order to assure order and progress (Moya, 1999). Its aim is simply prediction and control.

As such, predicting the costs of wage-labour-related injuries and deaths to collectively spread compensation among firms in related branches of industry is wcs s' information operations goal. In its normative function, injury information operations of constructing risk classes and experience ratings exclude principles of justice – i.e., depolitization. Insurance boards collect injury information to produce categories that reflect accidents' financial consequences (see Guinnane and Streb, 2015). wcs s' statistico-empirical injury information operations do not place the structural question of wage labourers' physical exposure and relation to particular physical risks at center stage; rather, they put the question of firms' economic exposure and relation to economic risks at center stage. Summing up, with statistics and probability constituting injury rates, the attributes of prediction, control, and the avoidance of historical background conditions and causes constitute essential elements of wcss' injury information-intensive operations.

6   Fifth Precondition: Money

As already shown, statistics and probability comprise the scientific and technical basis of the prediction and spread of compensation among the capitalist class. Only when society has met the aforementioned scientific means to predict and collectively spread the cost of compensation among firms in related branches of industry can an information-intensive mode of compensation be ready to function. Statistics and probability are preconditions for the processing of injury rates to construct risk classes and experience ratings. However, these rational scientific means do not solve the economic process of exchange among insurance boards and their associated firms in regard to risk premiums. Statistics situate injuries in relation to each other in order to be assessed and compared among firms in the same branches of industry. Through the number of working days lost, every injury can be effectively situated as the mirror and measure of themselves. But what makes every injury and death economically measurable and exchangeable is money. Money as a measure of value and medium of exchange is a vital precondition for insurance boards to price and realize risks. Risk classes and experience ratings, both the product of injury information-intensive processes, can only be exchanged when a universal equivalent – i.e., money – has appeared both as the main measure and medium of exchange of all values in society. wcss and their injury information operations are inextricably connected to one of the main relations of the capitalist mode of production: money. This is particularly the case with two of the three functions of money, namely, as a medium of measurement and a medium of exchange.

Money has historically been recognized as having three major functions (see Marx, 1993). One of them is to represent the amount of value – i.e., labour-time – of commodities as magnitudes of the same denomination (Marx, 1990). This function allows commodities to be compared qualitatively and quantitatively. Every commodity can be represented qualitatively as paper money – e.g., Canadian dollars – and quantitatively as a magnitude of paper money – e.g., 100 Canadian dollars. As a medium of the measurement of value, money has the capacity to act as a universal measure of value or as a universal equivalent

(Marx, 1990). As the universal measure of value, money represents the amount of labour time objectified in every commodity. As Marx (1990) points out, "Money as a measure of value is the necessary form of appearance of the measure of value which is immanent in commodities, namely labour-time" (p. 188).

As a medium of measurement, money is needed only as a category, as a mental relation, since the quantity of money actually available is utterly irrelevant (Marx, 1993). No existing money in any quantity is needed to perform this function. Now, in regard to risk – i.e., statistically-processed information that reflects the costs of compensation –, money plays a vital role as a measure of value. Risks are situated in relation to themselves on the basis of money rather than the type or kind of risks. The probability of suffering an electrical shock, a burn, a strain, a fall or a cut is represented as the amount of money needed to disburse compensation benefits to injured workers. As a measure of value, money allows different risks to be qualitatively represented as the same thing – e.g., paper money. As a measure of value, money enables the quantitative representation and comparison of different risks as a magnitude of the same thing – e.g., x quantity of paper money. Money makes different risks comparable. It is the magnitude of compensation in terms of money – i.e., cost of medical and wage-replacement benefits – that makes the probability of suffering falls, cuts and bruises the same, a comparable unit. Placed in a value relation, risks are nothing but money. As money, every risk can be effectively situated as the mirror and measure of themselves. Money situates risks in a value relation in order to be assessed and compared among firms of the same branches of industry. Firms are grouped together within a branch of industry based on the amount of money needed to compensate injured workers rather than the type of risks – e.g., cuts, falls, strains, burns. Money as a measure of value constitutes the unit of the risk class – i.e., the total expenditure of a class within five years –, and the experience rating – i.e., the relative share of a firm in the total expenditures of the year. And as a measure of value, money serves to convert risks into prices – in this case, the premium. Money becomes the very measure of risk.

Money also has a second function: it is a medium of exchange or an instrument of circulation (Marx, 1993). Money circulates commodities that have already been transformed into money as a measure of value. In this case, money must be physically present in a certain quantity to function as a medium of exchange (Marx, 1993). It is the material – e.g., paper or, more commonly these days, digital money – into which commodities can be exchanged. Rather than just being a mental relation, the quantity of existing available money is indispensable to performing the function of exchange. In addition, a price is needed for money to act as an instrument of circulation. Money as a medium of exchange needs to be posited in the form of the price of a commodity (Marx, 1993). As a medium of exchange, money is a realizer of prices; it circulates commodities in the form of prices (Marx, 1993). In regard to WCS s' main goal, to allocate compensation payments and compensation benefits among capitalists and wage labourers, respectively, money as a medium of exchange is an essential element of the system. Without money readily available the process of exchanging medical and wage-replacement benefits for premiums cannot be performed. Insurance boards collect money from associated firms at a price – i.e., the premium – to reconvert that money into medical and wage-replacement benefits to compensate injured workers.

Money as a medium of measurement and of exchange is central to the functioning of WCS s and their injury information-intensive operations. It is a vital precondition for the processing of injury rates in terms of economic equivalences in order to construct, represent and exchange risks for a guarantee against loss, and reconvert them into compensation benefits. Now, it is interesting to note how injury rates become reified in economic terms as money as an exchange value; that is, how much more or less money capitalists pay and wage labourers receive for the recorded and processed injuries. Put simply, injury rates – e.g., working days lost, the impairment rate – are transformed into physical money as an exchange value, enabling injured workers to receive their wage-replacement in the form of real money and capitalists to pay physical money in the form of premiums. Thus, only when money as a medium of exchange enables the conversion of risk into money at a price – i.e., the premium – and the reconversion of money in compensation benefits, is the purpose of injury information-intensive operations realized. Its goal is mediated by money as a medium of exchange. As a functioning category, injury rates are money and money is injury rates.

7   Sixth Precondition: A Capitalist State

A compulsory system for recording and processing injury information to allocate compensation payments and benefits among capitalists and wage labourers cannot operate without a significant amount of state power. Capitalists cannot coordinate themselves when it comes to the distribution of compensation payments. Wage labourers do not have enough social power to consistently demand compensation benefits from capitalists. The power of the state is essential. With this regard, state intervention is needed not only to enforce a WCS but to (a) legislate around issues such as risk classes, risk pricing (premiums), entitlement parameters, compensable injuries, (b) supervise insurance boards in regard to their methods of rating, rules and their accounts, and (c) exercise judicial functions settling disputes, adjusting claims during controversies, etc. The nation state is a necessary precondition for a state-sponsored or state-owned compulsory system. It is a major player within a WCS. However, it is not any kind of state but a capitalist state, whose main purpose is to run the capitalist economy through the assistance of capitalist enterprises (see Miliband, 2009).

It is not a coincidence that state intervention on behalf of the capitalist class preceded both the birth of capitalism (see Marx, 1990; McNally, 1993; Meiksins, 2002) and the birth of WCS s. The capitalist state, as a social form of state power peculiar to societies divided among classes – i.e., those who own and control the means of production and those who only own their labour power –, is paramount to the emergence and functioning of WCS s' injury information-producing operations. The capitalist state is constitutive to injury rates in regard to their class purpose – i.e., the allocation of compensation payments and benefits among classes – and their function of producing economic equivalences. Comparable to the general need of the capitalist state, namely, maintaining the relations of production and holding class struggle in check (Engels, 1978; Lenin, 1992), WCS s exist to repair, recover and maintain the reserve army of labour readily for exploitation. The reserve army of labour or the relative surplus population is key to maintaining wages at their lowest level thus a necessary part of capitalist exploitation (Marx, 1990).

First, it is important to note that the state is not just one entity. It is composed of a number of particular institutions that mutually interact with one another in the distribution of power in society (Miliband, 2009). These institutions are (a) the government, (b) the administration, (c) the military and the police, (d) the judicial branch, and (e) parliamentary assemblies (Miliband, 2009). As Miliband (2009) notes, "It is these institutions in which 'state power' lies [...]" (p. 40). So, to speak about the state is to speak about a number of institutions through which state power unfolds and manifests in society.

Second, power in a capitalist state is not diffused and balanced. In general, the capitalist state is not subjected to competing pressures. State power is substantially deployed to advance and protect capitalist interests from dissent that aims to undermine the capitalist order – i.e., private property, free markets, profit making (Miliband, 2009). Generally, the government, the administration, the judicial branch, and all the bodies that comprise the state tend to be loyal in serving and protecting the capitalist order. As Miliband (2009) explains, this occurs mainly because in capitalist societies, national interests are inextricably linked to the strength of capitalist enterprises. By helping business, the state naturally sees itself as fulfilling its role in advancing the common good. The capitalist state is essentially committed to the owners and controllers of the means of production and thus partial with respect to class. It is a misconception that free markets and capitalist states are in opposition (Panitch, 2009). State power is crucial in spreading capitalist relations around its confines.

Third, people who take positions in the state tend to have a bias in favour of capital. This disposition against labour and in favour of capital is due to the social origin, education and class situation of those who enter the ranks of the capitalist state (Miliband, 2009). The servants of the capitalist state are usually drawn from business, property, and the professional middle classes (Miliband, 2009). The social composition of the capitalist state is overwhelmingly represented by those who believe in the validity and virtues of the capitalist system. Broadly, it is the capitalist outlook of people drawn from upper and middle classes that governs, administers, judges, and represents the masses in capitalist societies. Now, this does not mean a capitalist state is absolutely and completely shielded from different pressures and interests, particularly those coming from the ruling classes. As already discussed, wcs s appeared in part as a response to German judges' activism in favouring the working class. German judges were interpreting the 1871 Liability Act to protect the working class rather than business. Here, the judicial branch was not loyal in protecting the capitalist order. Some commentators explain this behaviour as an attempt to keep liberals in check. As Kleeberg (2003) suggests, the Revolution of 1848 taught conservative German judges that without the support of the working class, it is not possible to succeed in staging a revolution. The judges' activism can thus be interpreted as a sectional attempt to keep liberals from exerting excessive power and control in society. Nonetheless, as Miliband (2009) argues, the pluralist view that sees the state as the arena of competing interests is exaggerated. Although there do exist historical instances such as the one portrayed, these tend to be rare cases conditioned by particular historical events. The capitalist state tends to overwhelmingly favour capital. In this regard, the appearance of wcs s as a state-sponsored scheme for the distribution of damage compensation in accordance with business interests constitutes a historical case of how the sum of institutions that organically compose the capitalist state react when capitalist interests are at stake. Let us look at this subject more closely.

In the nineteenth century, the German state transitioned from a police state, or one that secures the public order by protecting the land and its people, to a state of law primarily concerned with the economic order. The Capitalist Industrial Revolution pushed the German state to identify welfare and economic growth as its main duty. During this time, free trade, the standardization of currency, private property, the expansion of markets, and technological innovations began to be major concerns for the German state (Eghigian, 2000). In addition, the series of reforms that ended with the granting of free movement in 1867 were aimed at fostering economic growth rather than securing peace. In fact, the police state came into great conflict with political reforms aimed at the mobility of propertyless peasants (Eghigian, 2000). In this struggle, the economy as the new concern of the state would have the last word. As Eghigian (2000) points out, "by 1880 the state of law had become a regulatory institution in its dealings with society and economy, concerned primarily with the formal conditions for economic competition and productivity" (p. 37). Here, we are in front of the historical transition of the feudal state to the capitalist state, one that actively promotes and advances the social relations of the capitalist mode of production (see Meiksins, 2002). State power began to be deployed to advance capitalist relations – e.g., private property, free markets, wage labour, profit, capital accumulation, money, etc.

It is under a capitalist state that the German WCS came into existence. The German government, under the leadership of Otto von Bismarck, introduced the Act of 1884 as a way to integrate wage labourers into society as well as to undermine socialism and trade unions (Eghigian, 2000; Hobbs, 1939; Moses, 2018). Rather than a social-justice reform perspective, Bismarck followed what Holdren (2020) calls an instrumental-reform perspective, that is, a reform that aims at social stability. The Act of 1884 was part of two complementary, interrelated insurance funds to deal with the so-called "Worker Question". This technical approach was an attempt to depoliticize the social dilemma. Securing the wage labour/capitalist relation was a major concern for the German government. Here, the concern is instrumental. The well-being of workers is important as far as it is instrumentally valuable to preserve the capitalist mode of production. Wage labourers' health has to be managed to allow the production of profit at an increasing rate.

In addition, state intervention was not designed to solve the problem of mass accidents but rather that of their cost and distribution among society. In this regard, the German government followed a business-protection perspective. As Holdren (2020) explains, this perspective puts capitalists' interests in the forefront at the expense of wage labourers'. It enables the handling of work accidents as a business endeavour according to monetary matters. The German WCS appeared as a response to the high costs of the previous system – i.e., the liability system – as well as the proposal of expanding strict liability. It was proposed by a leading German mine owner and industrialist, Louis Baare, who feared that strict liability would be expanded, thus increasing costs to industry (Kleeberg, 2003; Moses, 2018). Miners and industrialists were meddling in state affairs from the beginning in order to protect their sectional interests. Wherever the state intervenes, businessmen will be ready to influence the nature of the intervention (Miliband, 2009). The capitalist class needs the power of the state not only to curb wages but to restrain compensation benefits into the limits suitable for making profit. In the end, Bismarck adopted Baare's proposal. Thus, rather than a social-justice reform perspective based on safety laws, tax reform, collective bargaining and prevention, the solution imposed by the government in line with capitalist interests was limited to damage compensation. Instead of introducing legislation to forcefully and effectively limit or inspect the revolutionized forces of production, state intervention took place at the level of physical damages and loss of wages. This was, above all, an instrumental and business-protection oriented decision. State power effectively shielded the revolutionized forces of production – i.e., productivity – from its destructive impact on the relations of production – i.e., in this case wage labour. Although there was agreement across every sector that capitalism was the chief cause of industrial accidents, the capitalist state opted for defending the capitalist economy rather than the life and wellbeing of wage labourers.

The collective character of the German government's intervention is worth noting. The German WCS was not designed to insure individual capitalists, but the capitalist class as a whole. Losses were spread among firms of the same risk class within a branch of industry. As Miliband (2009) argues, the capitalist bias of the capitalist state has immense policy implications, since the solution to many social problems requires governments to act sometime in opposition to individual capitalists. The collective quality of the 1884 Act should not be seen as damaging capitalist interests, but rather as the historical support needed from the capitalist state to allow firms to preserve their private character and keep wage labourers at their disposal. As Miliband (2009) explains, "The state must [...] engage in bastard forms of socialisation and assume responsibility for many functions and services which are beyond the scope and capabilities of capitalist interests" (p. 57). The socialisation of compensation payments can be seen as the ransom to be paid by the capitalist class for their inalienable right to exploit wage labourers without regard for their health and wellbeing. As has been shown, the German government was not subjected to different class interests. Capitalist interests were effectively safeguarded against the challenge of repercussions due to mass accidents. Bismarck's government proved to be loyal to the capitalist economy.

The other institution of the German capitalist state that played a major role was the administration. It was through bureaucracy that compensating work injuries was set apart from a juridical order and placed into an administrative one. It is interesting to note that the judicial branch, which was displaying clear signs of rebelliousness against capital, was replaced by a normative system. The judiciary system was a clear loser in terms of decision making regarding the allocation of compensation payments and benefits. In fact, a key and innovative element of the new system was its non-fault trait. A non-fault compensation system excluded the question of fault central to the judicial branch. Medical and wage-replacement benefits were to be awarded whether an injury met the conditions to be insured. The compensation problem was reduced to a contractual solution. As Eghigian (2000) correctly contends, the state's approach was an attempt to transform a social problem into an administrative matter. To do so, the state erected the Imperial Insurance Office as the chief legislative and executive body in insurance matters. One of the main legislation efforts of the Insurance Office was to precisely define the difference between compensable and non-compensable injuries. It was the bureaucracy that was in charge of determining what injuries were the result of a work accident and thus compensable. It was bureaucracy that was in charge of setting the professional parameters to convincingly explain an injury as the result of a work accident. In addition, this office was responsible for defining health in terms of the body's ability to function and its productive capacity, thus linking awarding wage-replacement benefits on the basis of a wage labourer's incapacity to work. In 1887, the Insurance Office indicated that disability was a relationship between injury, the individual, and work, and that the body was to be measured in how well the wage labourer could exploit his/her working potential monetarily (Eghigian, 2000). This was key to operationalizing health in terms of an economy of time and money and establishing entitlement parameters. Also, the office mandated insurance boards to invest in non-speculative assets such as mortgages, bank deposits, and real estate, and to allocate not less than one-quarter of its reserves in government bonds (Eghigian, 2000). Now, beside its executive and legislative role, the Insurance Office exercised judicial functions and was the highest judicial authority in insurance matters (Eghigian, 2000). It was composed of bureaucrats and representatives of employers and insurance boards (neither workers' representatives nor trade unions were represented) who arbitrated on coverage, compensations, pensions, etc. The office served as the final instance of appeal in insurance affairs. By 1912, before the office there were 42,795 appealable accident cases; 424,855 appealable accident pension decisions; and 192,379 appealable invalid pension decisions (Eghigian, 2000). In sum, the role of the Imperial Insurance Office in WCS issues was overwhelmingly significant to protecting capital. This is due to the fact that at the level of policy making, the administration is always political (Miliband, 2009). However, because of the type of involvement, the political aspect of bureaucracy takes a more subtle and nuanced form. By applying professional and technical criteria, contentious issues are depoliticized and judged in favour of business. This was the case with the professional and technical criteria used by the office for deeming work injuries compensable or non-compensable, establishing positivist parameters to prove an injury to be work related, defining disability in economic terms, linking wage-replacement compensations to wages and the capacity of work, etc. As Miliband (2009) contends, the administration may be independent from the government, "[...] but their members are not independent of ideological and political dispositions which make of the regulatory process more of a help than a hindrance to the interests regulated" (p. 92). Thus, although top civil servants of the Imperial Insurance Office did not rely on the government of the day, their decisions proved to be dependent on influences such as class origin, education, class situation, and professional tendency. High-ranking civil servants are likely to play a conservative role and thus administer state matters in favour of capital due to their class origin and professional bias (Miliband, 2009). The top civil servants of the Imperial Insurance Office showed themselves to be allies of existing economic and political elites. Bureaucracy, as part of state power, ensured that the WCS would work in affinity with the needs of capital. As Miliband (2009) states, bureaucracy is a crucial element in the maintenance and defence of the structure of power and privilege inherent in capitalist societies.

Overall, the relevance of the capitalist state to the WCS's injury information-producing operations can be summed up in relation to two distinct spheres: class purpose and class functioning. Following an instrumental and business approach, government power sets the recording and processing of wage-labour-related injuries to the class purpose of damage compensation. Injury rates' main task is directed to the construction of risk classes, experience ratings, establishing premiums, and, in general, the rationalization of costs to collectively insure the capitalist class as a whole against work injuries. In regard to class functioning, bureaucracy plays a legislative role in reifying injury rates as money and limiting its functioning to a set of official class definitions. State legislation on matters such as compensable and non-compensable injuries, establishing proof parameters, defining health in terms of productive capacity, and setting wage-replacement on the basis of working potential, is nothing more than the perspective of those drawn from superior classes who believe in the virtues and values of the capitalist mode of production. Bureaucracy in capitalist societies is simply a sophisticated expression of class interests. Thus, the injury information-producing operations in capitalist societies is essentially state power, both as the manifestation of government as well as the administration and its civil servants.

CHAPTER 3

Insurance Boards

The Landlords of the Circuit of Metamorphosis of Lost Labour Power

1   Introduction

This chapter addresses the main operative unit of WCS s, the insurance boards, state-owned (i.e., public) or state-sponsored (i.e., private) agencies that administer the compensation insurance fund to allocate costs and deliver medical and wage-replacement benefits to injured workers. It describes the functioning of insurance boards in present-day German-based WCS s. Following Mosco's (2009) ontological approach to analyze institutions as social processes, insurance boards are examined in terms of their economic process of exchange, which revolves around information. This vantage point does not avoid important distinctions among ownership matters – i.e., public/private – but rather emphasizes insurance boards' information-producing operations of recording and processing work injuries to distribute compensation costs and compensation benefits. It sets up a particular perspective for understanding insurance boards, one that establishes information as a priority and enables the understanding of insurance boards within a level of generality that brings into focus the relations of the capitalist mode of production. Since state-owned and state-sponsored insurance boards process injury information under the principles of exchange value to spread damage compensation under free market conditions, this vantage point lays bare the capitalist relations that condition both public and private insurance boards in their functioning under capitalism. As Garnham (2014) argues, extreme simplification in issues of ownership must be set aside when analyzing the operation of public and private informational industries.

The examination that follows analyzes insurance boards as information-producing agencies. Following Machlup (1962), insurance boards are conceptualized as information-intensive companies that are part of the information industry. This chapter examines insurance boards in terms of their information-producing operations of recording and processing work injuries in order to: (a) construct risk as a medium of measurement and a medium of exchange of expected lost labour power, (b) organize and classify firms in a branch of industry according to their contribution to the total mass of expected lost labour power, and (c) set the price of the guarantee against expected lost labour power. Drawing from a level of generality that brings into focus a set of interdependent capitalist relations that together form part of what insurance boards are and how they function, insurance boards are reconceptualized in their broader role in capitalist economies, namely, as the landlords of the circuit of metamorphosis of lost labour power. Through an information-intensive process, insurance boards transform the total mass of lost value produced in capitalist economies into money value, investment value, medical value, and wage-replacement value. The circuit of metamorphosis brings to light how lost labour power is converted by insurance boards into different forms thus disclosing how different elements become forms of one another. This perspective comprises a triad that links insurance boards, capitalists and wage labourers in a set of conflicting relations, ones that involve contestation over the transformation and value of lost labour power. Rather than complementary interests, the circuit of metamorphosis of lost labour power brings together conflicting interests that periodically erupt in the form of class struggle. Finally, insurance boards are presented as the informational landlords of lost labour power, monopolies whose revenue is linked to their exclusive control in the information-producing operations of recording and processing work injuries at every type of workplace. Rather than producing fresh value and realizing revenue through the exploitation of their own workforce, insurance boards appropriate value from individual firms through the selling of a guarantee against expected lost labour power. The circuit of metamorphosis of lost labour power involves unproductive labour, through which insurance boards appropriate value in the form of ground-rent from individual firms without directly producing it.

2 Insurance Boards as Part of the Information Sector

In the book *The Production and Distribution of Knowledge in the United States*, Fritz Machlup (1962) explores in detail industries whose main product is knowledge. Machlup identifies five major industries: (a) education, (b) research and development, (c) the media (ranging from books, films, radio, postal systems, etc.), (d) information machines, and (e) information services (financial and other business information services). Among the fifth industry, information services, Machlup identifies insurance companies (including insurance boards) as information enterprises. As part of the information industry, Machlup (1962) defines insurance boards as agencies whose main activity is the recording and processing of information to distribute risk. Insurance boards essentially offer risk pooling, and the information processing and transmission that goes with them cannot be divorced in practice (Machlup, 1962). As Mirowski and Nik-Khah (2017) acknowledge, Machlup has the merit of being one of the first economists to conceptualize information as a commodity, to map the information-producing sector, and to emphasize its relevance within the national economy. In addition, Machlup has the merit of conceptualizing information as the key commodity of insurance companies, thus theoretically identifying these risk-pooling agencies as part of the information sector.

This conceptualization has been followed by communication scholars such as Castells (1996) and Schiller (2007), both of whom also include insurance companies among the information sector. Despite this recognition, insurance boards have not been thoroughly analyzed in terms of their information-intensive process of exchange. In general, this sector has been narrowly understood as part of the service industry and viewed merely as institutions that trade medical treatment, prevention services and financial benefits. Yet while the abovementioned services are provided by insurance boards, they are not directly traded or exchanged for money. Client companies do not pay an amount of money in exchange for medical treatment, prevention services and financial benefits. The economic process of exchange, this book argues, takes place at the level of information-producing operations. The disbursement of both compensation payments and compensation benefits is mediated by information-producing operations. It is thus indispensable to examine insurance boards in terms of their economic process of exchange and their business relationship.

2.1   *Risk as Expected Lost Labour Power*

As identified by Machlup (1962), insurance boards' main activity is the spreading of economic loss through information-intensive risk assessment. Insurance boards informationally construct risk to spread compensation payments among firms. To do so, risk must be operationalized; that is, the manner in which it is quantified and measured has to be clearly established. Without a set of operational rules, risk can neither be measured nor constructed as a tool to spread economic loss. But, prior to the construction of risk the notion of risk has to be examined. What is risk? How do insurance boards understand risk? These questions cannot be answered by looking at that which is common to people as part of human society. That would be idealist and historically inadequate. The answers must be found by looking at what is peculiar to people and societies due to their functioning under capitalism and specifically by examining that which is specific to people during the capitalist labour process. In the lines that follow, I provide a succinct historical materialist view of risk based on the preconditions already expounded in Chapter 2. This analysis conveys crucial aspects of risk that are relevant to the understanding of today's insurance boards' informational process of spreading risk.

Risk as a social reality does not exist unless it is brought into being through the power of human abstraction and conceptualization. It cannot be found as a natural and immutable reality such as a wild animal, an earthquake or a lethal virus. These phenomena, of course, can be signified as risks to people's wellbeing, but first they must be conceptualized as such by the human mind. Risk is a social construct produced by people; however, it is produced by people under a set of social arrangements and conditioned by a definite development of productive forces. As something plastic, risk is shaped by historical, economic, political and social factors. As a social construct, it cannot be divorced from the material conditions already in place.

In capitalist societies, where workers produce commodities for a capitalist in exchange for a wage, risks to workers take the form of a wage-labour-related event or condition that can potentially damage labour power. Contrary to pre-capitalist societies, where labour risk assumes the form of something directly detrimental to peasants' health, labour risk under capitalism assumes the form of that which is detrimental to the exchange between wage labourers and capitalists: labour power. What distinguishes capitalist risk from pre-capitalist risk is its dependence on a labouring process with respect to a mode of production. Under a system of production for direct consumption, labour risks appear as the probability of damage to direct producers – e.g., peasants, artisans, independent workers. Under a system of production for exchange, labour risks appear as the probability of damage to labour power. Under capitalism, labour risk is not about the indeterminate and general destruction of labour but the determinate and historical destruction of labour power, the only thing owned by the propertyless wage labourers. Lost labour power – i.e., the temporary, permanent partial or total destruction of labour power during the labouring process – is the very object of risk assessment in capitalist societies. Risk is nothing but expected lost labour power. This act of reestablishing an absent concept might be viewed as negligible, but it has considerable theoretical consequences: in fact it is key to the understanding of how insurance boards construct and spread risk among their client firms. 'Lost labour power' is not only a concept but a theoretical concept, one which is representative of a theoretical system that brings into being a new object. Lost labour power, as a new object of knowledge, directly affects the understanding of risk spreading. It's importance relies on its capacity to shed light on an information-intensive mode of compensation the main goal of which is to exchange and distribute the economic costs of workplace injuries among different classes. Let us look at this in more detail.

The transformation of risk into expected lost labour power is peculiar to capitalist societies and the formulation of labour power within them. The concept of labour power, central to Marx's analysis, comes from Hermann von Helmholtz's laws of thermodynamics in 1847 (Foster and Burkett, 2008). Based on Helmholtz's law, Marx applied the law on the conservation of energy to the labouring process. He explained the wear and tear of wage labourers in terms of the inevitable and gradual decline of human energy. Similar to machine power, human labour power inevitably declines. As Moses (2018) points out, Marx's conception of labour power not only had tremendous significance for understanding work accidents – i.e., as part of the process of work – but to indemnify injured workers regardless of fault. Under this energetic formulation, fatigue rather than recklessness could be blamed for an accident or fatality (Moses, 2018). Rather than human agency or misfortune, the causes of work injuries became to be seen as emanating from the labouring process. As a finite resource, labour power could be drained thus leading to what this book defines as lost labour power. Therefore, in capitalist societies, risk takes the form of a measurement of expected lost labour power; that is, the expected destruction of wage labourers' capacity to work for a capitalist in exchange for a wage.

The emergence of risk as expected lost labour power is historically conditioned by two moments: (a) the build-up of the wear and tear of labour power under the capitalist industrial revolution and (b) the historical struggle for compensating for the deterioration of labour power that began in 1871 with the German Liability System (see Chapter 2). Risk as expected lost labour power appears together with damage compensation once society forces capitalists to take some responsibility for a labour process whose goal is production for exchange rather than direct consumption. In this regard, damage compensation as a social relation involves the separation of workers from the means of subsistence, the establishment of private property, the rise of the capitalist class, and the development of a market exchange economy. Why would workers be awarded damage compensation if they were producing for direct consumption rather than for exchange? Why would workers be indemnified for something else other than the labour power they have voluntarily sold?

Compensating lost labour power is rooted in the wear and tear of labour power during the production of commodities to be sold in the market; that is, production for exchange under the control of the capitalist class. It appears when the labour process is transformed to an activity aimed at the production of exchange values through the buying and selling of labour power as a commodity, when "[...] the labour process is nothing more than the consumption of the commodity purchased, i.e. of labour-power [...]" (Marx, 1990, p. 292). Thus, compensating lost labour power comes into existence when (a) the worker is the free proprietor of his own labour power, (b) the labour power takes on the form of a commodity, and (c) the owner of the means of production finds labour power available on the market. Only when the conditions for the sale, purchase, consumption and destruction of labour power have been socially met, compensation for lost labour power is ready to emerge.

The unity between compensation and labour power, which brings into focus the specific relations of the capitalist mode of production, is not only key to understanding the notion of risk but its informational construction and monetization. Risk under capitalism is not just a concept but an instrumental and fully functioning category. It is both an informational medium of measurement of lost labour power and an informational medium of monetization of lost labour power – i.e., the money value needed to compensate lost labour power. The purpose of constructing risk as a measure and monetization of expected lost labour power is simply to compensate the lost value of labour power and disperse its costs among the many capitalists in the form of money. Now, it is important to note that compensation excludes punitive and nominal damages. Only compensatory damages – i.e., damages awarded in respect of the actual losses suffered by an injured worker – are granted. Also, compensation is not directed to wage labourers' direct consumption – i.e., the medical and financial resources to fulfill wage labourers' needs – but to wage labourers' productive consumption – i.e., the medical and financial resources within the limits of what is absolutely necessary to keep labour power in motion. Productive consumption and direct consumption are totally different. As Marx (1990) explains, "In the former [productive consumption], he [the wage labourer] acts as the motive power of capital, and belongs to the capitalist. In the latter [direct consumption], he [the wage labourer] belongs to himself, and performs his necessary vital functions outside the production process" (Marx, p. 717). Compensation is therefore simply the replacement of the lost value of labour power. It takes the forms of (a) medical expenses – i.e., the value of the means of repair and recovery of labour power – and (b) wage-loss replacement – i.e., the value of the necessary means of maintenance to keep labour power alive during the days of disability.

As seen, the replacement of the lost value of labour power involves exclusively pecuniary damages or the financial costs of a work injury, that is, medical expenses and loss wages. Non-pecuniary damages – e.g., emotional distress, loss of quality of life, impaired appearance, loss of marriageability, aspirational losses – are not included in the value to be replaced. This decision can be historically traced back to the first liability system implemented in a capitalist economy. Early in 1857, when the liability system in Germany was established, the Supreme Court ruled that damage compensation for a given wage-labour-related accident would extend only to medical expenses and loss wages (Kleeberg, 2003). From the beginning, there was a clear aim to limit compensation exclusively to the lost value of labour power. Now, since the value of labour power in capitalist societies appears as the price, that is to say, wages (Marx, 1990), courts used the price of labour power or the wages an injured worker had been receiving at the time of the accident in order to rule the amount to be awarded. This put the value of compensation under the authority of the labour market. Lost labour power in the form of wage-replacement is in all respects established by the market. The same happens with medical expenses. The value to cover medical costs is also determined by the average price of medical resources available in society. Thus, it can be properly said that the total value of lost labour power is nothing but a market value, the sum of the prices of medical services and wages. It is also a value eventually shaped by class considerations, where high paying jobs are better compensated for the same injury than low paying jobs. Valuing persons' bodies and lives according to their wages is a key element for insurance boards to price and realize risk premiums.

With the rise of WCS s in Germany in 1884, the understanding of compensation as the market value equivalent to the lost value of labour power was reinforced. In 1887, the German Insurance Office indicated that compensation should be paid on the basis of a wage labourer's incapacity to work (Eghigian, 2000). Rather than an amount based on need, compensation would be disbursed to the extent a work injury constrained workers' ability to earn their usual wages. This policy forced German insurance boards to construct and monetize risk in terms of an economy of time and money and to establish differential compensation parameters. The labour market was giving primacy as the main architect of compensation payments and benefits. However, this did not mean the lost value of labour power would be fully compensated by insurance boards at their market value. In fact, disability payments were never enough to keep wage labourers alive for more than a few years (see Gerstenberger, 1985). This only meant that lost labour power, as a market value, would be used as the basic unit to construct risk levels to spread the payment of compensation benefits across firms. Mainly, this decision imposed market limits and pressures. From the beginning, insurance boards intended to limit the payment of compensation benefits to a strict measure of the lost value of labour power in market value terms.

Risk as a measure and monetization of lost labour power did not change under the administration of WCS s and insurance boards. However, what did profoundly change was the manner of measuring, monetizing and awarding compensation payments and benefits. Rather than a juridical order based on a liability system and the common law defense, where judges awarded compensation benefits and costs according to their own assessment of the lost market value of labour power, insurance boards' information systems provided a business solution to the measurement, monetization and disbursement of compensation benefits (see Chapter 2). Lost labour power became commodified through the capitalist logic of property exchanges. In the form of an insurance guarantee, risk or lost labour power was set to be exchanged at a market value among insurance boards and individual capitalists. On the one side, insurance boards produce expected lost labour power as an insurance guarantee and sell it to individual capitalists. On the other, capitalists buy expected lost labour power in the form of a guarantee to shield themselves against disputes in courts and the direct costs of compensating injured workers. Instead of constructing risk in terms of an absolute principle, risk was informationally constructed in relation to the total mass of expected lost labour power in a branch of industry. Insurance boards began to systematically record information on wage-labour-related accidents and subsequently to process it based on the science of statistics and probability. These information-intensive operations enabled insurance boards to organize firms according to risk levels – i.e., levels of expected lost labour power – and differentially spread compensation payments among the capitalist class.

2.2   *Risk as Information*

Risk spreading or the distribution of expected lost labour power in relation to aggregates, is information dependent. Insurance boards spread risk or expected lost labour power among the capitalist class through the intensive manipulation of injury information at work. In this regard, Machlup (1962) correctly points out that risk pooling is a practice that cannot be divorced from information-producing operations. He acknowledges that risk is conditioned by the quantity and quality of the information recorded and processed. As Guinnane and Streb (2015) point out, from the beginning, the lack of long-term accident statistics was a problem facing insurance boards in their efforts to construct risk – i.e., expected lost labour power – and assign risk levels to firms. Insurance boards' databases are crucial to construct risk levels and spread payments among aggregates. However, what Machlup (1962) misses is that information in the insurance sector is constitutive of risk. It is not just that risk cannot be divorced from information-operations but that risk itself is nothing but wage-labour-related injury information. Risk as the expected lost value of labour power is an informational construct. As such, it can be simply described as statistically-processed injury information at work – e.g., working days lost, total wages, the permanent impairment rate, the fatality rate, the loss of earnings pension – produced to measure and monetize expected lost labour power in order to spread compensation payments and benefits. As a social reality, risk comes into being when injury information has been recorded and statistically processed for the purpose of exchange. It is insurance boards' material practice of recording and process-ing injury information that brings risk as lost labour power into existence. In this regard, in a subtle twist to Machlup's definition of the insurance sector, I propose the following: rather than it being companies whose main activity is the recording and processing of information to distribute risk, I reconcep-tualize insurance boards as the agencies whose main activity is the recording and processing of injury information at work to construct risk and spread the lost value of labour power at a market price. This reconceptualization is not innocuous. By naming insurance boards as the agencies that construct risk based on injury information, the function of producing risk is not only distin-guished and separated from the function of distributing risk, but it is assigned a primary position with respect to the latter. This is key because the produc-tion of risk governs the distribution and consumption of risk. The focus here is on the construction of risk, a move that puts information at the forefront. In addition, by conceptualizing insurance boards as agencies that spread lost labour power rather than simply risk, the historical subject of risk in capitalist societies – i.e., lost labour power – is put forward. Risk as an informational construct aims to measure, monetize and spread expected lost labour power at a fair or average price. This brings into light that: (a) risk is a particular unit of information constructed under a specific set of social, economic and insti-tutional arrangements – i.e., insurance boards; (b) risk comprises a particular type of injury information that enables it to function as a medium of mea-surement and exchange; (c) risk is an informational construct that measures and monetizes lost labour power; and (d) risk is an informational construct that enables the exchange of lost labour power in a business relationship at a market price.

2.2.1   Risk as Class Information

As has been argued thus far, risk is an informational construct, a particu-lar unit of information. However, it is a unit of information peculiar to the functioning of the labour process under the capitalist mode of production. First, risk as information has the character of what Bolaño (2015) dubs "class information". This is a type of information that is "[...] hierarchical and bureaucratic, compatible with the structure of power in the factory" (Bolaño 2015, p. 19). As a unit of class information, risk is hierarchically and bureaucratically produced by insurance boards' information-operations of recording wage-labour-related injuries, disabilities and fatalities and is processed based on principles of statistics and probability. This information ceases to be information produced between peers. Wage labourers have no participation in the construction of risk. It is the capitalist state – i.e., public insurance boards – or capitalist themselves – i.e., private insurance boards – who on behalf of the collective interest of the capitalist class engage in the construction of risk.

Second, as class information, risk acquires what Bolaño (2015) describes as a character in reference to the labour process peculiar to the capitalist mode of production. It is under the capitalist labour process that risk as a unit of information aims at the measurement and monetization of lost labour power for productive consumption. Here, the focus is on the replacement of the lost value of labour power due to a work accident or disease; that is, the necessary means of repair, recovery, and maintenance of labour power during the disability period. Risk is a unit of class information without which the spread of compensation payments among many capitalists is not conceivable. It functions according to the needs of capital accumulation, another trait that Bolaño (2015) identifies as part of class information. In this regard, risk's main purpose is to function as a medium of exchange or to spread the lost value of labour power at a market price. Risk under a collective liability system simply protects capitalists from the full cost of compensating lost labour power. Individual profits are shielded by socializing compensation payments (see Chapter 4).

Third, risk information is shaped by class considerations. As Moses (2018) points out, the construction of risk classes is guided by assumptions about class divisions. Based on the total expenditure among enterprises of the type in a branch of industry – e.g., construction, transportation, forestry – insurance boards come up with differential risk levels to construct risk classes or rating groups. In this regard, the fact that firms are required to share the financial burden within risk classes is a tacit assumption of the class structure of society, where some workers are exposed to higher hazards. By grouping enterprises of the type based on their expected lost labour power, risk information produces class divisions. In addition, by setting the rate of compensation in relation to the wage bill, namely, the market price of labour power, risk information reinforces class differences. As Holdren (2020) sarcastically puts it, managers with higher wages get more compensation for their broken bones during the same period of time than low paid workers. In sum, at the level of the labour process in a class divided society and in tandem with capitalist needs, risk as a unit of information unmistakably acquires the character of class information. As such, risk cannot conceal its traits of power and the domination of the working class by the capitalist class.

2.2.2   Risk as Lost-Time Injury Rates

As a unit of injury information, risk comprises a particular type of information, one that enables lost labour power to be measured and monetized for exchange purposes. Information on work injuries must be recorded and processed to serve a process of economic exchange. In this regard, many scholars describe risk levels as being constructed by recording and comparing the number of on-site accidents with the average number of accidents in a similar branch of industry (see Eghigian, 2000; Guinnane and Streb, 2015). This description is not accurate. Insurance boards do not process injury information that derives from accidents but from lost-time injury accidents. Injury information is only processed from those events that effectively render a loss on the value of labour power – accidents and diseases leading to temporary disability, permanent partial disability, permanent total disability, and, of course, death. Insurance boards aim to record lost-time injury information to construct risk levels and organize firms around risk groups for the purpose of exchange – i.e., to spread the cost of compensation payments. Let us delve into this matter more closely.

As the representation of expected lost labour power, risk extends only to the financial costs of a work injury – i.e., medical expenses and loss wages. Non-pecuniary damages and nonwage losses do not enter insurance boards' calculations for compensation. Out-of-pocket payments, time lost from leisure, time spent by others assisting the worker, and the loss of quality of life, which total between 1 to 1.5 times medical and wage-replacement benefits, are borne by the wage labourer and his family (Guzman et al., 2013). In this regard, risk is not just an equivalent to medical and wage-replacement benefits due to work injuries but chiefly due to lost-time injuries. This distinction is key to the understanding of how insurance boards allocate compensation payments and benefits. Let us remember that since the inception of wcs s, the presence, absence or degree of disability has been the central criterion for compensation (see Eghigian, 2000). In fact, wcs s' accident insurance was designed to work together with the Sickness Insurance fund (see Chapter 2). While the Sickness Insurance fund provided benefits from the fourth day of disability until the thirteenth week, the wcs s' insurance fund provided benefits beyond 13 weeks (see Hobbs, 1939). Today, insurance boards provide medical care from the first day of disability and wage-replacement benefits from the first to the fourth day of disability – depending on the waiting period – until the worker returns to work. The important fact to note is that wcs s were "[...] conceived primarily as an insurance against risks to employees' health and their ability to work" (Eghigian, 2000, p. 19). Insurance boards' key objective is to provide compensation for lost earnings to injured workers who cannot get back to work. These systems are procedurally designed to cover medical and wage-replacement benefits due to lost-time injuries, which are injuries that result in workers' inability to work.

Risk is not constructed to prevent the occurrence of work injuries, as is commonly assumed, but to exchange lost labour power resulting from work injuries with lost time. This misrecognition is born from an indeterminate and ahistorical conceptualization of risk, one that conceptualizes risk from a level of generality that excludes the specificities of the capitalist mode of production. The fact that lost-time injuries are used for prevention purposes does not alter the fact that this type of information is produced for exchange purposes rather than prevention purposes. In the mid-twentieth century, Heinrich (1950) noted this dilemma. He claimed that since insurance boards process only lost-time injury information rather than information about accidents with no injuries and time lost, there is a lack of significant and valuable data to prevent work accidents and diseases. "[...] thousands of accidents having the potentiality of producing serious injuries do not so result. [...] in prevention work, the importance of any individual accident lies in its potentiality of creating injury and not in the fact that it actually does, or does not, so result" (Heinrich, 1950, p. 25). Being aware of this, Heinrich (1950) proposed to record and process information at the level of the firm rather than relying on insurance boards in order to prevent work accidents and diseases from taking place. In this regard, Heinrich (1950) noted, "When lost-time or so called 'major' accidents only are selected for the study, as a basis for records and for guidance in prevention work, efforts are often misdirected, valuable data are ignored, and statistical exposure is unnecessarily limited" (p.25). The important thing to note here is not only that insurance boards construct risk on the basis of lost-time injuries but that under insurance boards, injury information at work takes the dominant form of lost-time injury information. Injury information appears as lost-time injury information due to the function of constructing risk for exchange rather than risk for prevention. It is the need to exchange lost labour power for money that conditions injury information to take the form of lost-time injury information. This brings into focus the dominant specific form it takes in capitalist societies, where insurance boards, as information-intensive agencies, construct risk to spread the expected lost value of labour power among the capitalist class. By referring to injury information as lost-time injury information, the social functions of health protection, disease prevention and health promotion are de-prioritized with respect to the function of exchanging and spreading lost labour power. Here, the labeling occurs from the vantage point of the type of information collected and its specific function: to construct risk for exchange.

As lost-time injury information, risk can be divided on the basis of insurance boards' main information-producing operations: record keeping and processing. Record keeping information is simply the type of information gathered through the reporting of injury claims. It comprises all the different pieces of information of a work-related injury, disease or fatality leading to temporary lost labour power, permanent partial lost labour power, or permanent total lost labour power. It includes (a) the name, age, sex and wage of injured workers, (b) the name of the company and economic activity, (c) the date and time of the event, (d) the type of event (injury, disease, death), (e) the type of injury, (f) the type of disease, (g) the participating agents, etc. Processed information is the information resulting from computing and combining the aforementioned different pieces of information. Based on particular processing rules, the processing moment changes both the form and content of record keeping information and comes up with an aggregate type of information: numbers and rates. Processed information includes (a) the number of injuries per branch of industry, (b) the number of diseases per branch of industry, (c) the number/average of working days lost, (d) the injury rate, (e) the fatality rate, (f) the disease rate, (g) the permanent impairment rate, (h) the wage rate, and (i) the loss of earnings pension.

Recorded and processed information are two different moments in time in the becoming of lost-time injury information, where record keeping operations precede processed operations in the production of quantitative units of information for the purpose of measurement and exchange. In this regard, processed information assumes supremacy due to its capacity to subsume recorded information and to function both as a medium of the measurement of risk – i.e., a measurement of expected lost labour power – and a medium of exchange – i.e., a medium to exchange expected lost labour power for money. Here, the purpose is to instrumentally come up with quantitative units of information, in this case, lost-time injury rates, to enable the measurement and exchange of lost labour power. Now, since the final product is nothing more than rates, risk as a particular unit of injury information can be simply conceptualized as lost-time injury rates. This is the definitive historical form that risk takes under the conditioning pressure of insurance boards in capitalist societies. As a unit of injury information, risk is a quantitative unit, lost-time injury rates, without which the exchange of expected lost labour power cannot be accomplished. This new labeling brings into focus the quantitative and instrumental form of risk.

2.2.3   Risk as an Informational Medium of Measurement and
           Monetization

Lost-time injury rates are processed by insurance boards to construct risk both
as a medium of measurement and as a medium of monetization. As a medium
of measurement, risk aims to measure the expected lost value of labour
power at a firm level, a subset of firms of the type, a branch of industry and all
branches of industry. As a medium of monetization, risk aims to measure the
lost value of labour power in the form of money; that is, the money value or
simply the cost of the necessary means of repair, recovery and maintenance to
keep injured workers alive during the days of disability. Now, risk as a medium
of measurement and monetization cannot be set apart due to the fact that they
are bound together. Risk is a measure of the lost value of labour power in terms
of money. It is constructed not just to measure the lost value of labour power
but to situate the lost value of labour power in relation to money. Money as
the universal equivalent of value plays an indissoluble role in the construction
of risk as a medium of measurement. It makes risk economically comparable between firms and branches of industry. As stated in the previous chapter,
money is a key precondition for insurance boards' process of constructing risk
as a medium of measurement. In this regard, risk is a unit of information that
measures the expected lost value of labour power as money value, a quantitative mathematical expression that represents the amount of money needed
to pay for the lost value of labour power due to work accidents, diseases, or
fatalities. For the purpose of simplification, the expression "medium of measurement" will signify both medium of measurement and medium of monetization. Henceforth, risk as a medium of measurement includes the function of
the medium of monetization.

   As a medium of measurement, risk works as what Mirowski and Nik-Khah
(2017) call a technology of inductive inference. As such, it allows a conclusion
to be reached on the riskiness – i.e., the magnitude of expected lost labour
power – of an enterprise, a group of enterprises, a branch of industry and all
branches of industry, based on evidence provided by particular instances –
i.e., record keeping on lost-time injury rates. It can be simply understood as
the sum of signals emitted by every workplace in the form of accidents, diseases and fatalities leading to temporary lost labour power, permanent partial
lost labour power, or total destruction of lost labour power. As a medium of
measurement, risk establishes levels in order to organize and classify enterprises according to expected lost labour power within a particular branch of
industry. Based on statistics and probability, insurance boards combine lost-
time injury rates from a branch of industry – e.g., construction, transportation,
forestry, mining – and come up with risk levels. These are numerical units of

information that estimate the differential cost of compensation based on each firm's expected contribution to the total mass of lost labour power in a branch of industry in a period of time. Based on risk levels – i.e., differential expected lost labour power – insurance boards construct risk classes or rating groups to classify, organize and assign firms. In simple words, enterprises are grouped among firms of the type based on their expected contribution and charged a group rate.

Insurance boards' group classification varies considerably among countries and jurisdictions. For example, while the insurance board of Ontario, Canada has approximately 200 rating groups classified into eight branches of industry (forest products, mining and related products, other primary industries, manufacturing, transportation and storage, retail and wholesale trades, government and related services, and other services) in exclusion of the construction sector, the insurance board of British Columbia, Canada, had 67 rating groups classified in all branches of industry including the construction sector (see Tompa et al., 2016). Different systems for rating group classification yield a high variance in the number of rating groups. Notwithstanding this variability, rating groups allow the burden of payments to be distributed more equitably across a branch of industry. High-risk rating groups exhibit higher lost labour power and compensation costs, while low-risk rating groups exhibit lower lost labour power and compensation costs. Divided into rating groups, firms are collectively held liable for the group contribution to the total mass of lost labour power in a branch of industry.

Although the majority of insurance boards organize a subset of firms based on differential risk levels, some insurance boards construct risk simply based on all the member firms of a branch of industry. Firms are simply assigned to their own branch of industry and measured in relation to the average mass of lost labour power in all branches of industry. This process renders a general risk rate per each branch of industry. Whether differential compensation payments based on expected differential lost labour power are constructed based on a subset of firms – i.e., a group rate – or all the member firms within a branch of industry – i.e., an industry rate –, it is important to note that risk is not an absolute measurement but a relative one. Risk as a relative measurement can only be constructed with information on all individual cases, be it the total mass of lost-time injury rates from a subset of firms within a branch of industry or the total mass of lost-time injury rates of all members within a branch of industry. Risk as a medium of measurement is above all a relative measure, one that is brought into existence by insurance boards' statistically information-intensive operations. Also, as a medium of measurement of lost labour power, risk allows the qualitative representation of lost labour power as a unit of the same thing, that is, simply as risk, and the quantitative representation of lost labour power as a magnitude of risk. Risk makes lost labour power mathematically and economically comparable to the aggregate, but in exclusion of its own peculiarities. Under risk, lost labour power assumes a magnitude of differential compensation payment based on the aggregate in disregard of the type of accident or disease. The economic magnitude of lost labour power of a firm due to cuts, falls, bruises, depression or dermatitis is rendered exactly the same. Workers' injuries are uniformly evaluated in terms of the lost productive potential or lost labour power. Placed in economic relation to the total mass of lost labour power in a branch of industry, risk makes lost labour power an expression of the aggregate. It is the economic equivalent of the aggregate – i.e., the economic equivalent of the total mass of lost labour power – that conditions the magnitude of risk as a medium of measurement. It is the aggregate that gives meaning and importance to risk as a medium of measurement.

In addition, risk as a medium of measurement is a probabilistic measurement. Firms are probabilistically gathered in a rating group of the type that reflects its expected contribution within a branch of industry. Risk as a probabilistic measurement aims to quantify the expected lost value of labour power based on historical lost labour power. From this perspective, risk can be understood as firms' historical claim cost performance or compensation payments. Lost-time injury rates of the present are combined and processed by insurance boards to come up with group rates that will be applied in the future. Thus, present risk levels never match the effective contribution to the total mass of lost labour power of the aggregate in a particular period of time. There is a temporal incongruity between risk levels and the magnitude of lost labour power that makes present risk levels not just an expression of the aggregate but of an historical aggregate.

Beside constructing risk as a medium of measurement to quantify each firm's expected contribution to the total mass of lost labour power in an aggregate, modern insurance boards construct risk as an individualized measure to quantify the deviation from the expected contribution to the aggregate. This measure, dubbed the experience rate, provides information on lost labour power at the firm level. It is constructed on the basis of the firm's lost-time injury rates in relation to the lost-time injury rates of the aggregate. This measure appears in the last decades of the 20th century in order to align payments more closely with the firm's own performance (Tompa et al., 2012a). It has become prevalent among many countries and jurisdictions, including Canada, the USA, Australia, and New Zealand (Mansfield et al., 2012). Although the design of this measure varies among insurance boards, most have common features. As a technology of inductive inference, and similar to group rates, it allows a conclusion to be reached on the riskiness – i.e., the mass of expected lost labour power – of a firm based on particular instances – i.e., record keeping lost-time injury information – when compared to the total mass of lost labour power in an aggregate. The purpose of the experience rating is to measure the proportion of the deviation of an individual firm from the expected contribution to the total mass of lost labour power in an aggregate. The experience rate is a measure of lost labour power that reflects the firm's deflection to the expected cost of compensation based on quantifying the production of lost labour power at the firm level. Essentially, it identifies the firm's performance relative to the aggregate. The magnitude of the deflection is sometimes described as the degree of experience rating; a higher degree of experience rating implies a higher degree of firm-level responsibility for its own costs (Tompa et al., 2013). If the assessment is done at the beginning of a period (prospectively) the measure will render an expected deviation of lost labour power and thus compensation costs in the form of premiums or discounts. In this case, the firm's historical lost-time injury rates are key to establishing the experience rating, which takes the form of an economic estimate of the deviation, a probability. If the assessment is done at the end of a period (retrospectively) it will render the actual deviation of lost labour power and compensation costs, which will take the form of rebates and surcharges. In addition, within each rating group there is a rating factor applied to every firm. Usually, larger firms are assigned a higher rating factor. In general, the formula for the experience rating is simple and usually looks like the following. For prospective programs: premium/discount = (historical costs at the firm level – expected contribution to the aggregate) x rating factor. For retrospective programs: rebate/surcharge = (costs during the year at the firm level – expected contribution to the aggregate) x rating factor (see Tompa et al., 2013). In both cases, positive values are premiums and surcharges respectively and negative values are discounts and rebates respectively (Tompa et al., 2013). Usually, there are cost caps at the individual level and other mechanisms – e.g., cost relief, cost adjustment period, total claim levels – that prevent firms from being charged 100% of the total lost value of labour-power produced at their level (personal communication with E. Tompa, October 9, 2018).

In sum, as a medium of measurement, risk can be conceptualized as two distinctive measures of lost labour power: normative and deviate. It is a normative medium of measurement – i.e., group rate – when constructed to quantify each firm's expected economic contribution to the total mass of lost labour power produced in an aggregate. It is a deviate medium of measurement – i.e., experience rate – when constructed to quantify every firm's departure from the expected contribution to the total mass of lost labour power in an aggregate.

Although their function is different, risk as a normative and deviate measure is (a) a mathematical and monetized representation relative to the total mass of lost labour power in an aggregate, and (b) the product of lost-time injury rates in an aggregate. Risk is a collective measure relative to all the individual cases in an aggregate, whether it is used to set the standard contribution to the aggregate – i.e., group rate – or the deviation from the aggregate – i.e., experience rate. As a unit, risk as a medium of measurement can be summed up as the firm's contribution to and deviation from the total mass of expected lost labour power in an aggregate. As a unit that expresses both a normative and deviate value, risk includes the total mass of lost-time injury rates in an aggregate; that is, the total mass of information of wage-labour-related accidents, diseases and fatalities leading to temporary lost labour power, permanent partial lost labour power, or permanent total lost labour power. Without insurance boards' statistically information-intensive operations, risk as the measure of normative and deviate lost labour power does not exist because risk in any of its forms – e.g., risk level, group rate, experience rate – comprises the processing of the total mass of lost-time injury rates.

2.2.4   Risk as an Informational Medium of Exchange

As a unit of class information peculiar to the capitalist mode of production, risk's main purpose is to function as a medium of exchange rather than solely as a medium of measurement. This does not eliminate risk's function as a medium of measurement since for something to be exchanged it first has to be measured. This, however, makes the function of measurement secondary to the function of exchange. Risk functions as a medium of measurement in order to function at a later stage as a medium of exchange. Exchange is the dominant function; exchange subsumes measurement. Here, the totality – i.e., the historically capitalist mode of production – conditions and expresses itself through risk. Risk as a medium of exchange is not something common to any society but is peculiar to capitalist societies where a system of production for exchange is in place. Risk for exchange is consonant with the mode of production where it operates. Insurance boards construct risk as a medium of exchange to draw money from firms to reconvert that money into medical and wage-replacement benefits – i.e., the value of the necessary means of repair, recovery and maintenance of labour power during the disability period. As an informational medium of exchange, risk aims to exchange the lost value of labour power for money, the universal equivalent.

As a medium of exchange, risk is constructed by transforming the measure of risk – i.e., the firm's contribution to and deviation from the total mass of expected lost labour power in an aggregate – into a mathematical representation that enables the exchange in the form of money. To trans-form these measures into a medium of exchange, insurance boards calculate these figures in relation to the total wages of members' firms in an aggregate. Although the construction of risk as a medium of exchange varies among insurance boards, most share a wage-relation formula based on the transfor-mation of normative and deviate lost labour power into a percentage of the wage bill. The basic steps to arrive to a wage-relation formula can be described as follows. First, the amount of normative lost labour power to be exchanged in the form of money is set by (a) summing the total mass of the lost value of labour power in an aggregate, (b) dividing it by all the wages of the member firms in an aggregate, and (c) multiplying the number by a risk factor – i.e., risk level – that expresses the relative share of an individual firm to the aggre-gate. This yields a percentage of the wage bill that represents the individual firm's expected contribution to the aggregate. If the percentage is, for example, 1.6%, it means an individual firm will pay a rate of 1.6% of its total wages as its contribution to the lost value of labour power in an aggregate. Second, the amount of deviate lost labour power to be exchanged in the form of money is set by (a) summing the total mass of the lost value of labour power at the firm level, (b) calculating its deviation from the firm's expected contribution to an aggregate, (c) multiplying the number by a rating factor, and (d) dividing the number by all the wages at the firm level. This yields a percentage of the wage bill that represents the firm's deviation from its expected contribution to the aggregate. If the percentage is, for example, 0.2%, it means an individual firm will pay an additional rate of 0.2% of its total wages to compensate its posi-tive deviation from the expected contribution to the total mass of lost labour power in an aggregate. Now, let us remember that there are caps and other mechanisms used to control the reduction or increase costs of the deviation from the aggregate. Firms' contribution is usually kept within the aggregate, and the proportion of the deflection shall never put at risk the viability of a particular firm. However, as Tompa et al. (2012) point out, the adjustment of the contribution at the firm level reduces the pooling of the economic bur-den. Third, once the normative and deviate measures are transformed into percentages of a firm's wage bill, both percentages are summed to come up with the rate of compensation or risk as a medium of exchange. The rate of compensation – i.e., risk as a medium of exchange – is just a wage expression of a firm's contribution to and deviation from the total mass of expected lost labour power in an aggregate. So, if the expected contribution yields a rate of 1.6% and the deviation from the expected contribution yields a rate of 0.2%, the individual firm will pay a total rate of compensation of 1.8% of the wage bill in a given period.

As an informational medium of exchange, risk is not just a wage-relation formula that facilitates the exchange of expected lost labour power among insurance boards and capitalists. It is also a statement of principles, a moral rule. On the one hand, it implies that no one has been wrong or unjust; on the other, risk suggests that it is right to exchange workers' suffering due to injuries, diseases, disabilities and fatalities for money. As Barnetson (2010) correctly claims, this approach assumes that the major consequence of injuries is economic rather than human. As a medium of exchange value, risk rationalizes and normalizes the consequences of a work accident and disease in economic terms. Consonant with the capitalist mode of production, which has the ability to transform everything into exchange values (see Marx, 1990), risk as a medium of exchange enables the conversion of lost labour power into a percentage of the wage bill for exchange purposes. The exchange function of risk discloses its main attribute, its essence. Insurance boards' construction of risk does not emphasize the question of wage labourers' health and safety; rather it puts the question of firms' economic exposure at center stage. They impose the moral norm that wage labourers' health is a game of economic trade-offs like any other. Risk in capitalist societies turns workers' health and safety into a process of exchange.

Once risk appears as a medium of exchange, that is, as the rate of compensation, the exchange of the lost value of labour power for money can take place. The process of exchange is not a collective but an individual process. It is between an insurance board and an individual firm. Although the construction of risk as a medium of exchange is a collective process, since it involves the total mass of lost-time injury information of an aggregate including the total wages, the process of exchange is always an activity that pertains only to the insurance board and a capitalist. This process of exchange takes place as the selling of a guarantee against expected lost labour power. The guarantee acts as financial protection against the costs of compensating for injured workers' lost labour power. This contractual solution allows capitalists to ruin labour power without the inconvenience of going to court. The insurance boards' guarantee keeps costly and lengthy disputes out of courts. As already explained in Chapter 2, rather than exchanging lost labour power based on the common law defense, where judges arbitrarily assess the lost value of labour power, insurance boards provide an informational system based on statistical principles of normativity to exchange expected lost labour power. This guarantee against the expected lost value of labour power is sold at a value that represents the relative share of an individual firm to the total mass of lost value of labour power in an aggregate.

The price of the guarantee, the informational representation of the money value to be paid by an individual capitalist for a contract of insurance, is called the premium. The premium represents the money value of the guarantee, the money expression of the compensation rate without which it is not possible to know the exact money value to be exchanged. The premium is a category, a mental relation, that discloses the exact money value represented by the compensation rate. No existing physical money in any quantity is needed for the premium to exist as a representation. If the total wages of a firm are equal to $100,000,000 and the compensation rate is equal 1.8%, the monthly premium to be paid by a firm would be equal to $1,800,000. It is under the premium as a mental relation that the money value of lost labour power – i.e., price – is finally brought into light. While the compensation rate is a representation of lost labour power in the form of wages, the premium is a representation of lost labour power in the form of money. In the same way, while the compensation rate is a representation of the guarantee in the form of wages, the premium is a representation of the guarantee in the form of money. Money as the universal equivalent, as the universal measure of value, becomes the main denomination of risk.

The premium reifies lost labour power in terms of money. The lost value of labour power is converted into physical money as an exchange value, enabling firms to pay in physical money an equivalent of their contribution to and deviation from the total mass of expected lost labour power in an aggregate. Lost labour power is successfully converted into money due to insurance boards' information-intensive construction of risk as a medium of exchange. Just as lost labour power is money, money is lost labour power. Now, although the conversion of lost labour power into money is performed at its value, its distribution among individual capitalists does not match their effective production of lost labour power. This is a system that exchanges lost labour power at its value but spreads it disproportionately among firms, that is, uneven to the effective amount produced by an individual capitalist. It imposes upon the capitalist class the obligation of sharing the burden of lost labour power. The premium to be paid by an individual capitalist could be either too large or too small in relation to the concrete lost labour power produced at his own firm. By design, the system implies a disparity between premiums and the mass of lost labour power produced at the firm level. This occurs mainly due to the collective character of the construction of risk as a medium of exchange. Let us have a look at this in detail.

As a medium of exchange, risk is the result of transforming every firm's contribution to and deviation from the mass of expected lost labour power into a percentage of its wage bill, but in relation to the total mass of expected lost labour power and the total wages in an aggregate. The rate of compensation and its price – i.e., the premium – is always collective, relative to an aggregate, in disproportion to the performance of an individual firm. In this regard, there are three ways through which the rate of compensation and its price is equalized among all the firms, thus enabling the disproportionate distribution of lost labour power in money value. First, by constructing the rate of compensation on the basis of the share to the total mass of lost labour power in an aggregate, every individual firm is fastened to the outcome of the aggregate. Second, by adjusting the rate of compensation to the degree of departure from the contribution to the mass of lost labour power in an aggregate, the individual firm is economically discouraged to divert itself from an aggregate. Here, the deviation of the firm is controlled by the standard itself. And third, via multiple mechanisms that act as cost caps and cost relief that keep the deviation of the individual firm at bay. No matter the amount of concrete deviation of lost labour power produced at the firm level, it will never be reflected in the rate of compensation and the premium. This triple tendency towards the equalization of the rate of compensation in relation to an aggregate allows the disproportionate distribution of the lost value of labour power among capitalists. Independently of the amount of lost labour power produced at the firm level, the rate of compensation does not confront the individual firm as the costs of compensating the lost value of labour power effectively produced during their own labour process. Capitalists are collectively liable rather than individually liable by a rate of compensation that equalizes the distribution of the lost value of labour power. The conversion of lost labour power into money at its value and its disproportionate distribution among the many capitalists is one of the main feature of wcss' insurance boards. This trick can only be done through an information-intensive process operating behind the scenes, one that equalizes the rate of compensations among the flux and reflux of lost labour power in different branches of industries and rating groups. Insurance boards' information-intensive operations do not function only as a way of constructing risk as a medium of exchange in order to exchange lost labour power in the form of money at its value. Insurance boards' information process functions as well as an equalization process, one that erases individual differences among firms and disproportionately spreads the lost value of labour power across the capitalist class. This is the collective character of risk as a medium of exchange. Disparity in the allocation of lost labour power in the form of money is what makes the rate of compensation a social category rather than an individual one.

3   The Informational Landlords of the Circuit of Metamorphosis of
       Lost Labour Power

Now that the information-intensive construction of risk has been examined
in detail, it is possible to offer a conceptual and historical definition of risk
and reconceptualize insurance boards in terms of their broader social role.
By doing this, I aim to lay bare not only the many connections that insurance
boards' construction of risk establish, but to make sense of their social function in capitalist economies. The process of reconceptualization, as a labeling
process, is vital to bring to light hidden aspects that are necessary to the understanding of the nature and function of complex social processes like the one
performed by insurance boards.

    As has been unveiled thus far, risk as a unit of information has a definitive
nature and a series of definitive attributes. This nature and series of attributes
are the results of its functioning under insurance boards and the conditioning of the historically capitalist mode of production. Above all, risk's definitive
nature is exchange. Risk for exchange is not something common to every society but peculiar to capitalist societies where insurance boards operate. Just as
production in capitalist economies is organized in terms of exchange, risk is
constructed by insurance boards based on a series of characteristics to enable
exchange. As an enabler of exchange, risk has a definitive character, form, purpose and function. These four traits are the expression of its exchange nature.
First, as hierarchically and bureaucratically produced by insurance boards
rather than between peers, risk acquires the character of class information,
reflecting the class structure of capitalist societies. As class information and
in accordance with capitalists' interests, risk is peculiar to the labour process
of the buying and selling of labour power, particularly to the exchanging of
lost labour power. It is the embodiment of power and the domination of one
class over another. Second, risk takes the form of a particular type of injury
information; that is, lost-time injury rates, a quantitative unit that enables lost
labour power to be measured and monetized for exchange purposes. Lost-
time injury rates, as the definitive historical form of risk, is processed information of injury claims leading to temporary lost labour power, permanent
partial lost labour power, permanent total lost labour power and the extinction of lost labour power – i.e., deaths. Third, the definitive purpose of risk
is to compensate injured wage labourers for their lost value of labour power
and spread compensation payments among the many capitalists. Rather than
health protection, accident prevention or health promotion, risk's driving goal
is the exchange and distribution of lost labour power in the form of compensation benefits and payments. Fourth, risk is constructed to perform two main

definitive functions: as a medium of measurement and a medium of exchange. As a medium of measurement, risk is a relative measure, one that quantifies the individual firm's share to the total mass of expected lost labour power in an aggregate – i.e., group rate –, and the individual firm's deviation from the total mass of expected lost labour power in an aggregate – i.e., experience rate. As a medium of exchange, risk aims to exchange the lost value of labour power for money and distribute it in disproportion among the capitalist class. This is done by calculating the group rate and the experience rate in relation to the total wages of member firms in an aggregate and the total wages at the firm level. The result is the rate of compensation in its money form: the premium. These are the four definitive traits of risk, which bundled together constitute the true manifestation of risk for exchange.

Now, it is interesting to note that risk for exchange not only results in the exchange of lost labour power for money but in the actual conversion of the lost value of labour power into money value. The lost value of labour power is successfully transformed into money value. Here, we are in the midst of a process of metamorphosis of value. Insurance boards record and process lost-time injury rates to construct risk into its many configurations – i.e., risk level, experience rate, group rate, rate of compensation, premium – to enable the metamorphosis of the lost value of labour power into money value. The metamorphosis of the lost value of labour power into money value takes place among insurance boards and individual capitalists as the selling and buying of a guarantee against expected lost labour power. This is, however, the first stage in the process of metamorphosis of lost labour power. Once the lost value of labour power is converted into money value, it is reconverted at a later stage into medical value and wage-replacement value for injured workers. The lost value of labour power changes its form three times. This whole process of the metamorphosis of lost labour power not only involves insurance boards and capitalists but also wage labourers. It reunites the two classes of society: those who own the means of production and those who only own their labour power and their lost labour power. In this respect, Machlup's (1962) exclusion of wage labour in his general definition of insurance boards is perhaps one of his biggest flaws. For Machlup (1962), insurance boards are nothing but a business between a seller and a buyer. This might be true for insurance companies in maritime, personal life and natural disasters, but not for WCSs' insurance boards, where the buyer is not the same person as the consumer. Machlup (1962) is not aware that WCSs' insurance boards are a distinctive type of insurance business. It is a business that takes place among three actors: insurance boards – i.e., the seller –, the capitalist – i.e., the buyer – and the wage labourer – i.e., the consumer. The consumer and the buyer are split up in two different classes. Here, the buyer is not only different from the consumer, but they find themselves in opposition in capitalist societies. So, what insurance boards actually perform is a much more complex function in capitalist societies. They mediate and perform the metamorphosis of lost labour power in a class structured society. Through an information-intensive process, insurance boards manage the circuit of metamorphosis of lost labour power among capitalists and wage labourers. This information-intensive process stands in a dialectic relation to capital and wage labour; it mediates both. The circuit of metamorphosis of lost labour power, or the series of metamorphoses the lost value of labour power undergoes to allocate compensation payments and deliver compensation benefits, is the definitive historical function of insurance boards in capitalist societies.

Drawing from a broader level of generality, one that brings into focus the specific relations of the capitalist mode of production, I will offer a historical conceptualization of insurance boards. Rather than agencies whose main activity is the recording and processing of lost-time injury rates to construct risk and spread the lost value of labour power, I reconceptualize insurance boards as agencies that record and process lost-time injury rates to construct, measure, monetize and exchange lost labour power in order to administer the circuit of metamorphosis of lost labour power in capitalist societies. This new conceptualization brings into light not only that lost labour power can be informationally constructed, measured, monetized, exchanged – functions already covered under the notion of risk – but that it can be transformed into four different forms: (a) money, (b) non-speculative and speculative assets, (c) medical benefits, and (d) wage-replacement benefits, thus disclosing how different elements can become forms of one another. Now, to say that lost labour power can be transformed into four different forms is simply to put an emphasis on the value form of lost labour power and its capacity to change into money value, investment value, medical value and wage-replacement value. This vantage point focuses on the underlying value form of lost labour power and its ability to mutate into other value forms. In addition, it brings together a triad that links insurance boards, capitalists and wage labourers in a set of conflicting relations that are central to the capitalist mode of production, thus inviting a dynamic view of the struggle for the transformation and distribution of the lost value of labour power. This involves contestation between capitalists and wage labourers over control of the circuit of lost labour power.

3.1   Stages of the Circuit of Metamorphosis of Lost Labour Power

The circuit of metamorphosis of lost labour power consists of three stages (see Figure 1). The first stage is the transformation of the lost value of labour power – i.e., the necessary means of repair, recovery, and maintenance of labour power during the days of disability – into money value. Insurance boards record and process lost-time injury rates to construct risk in order to measure, monetize, exchange and transform the lost value of labour power into money value. This is represented by C – M, where C is commodity production – i.e., commodification of lost labour power – and M is money. This act of processing lost-time injury rates to convert the lost value of labour power into money value appears as the selling and buying of a guarantee against expected lost labour power. While insurance boards appear as the sellers of the guarantee, capitalists appear as the buyers of the guarantee. The second stage is the transformation of money value into the invested compensation fund. Insurance boards invest the money value in non-speculative assets – e.g., bank deposits, government bonds, municipal bonds, real estate – and speculative assets – e.g., corporate securities, currency trade, derivatives. This act is represented by M – I, where M is the money value from the first stage, and I is the investment value. This is the act of valorizing money value through the invested insurance fund. This stage appears in the market as the buying and selling of financial products between insurance boards as buyers, and banks, financial corporations, hedge funds and the alike – i.e., interest-bearing capitalists – as sellers. The third act is the transformation of a portion of the investment value into medical value and wage-replacement value. This is the act of compensating injured workers for their lost value of labour power. It is represented as I – MW, where I is investment value from the second stage, and MW is medical value and wage-replacement value. This third act appears on one side as the business between insurance boards and medical institutions and, on the other, as the delivery of insurance boards' wage-replacement benefits – i.e., temporary wage-loss benefits, permanent wage-loss benefits, and pensions – to injured workers. Thus, the formula for the circuit of metamorphosis of lost labour power can be read as follows: C – M – I – MW (see Figure 1). In this circuit, the lost value of labour power changes its form four times. First, from its commodity value – i.e., commodification of lost labour power – to money value; second, from money value to investment value; and third, from investment value to medical value and wage-replacement value. (Note that the third stage involves a dual transformation into medical value and wage-replacement value). The purpose of the circuit is to transform the lost value of labour power into compensation value. Money value and investment value are mediators, vanishing moments, mere forms in the transformation of the lost value of labour power into medical and wage-replacement value.

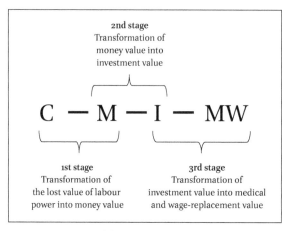

FIGURE 1   Stages of the circuit of metamorphosis

3.1.1   The First Stage: C – M

C – M represents the act of transforming the lost value of labour power into money value. Insurance boards convert the lost value of labour power into money value, while capitalists convert money value into the lost value of labour power. This act appears as the selling and buying of a guarantee against expected lost labour power. Insurance boards sell a guarantee against expected lost labour power to capitalists, while capitalists buy the guarantee from insurance boards to shield themselves against lengthy disputes in courts and the direct costs of compensating lost labour power. To perform this transformation, lost labour power must first be constructed, measured and monetized, and prepared for exchange. In other words, lost labour power needs to be commodified; that is, organized and produced as something exchangeable. Now, since lost labour power cannot be found as a natural and immutable reality, it has no physical body or shell, it has to be brought into life through information as a representation. Here, we are facing an informational process of commodification, one that involves recording, processing, calculating and combining different pieces of information (see Mosco, 2009). This is precisely what insurance boards do in the first stage. Their information-intensive operations of recording and processing lost-time injury rates to construct risk into its many configurations – i.e., risk level, group rate, experience rate, rate of compensation, premium – is an informational process of commodification to enable the exchange of lost labour power for money. In this regard, insurance boards' information-intensive process can be conceptualized as the informational commodification of lost labour power. Lost labour power comes into life as an informational commodity as the result of insurance boards' information-producing operations. The informational commodification of lost labour power, or the transformation of lost labour power into a commodity, is represented as C in this first act. The first stage of the circuit of metamorphosis of lost labour power begins with the lost-labour-power commodity (C) ready to be sold as a guarantee. Once lost labour power is begotten as a commodity, as something exchangeable for money, it can be actually exchanged and transformed into money value. The lost-labour-power commodity is exchanged at the rate of compensation and its price, the premium. Once the premium is set by insurance boards, the lost value of labour power in its commodity form can be effectively exchanged and converted into money value. Only then is the conversion C – M realized. This act does not appear only as the selling and buying of a guarantee against expected lost labour power but also as rent, a premium to be paid monthly to insurance boards. The first metamorphosis of lost labour power takes the social form of a rent collected by insurance boards. Let us look at this more closely.

As already expounded, insurance boards record and process lost-time injury rates to construct risk into its many configurations to commodify lost labour power and enable its exchange and metamorphosis into money value. This informational process is represented by C, the lost-labour-power commodity. The price of C is set by the premium, which, as already explained, is the money expression of the rate of compensation. Insurance boards' revenue is directly linked to the value of premiums. Rather than the value produced by their workers, their revenue comes from the premium paid by corporations. The labour involved in this industry does not stand in relation to the amount of revenue collected by insurance boards. Insurance boards' revenue does not take the form of profit, or the difference between the total mass of value extracted from wage labourers and the total wages. Their revenue takes the form of ground-rent. It does so because it does not arise from the direct exploitation of labour – i.e., the difference between the wages and the total mass of value produced – but from a monopolized item. In this case, rather than having a monopoly on a piece of earth such as agricultural land, a waterfall, a mine, or fishing grounds, insurance boards have a monopoly on the informational construction of risk and the commodification of lost labour power in society. As Harvey (2002) explains, "[...] rent is based upon the monopoly power [...] by virtue of their exclusive control over some directly or indirectly tradable item [...]" (p. 94). These agencies collect a rent based on the total mass of lost labour power produced by workplaces. Similar to Marx's (1991) differential rent concept, which depends on the varying fertility of the land, the assessment of insurance boards' rents is an assessment of varying risks between types of workplaces in general. In the insurance boards' terminology, a type of workplace is called a rating group, which comprises a subset of firms with similar risks within a branch of industry. Firms are placed by insurance boards within a rating group to estimate each firm's contribution to and deviation from the total mass of expected lost labour power in the aggregate and to come up with the rate of compensation and its money form: the premium. As the money expression of the rate of compensation, one that includes both the contribution to and deviation from an aggregate, the premium is divided into the base premium and the experience premium, respectively. While the base premium is determined by the firm's expected contribution to an aggregate, the experience premium is determined by the firm's expected deviation from an aggregate. Thus, the total rent appropriated by insurance boards as rentiers – i.e., the premium rate – is determined both by the base premium and the experience premium, which respectively reflect the incremental risk of the type of workplace and every firm's workplace. From this view, insurance boards are literally the landlords of the construction of workplace risks and the commodification of lost labour power. As with every landlord, their revenue neither takes the form of profit nor interest, but of ground-rent (see Marx, 1991). As informational rentiers, insurance boards make rent through the provision of a guarantee against expected lost labour power by virtue of their monopoly power over the informational commodification of lost labour power, a process that involves the recording and processing of lost-time injury rates and the construction of risk into its many configurations. These agencies have exclusive control over determining the riskiness of every workplace and transforming the lost value of labour power into money value based on their monopoly to track signals emitted by every workplace in the form of work injuries, diseases and fatalities.

In conclusion, the first stage in the metamorphosis of lost labour power not only represents the act of transforming the lost value of labour power into money value but the appropriation of surplus value already produced by individual firms as rent. Insurance boards appropriate value as a share in profit from firms rather than directly producing fresh surplus value through the exploitation of their workforce. The first stage C – M involves unproductive labour; that is, an amount of money that does not stand in direct relationship to the difference between the wage paid to wage labourers and the excess labour extracted from them. It is unproductive because insurance boards appropriate a fraction of surplus value from firms without producing surplus value, thus they do not add to the total mass of surplus value in society (see Finkelstein, 2018; Foley, 2013; Mandel, 1992; Marx, 1991). Therefore, the metamorphosis of the lost value of labour power into money value (C – M), is a process of the appropriation of value without producing value. It appears as a monthly payment at a price – i.e., premium rate – that represents the lost value of labour power, a form of rent to be paid by capitalists to avoid disputes in courts and the direct costs of compensating injured wage labourers. Thus, in the stage C – M, lost labour power not only confronts capitalists as money but as rent.

3.1.2   The Second Stage: M – I

The stage M – I represents the act of transforming lost labour power in the form of money value (M) into investment value (I). Here, it is important to note that insurance boards do not store money. They invest the money appropriated as rent from individual firms into non-speculative assets – e.g., bank deposits, government bonds, municipal bonds, real state – and speculative assets – e.g., corporate securities, currency trade, derivatives. Insurance boards are agencies that do not administer a compensation fund but an invested compensation fund to deliver medical and wage-replacement benefits to injured workers. This distinction is not superficial. It implies that insurance boards try to valorize the money appropriated from firms; in other words, to increase the value of the rent by investing in financial assets. To do so, insurance boards need to show up at the financial marketplace and buy financial assets from interest-bearing capitalists – e.g., banks, financial corporations, hedge funds – and the government. The amount of freedom insurance boards enjoy at this stage varies depending on state legislation. For example, the German state in the 19th century was very conservative in regard to insurance boards' investment portfolios. It mandated that they must only invest their reserves in non-speculative assets and at least 25% in government bonds (Eghigian, 2000). This was quite restrictive if we consider that early German insurance boards were all privately owned. In this regard, one would reasonably anticipate that issues of ownership – i.e., state owned or privately owned – would have had a strong influence on insurance boards' liberty to invest their reserves. However, beyond the restrictions placed on insurance boards' investment portfolios, the amount of value invested was enormous. Billions of dollars of lost labour power in the form of money value were transformed into financial assets. In the late 1970s, Canadian insurance boards from Alberta, British Columbia and Ontario had a combined investment portfolio well in excess of $2 billion dollars (Reasons et al., 1981). In the case of Canadian insurance boards, their portfolio distribution varies depending on provincial legislation. For example, in 1978, the insurance board of Alberta transformed the money appropriated as rent from individual firms into Government of Canada bonds (30%), provincial securities – including telephone, hydro, and municipal bonds – (46%), and in corporate securities (20%), totaling a value of $260 million (see Reasons et al., 1981).

In contrast, the insurance board of British Columbia not only invested a higher proportion of its total funds – approximately $570 million – in provincial securities (55%) but allocated its majority into one company, BC Hydro (see Reasons et al., 1981). This massive amount of value invested by Canadian insurance boards in provincial securities does not come from productive labour but rather unproductive labour. The total mass of value invested in provincial securities stands in direct relationship to the amount of value collected in the form of premiums from individual firms rather than the value produced by insurance boards' wage labourers. Does this mean that provincial business in Canada is ultimately subsidized by individual firms? Certainly not. If we take into account the first stage of metamorphosis, C – M, the one that precedes this second stage, it can be seen that it is wage labour that subsidizes provincial business. The amount of value collected in the form of premiums from individual firms and invested in provincial securities is nothing more than wage labourers' expected lost value of labour power. Let us remember that the premium is the money expression of the compensation rate; in other words, a percentage of the wage bill that represents the total mass of expected lost labour power. It is then the future lost value of labour power that is funneled in the form of money to provincial, government and corporate businesses. Thus, the billions of dollars invested by insurance boards into non-speculative assets and speculative assets is simply future lost labour power; that is, the future value of the necessary means of repair and recovery of labour power – i.e., medical benefits – and the future value of the necessary means of maintenance to keep labour power alive during the days of disability – i.e., wage-replacement.

The metamorphosis of money value into the invested compensation fund not only immensely benefits public businesses but indirectly a large number of capitalists that depend on hydro, roads and railways. Although a large quota of state-owned insurance boards' funds might end in government and provincial assets, the capitalist class is well served by insurance boards (see Reasons et al., 1981). In addition, as Reasons et al. (1981) point out, "Not only are the collected funds invested in enterprises which benefits overall economic development but the increased returns on investments are used to keep assessment rates down" (p.171). In other words, the return on investment subsidises the capitalist class. This occurs because the return in the form of interest allows insurance boards to pay compensation benefits – i.e., medical and wage-replacement benefits – without increasing the value of premiums; that is, the rent paid by capitalists to insurance boards. Thus, the second act in the metamorphosis of lost labour power, the transformation and valorization of the money value (M) into investment value (I), comprises a stage that largely benefits the capitalist class. As a process of valorization of lost labour power, this stage services the capitalist class, who control the means of compensation or the informational means to commodify lost labour power, rather than the working class, the real owners of both labour power and lost labour power.

3.1.3   The Third Stage: I – MW

The third and final stage of the circuit of metamorphosis of lost labour power is represented by I – MW, where I stands for the invested compensation fund and MW for medical and wage-replacement benefits. In this act, the lost value of labour power comes back to its real owners – i.e., wage labourers – in the form of compensation benefits. Insurance boards liquidate a portion of their financial assets in order to compensate injured workers by paying their medical expenses and their wage-loss during the days of disability, be it temporary, permanent partial, permanent total or death. A portion of the investment value (I) is transformed into the medical value and wage-replacement value (MW). To be precise, it is not just a portion of the investment value (I) that is transformed into medical value and wage-replacement value (MW), but a portion of the investment value plus interest (I'). Let us remember that the preceding stage is not only a process of transformation but of valorization that subsidises the capitalist class by keeping premiums down. So, in reality, the third stage should be represented as I' – MW, where the apostrophe stands for interest. Thus, what returns to wage labourers is their valorized lost value of labour power in the form of medical and wage-loss benefits. The circuit of metamorphosis of lost labour power is not only a process of reconversion but of valorization of lost labour power. It begins with the transformation of the lost value of labour power into money value through insurance boards' informational process of commodification, then continues by transforming money value into investment value, and ends up with valorized lost labour power in the form of compensation benefits, medical value and wage-replacement value. Lost labour power changes form four times to finally finish as valorized lost value.

It must be stressed that the valorized lost value of labour power never matches wage labourers' direct consumption needs, specifically, their individual needs, those that spring from the sociocultural context of society. The amount of compensation benefits are not disbursed on the basis of factual needs but on the market value of lost labour power – i.e., medical value and wage-replacement value. This circuit is not about satisfying real needs – i.e., direct consumption – but about reconverting the lost value of labour power – i.e., productive consumption. The circuit of metamorphosis provides the medical and financial resources needed to keep labour power fully functioning. It must be sufficient to compensate wage labourer's wear and tear and keep them in motion. It is intended to replace the value of the necessary means of repair, recovery and maintenance of labour power during the time of disability, nothing more. To be clear, compensation benefits in the form of medical and wage-replacement benefits have the same significance as the repair and maintenance of any other productive instrument.

In relation to wage labourers' needs, at least three levels of needs can be identified: (a) physiological needs, (b) necessary needs and (c) social needs (see Lebowitz, 2003). The transformation of the lost value of labour power into the medical value and wage-replacement value (MW) targets the two first levels of needs. It replaces the value of the necessary means of repair, recovery and maintenance required to produce the wage labourer as a natural subject, the physical minimum, the barest level of subsistence – i.e., physiological needs – and those needs "[...] necessary by habit and custom ... [which] normally enter into the consumption of workers" (Lebowitz, 2003, p. 40), what Marx (1990) identifies as necessary needs. However, the level of social needs is never met. Medical value and wage-replacement value are not intended to satisfy social needs, the "[...] needs of the worker as a socially developed human being at a given point" (Lebowitz, 2003, p. 40). Social needs not only spring from the social conditions in which people are raised but are conditioned by the social organization of society (Lebowitz, 2003). Social needs are not naturally determined but conditioned by social life; these are "historic needs" (Marx, 1993).

In regard to social needs, it can be argued, for example, that the loss of a hand or fingers is not just a biological matter but a social one. As described by Murray (cited in Holdren, 2020), the loss of her fingers makes it harder for her to being feminine and attractive to men. She felt she should be compensated for her impaired appearance and the reduction of her chances in entering an advantageous marriage. In this case, her physical disability and having been maimed resulted in a social exclusion: the closing of the doors of marriage. However, compensating a limb within the circuit of metamorphosis of lost labour power – i.e., medical value and wage-replacement value – does not take into account the social context of a work injury. There is no cultural value, social value or moral value to be quantified, transformed and fairly compensated. For Murray, losing her fingers also meant extinguishing her career aspirations of being a piano teacher and the enjoyment of her musical life (see Holdren, 2020). These aspirational and enjoyment losses are also left aside by considerations undertaken within the circuit of metamorphosis. In addition to the social context of an injury, medical value and wage-replacement value do not include those losses embedded in particular relationships and social positions such as being a mother or a father. For example, losses such as the disolution of the family, the destruction of domestic peace, the loss of a wife's affection and comfort or the loss of the simple ability to hold your own kid. Non-pecuniary damages or social needs, namely, those which are a matter of social, cultural and moral conventions, are excluded from compensation.

While the satisfaction of physiological and necessary needs is met by compensation benefits, workers' social needs or direct consumption needs are completely neglected. This in part happens because, as Lebowitz (2003) explains, "[...] it is not the intrinsic properties of an object that determines whether it meets social needs" (p. 37) but the judgement made by society. In this respect, the object that serves wage labourers' satisfaction, the amount of medical and wage-replacement benefits, is established by insurance boards' circuit of metamorphosis of lost labour power. The intrinsic value of medical and wage-replacement benefits is conditioned by insurance boards' information-intensive operations rather than workers' social needs. Therefore, the final stage of the circuit of metamorphosis (I – MW) is not only the metamorphosis of a portion of lost labour power in the form of investment value (I) into medical and wage-replacement value, but at the same time the non-realization of the social needs of wage labourers.

CHAPTER 4

The Lost-Labour-Power Commodity

1   Introduction

Insurance boards are informational agencies that manage the circuit of meta-morphosis of lost labour power in capitalist societies. Through an information-intensive process, these agencies transform the total mass of lost value pro-duced in capitalist economies into money value, investment value, medical value, and wage-replacement value in order to exchange and distribute lost labour power in the form of compensation payments and compensation ben-efits. The circuit of metamorphosis begins with the informational commod-ification (C) of lost labour power or the act of producing lost labour power as something readily exchangeable. Through the information-producing operations of recording and processing wage-labour-related injuries, diseases and fatalities to construct risk into its many configurations – e.g., group rate, experience rate, rate of compensation – lost labour power is transformed into a commodity. The informational commodification of lost labour power for the purpose of exchange constitutes WCS s' biggest innovation. What exactly comprises the insurance boards' commodity however? Is it lost labour power? Is it lost-time injury rates? Is it the group rate and the experience rate? Is it the rate of compensation and the premium? Is it all of them? No one to my knowledge has developed a theoretical exposition of what insurance boards' commodity is. Although Machlup (1962) recognizes the information com-modity in the insurance sector, he fails to abstract and conceptualize it, much less put it into the context of a level of generality that focuses on the capitalist mode of production. Besides classifying the information commodity into dif-ferent types of goods, such as investments or goods for intermediate and final consumption, Machlup (1962) eludes the complexities of providing a compre-hensive explanation of insurance boards' commodity. In addition, contem-porary information scholars such as Castells (1996) and Schiller (2007) also ignore this question. This chapter aims to fill this gap by providing a com-prehensive examination of insurance boards' commodity and its commodi-fication process. It goes back to Marx's (1990) analysis of the commodity and discusses some current theories about information commodities in order to come up with a provisional theory to make sense of insurance boards' com-modity. It proceeds by describing insurance boards' commodity as a means of production, a use value, an exchange value, and a value. Based on Marx's

(1990, 1991, 1992) value theory, the chapter goes on to account for the capacity of insurance boards' commodity to transform lost value into value in order to exchange expected lost labour power for money at equivalent proportions. The chapter ends with a portrayal of the process of commodification, in other words, the information-intensive moments that lost labour power passes through to become a commodity. It includes the abstraction, conceptualization and description of five consecutive moments: (a) the working-day-lost moment, (b) the reporting moment, (c) the recording moment, (d) the processing moment and (e) the programing moment.

2   The Commodity

Marx's (1990) analysis of the commodity is still the most comprehensive examination on the matter. Marx goes to great lengths to abstract and conceptualize the nature of commodities as use value, exchange value and the embodiment of value or labour power. However, Marx's analysis of the commodity concentrates on the industrial moment of capitalist production, when world trade was still in its manufacturing and industrial phase based on the production of physical commodities such as cotton, wool, timber, steel, tea, meat and products in general. In line with an industrial economy rather than the informational economy we have today, Marx analyzes the commodity as a physical object. He begins by defining the commodity as "[...] an external object, a thing which through its qualities satisfies human needs of whatever kind" (Marx, 1990, p. 125). He explicitly addresses the commodity as a "sensuous thing" with a "physical body" conditioned by "physical properties". Although in *Capital volume I*, *Capital volume II* and *Capital volume III* Marx (1990, 1992, 1991) does go over the activities of the singer, the schoolmaster, the literary proletarian, the commercial capitalist and the interest-bearing capitalist, which at the time were information-producing commodities, he does not theorize about information commodities as such. In addition, Marx's examination of the commodity is restricted to the process of production and excludes the process of circulation in which commercial and financial capital were producing at the time information commodities in the form of marketing products, loans, bonds, financial instruments, etc. Thus, to understand the commodity of insurance boards, it is necessary to go beyond Marx's theorization of the commodity. Nevertheless, it is key to include Marx's major contribution to the theory of the commodity, namely, the theoretical trinity of use value, exchange value and value.

3   The Information Commodity

The analysis and theorization of information as a commodity has mostly been performed by political economists linked to the academic fields of the mass media, mass communication and information studies (see Fuchs, 2011; Garnham, 1990; Horkheimer and Adorno, 2006; Meehan, 2012; Murdock and Golding, 1973; Mosco, 2009; Schiller, 2007; Smythe, 1977). Although it has been examined by a multitude of scholars there is no comprehensive theory of the information commodity applicable to all information industries, including the insurance sector. It is still largely untheorized, in part due to the far greater complexity of analysis required by the information commodity compared to the physical commodity.

One of the main theoretical challenges posed by informational commodities is related to their abstraction and conceptualization. While the process of abstraction aims to break down a concept into manageable units and establish boundaries, the process of conceptualization is aimed at the labeling of a concept in terms of its particular connections, which are the attributes of what the concept really is. Specifically, the great problem of abstracting and conceptualizing an information commodity is that, unlike a physical commodity, it can take more than one form. In his book *The Political Economy of Communication*, Mosco (2009) acknowledges this dilemma. Based on the analysis of the commodity from the field of media and communication studies, Mosco (2009) points out that the information commodity can be thought of as content and as an audience. As content, an information commodity is a group of messages, ideas, symbols, images, stories, motion pictures, music, and data that are made into marketable products (Mosco, 2009, p. 133). Here, the information commodity is similar to a traditional physical commodity, where its physical body, that is, its packaged information content – e.g., a book, music album, or video – comprises that what is exchanged for money. Through the commodification of content into an information commodity, capitalists are able to put a packaged-information commodity on the marketplace and sell it for profit. However, as noted by Mosco (2009), the information commodity in the media can also take the form of an audience (see Smythe, 1977). This occurs when the media system is highly privatized and companies' revenue is made through advertisements. In this case, the content is produced in an instrumental way only to attract audiences, which, in the words of Smythe (1977), are sold to advertisers for a profit. Here, the construction of audiences as a commodity through programing takes the lead. It is not content but audiences that are constructed through an informational process and sold to advertisers.

TABLE 1   Audience commodity

Ratings	Audience
I. Representation	II. Reference
Audience Commodity	

Meehan (2012) added complexity to the audience commodity by claiming that ratings are what is really exchanged. Advertisers purchase audience ratings from an oligopoly of agencies that comprise the market of commodity ratings (Meehan, 2012). The ratings industry produces statistical reports to define and differentiate the audience commodity based on size, gender, age, composition, demographics, purchasing power and patterns of media usage. The important thing to note about the audience commodity is that information acts in a dual-order commodification process in which the physical body of information – i.e., ratings – represents that what is actually exchanged: the audience. In this case, the information commodity is split into representation and reference. Audience ratings – i.e., the physical body of information – are the representation of a reference, the real people that consume media content – i.e., the audience. This split between representation and reference happens because advertisers cannot directly exchange audiences – i.e., real people consuming media – for money (see Lebowitz, 1986) but indirectly exchange money for that which represents a particular audience – i.e., audience ratings. The selling and buying of the audience is mediated by an information process that represents the audience in terms of its quantitative and qualitative traits. This dual-order commodification process implies a dual movement by which an information commodity is divided into representation and reference. The audience commodity can be thought of as a twofold commodity; the representation – i.e., ratings – and the reference – i.e., the audience (See Table 1).

Now, in the case in which the content is the form of the information commodity and is similar to any physical commodity, the information commodity appears as a unity. There is no split between representation and reference. The physical body of the content commodity, whether it be messages, data, symbols, bits, music or films in the form of a marketable product, comprises at the same time the representation and the reference. As Table 2 depicts, the representation and reference collapses into the thing itself. Similar to physical commodities, the content commodity implies a traditional single-order commodification process in which the representation and the reference is the thing being commodified.

TABLE 2   Content commodity

Messages, data, symbols, music, films, bits, etc.
I. Representation – Reference
Content Commodity

As a provisional theory, I abstract and conceptualize those information commodities whose physical bodies – e.g., numbers, rates, signs, text – are exchanged in the market in virtue of what they represent rather than packaged and sold for what they physically are as twofold information commodities. This provisional theory will aid in making sense of the insurance boards' information commodity, which is also exchanged based on what it represents rather than its physical body and is therefore split into representation and reference. Like media companies that exchange audiences via ratings based on size, gender, age, and composition, insurance boards exchange lost labour power via rates based on working days lost, permanent impairment rates, loss of earnings, wages and fatalities, among other variables. Insurance boards need to transform lost labour power into a commodity to perform the first act of the metamorphosis of lost labour power, which is the transformation of lost value into money value. To do so, these agencies commodify lost labour power through an informational process, that involves recording, processing, calculating and combining work injuries, diseases and fatalities to construct risk into its many configurations – i.e., group rate, experience rate and rate of compensation. As a commodity, lost labour power is not just created by information-intensive operations but represented and objectified by information itself. As an information commodity, lost labour power is the reference of lost-time injury rates, and lost-time injury rates are the representation of lost labour power. The insurance boards' commodity is therefore at the same time its reference and its representation, lost labour power and lost-time injury rates respectively (See Table 3). In this case, lost-time injury rates – e.g., the average number of working days lost, the fatality rate, the permanent impairment rate, the loss of earnings rate – represent the amount of lost labour power produced at a firm level, a subset of firms, a branch of industry and all branches of industry.

The commodity of insurance boards is a twofold information commodity, its material shell – i.e., lost-time injury rates – and its immaterial substance – i.e., lost labour power. Henceforth, I will label this particular twofold information commodity as the lost-labour-power commodity. I have chosen to name it

TABLE 3   Insurance boards' commodity

Lost-Time Injury Rates	Lost Labour Power
I. Representation	II. Reference

Lost-Labour-Power Commodity

as its immaterial substance or reference due to the fact that insurance boards process lost-time injury rates to perform the circuit of metamorphosis of lost labour power rather than packaging lost-time injury rates as a final product to be sold for a profit. Nonetheless, the commodity of insurance boards comprises at the same time its representation – i.e., lost-time injury rates – and its reference – i.e., lost labour power (see Table 3). Both elements must always be present to bring into existence this commodity. Without an accident, disease or death leading to temporary, permanent or total disability, there is no lost labour power available to produce this commodity. On the other hand, without insurance boards' information-producing operations of recording and processing work accidents, diseases and deaths, there are no signs to represent this commodity.

4   The Lost-Labour-Power Commodity

As already conceptualized, the lost-labour-power commodity is a twofold information commodity: a material object and an immaterial substance. First, as a material object it is processed information resulting from computing and combining information of wage-labour-related accidents and diseases leading to the temporary, permanent, or total extinction of lost labour power. It is the object of lost labour power, a physical representation, that determines the manner of measuring, exchanging and replacing lost labour power. As an external object, this commodity takes the physical form of a group of signs in the form of numbers and rates that can be written, typed, deleted and circulated independently of human beings. It comprises (a) the number of working days lost at a firm level, (b) the average number of working days lost in a subset of firms, (c) the injury rate, (d) the fatality rate, (e) the disease rate, (f) the permanent impairment rate, (g) the wage rate, and (h) the loss of earnings, among other numbers.

Second, as an immaterial substance this commodity is abstract lost labour power or wage labourers' incapacity to work for a capitalist due to a work

accident, disease or fatality. It is the subject of lost-time injury rates, an immaterial reference, one that creates the need for the recording and processing of
lost-time injury rates. As an immaterial substance, this commodity specifically
creates the purpose for producing itself as an external representation equivalent to the value of repairing, recovering and maintaining labour power during
the period of disability. Therefore, as a unity, the lost-labour-power commodity can be thought of as a group of signs – i.e., lost-time injury rates – that
represent wage labourers' incapacity to work – i.e., lost labour power – whose
quantity is equivalent to the value of repairing, recovering and maintaining
the injured worker during the time of incapacity.

   As with any commodity, the production of the lost-labour-power commodity aims at satisfying the needs of others rather than those of the
producers (see Marx, 1990). Insurance boards perform the information-
intensive operations of recording and processing wage-labour-related
accidents, diseases and fatalities to produce the lost-labour-power commodity and sell it to individual firms. The commodity, as a group of signs
that represent wage labourers' lost labour power or incapacity to work, is
transferred to firms for whom it satisfies a specific need. Now, what exactly
is the need that this commodity fulfills? What is the use value or utility
of the lost-labour-power commodity? What is the value or the amount of
labour power objectified in the commodity? What is the exchange value
or the quantitative relation through which this commodity is exchanged
for money? As Marx (1990) warns us, "[a] commodity appears at first sight
an extremely obvious, trivial thing ... [b]ut its analysis brings out that it is
a very strange thing, abounding in metaphysical subtleties and theological
niceties" (p. 163). Let us delve into the matter more deeply.

4.1   The Satisfaction of Needs as a Means of Production

Foremost, it is necessary to locate this commodity in relation to the satisfaction of needs. Although Marx (1990) dismisses the nature of commodities'
needs as a relevant category for the analysis of commodities, I claim it is a
fundamental category to make sense of this particular commodity. The lost-
labour-power commodity does not satisfy needs as an object of direct consumption but indirectly as a means of production or a producer good. It is
not created as a product for final consumption, packaged information of lost
labour power in the form of lost-time injury rates for knowledge purposes,
one that directly aims to capture profit. It is produced by insurance boards
as a means of production, a cost element required for the production of all
commodities in a capitalist economy. In Marxist terminology, this commodity
is produced by 'Department I', devoted to the reproduction of the conditions

of production on a simple or extended basis. As a product of 'Department I', the lost-labour-power commodity is exchanged between the members of the capitalist class and its representatives – i.e., the capitalist state – who have the monopoly of the means of production.

Insurance boards' information-intensive process yields an information commodity employed in the labour process of other goods and services performed by individual capitalists. The lost-labour-power commodity constitutes neither consumption nor investment, but rather a compulsory intermediate commodity for the production of anything else. It is a mandatory commodity to be purchased by every firm that consumes labour power – i.e., wage labourers' capacity to work in exchange for a wage. The buying and consumption of the lost-labour-power commodity can thus be regarded as a cost of running companies. Capitalists purchase and consume the lost-labour-power commodity as an input for the capitalist labour process of production, a process that involves both the consumption of labour power and the production of lost labour power. Similar to the traditional wage that pays for the consumption of labour power, the lost-labour-power commodity allows capitalists indirectly to pay for the consumption of lost labour power. While the traditional wage directly replaces the value of labour power – i.e., the value of the means of subsistence for the production, reproduction and maintenance of labour power – the lost-labour-power commodity indirectly replaces the lost value of labour power – i.e., the value of the means of repairing, recovering and maintaining labour power during the incapacity to work period. As with any means of production, the lost-labour-power commodity is consumed by being used up in the labour process, that is, by producing work accidents, diseases and fatalities, and indirectly compensating injured workers through insurance boards with an equivalent value to the lost value of labour power in the form of medical and wage-replacement benefits. From capitalists' vantage point, the cost of consuming the lost-labour-power commodity is viewed as an externality, similar to pollution or other social costs of production. Rather than enforcing effective preventive measures – e.g., engineering controls and administrative controls – through government regulations, companies are left to absorb the costs of destroying labour power through insurance boards' market-oriented mechanisms. Thus, from the capitalist perspective the consumption of the lost-labour-power commodity is nothing but a market externality. Just as carbon taxes are consumed to efficiently distribute the costs of pollution, the lost-labour-power commodity is consumed to efficiently distribute the value of the means of repairing, recovering and maintaining labour power during the incapacity to work period.

4.2   *Use Value*

Marx (1990) claims that the use value or utility of a commodity "[...] does not dangle in mid-air" (p. 126) and has no existence apart from its physical properties. He is adamant in locating the use value of a commodity around its materiality. Although this definition works well for physical commodities, it does not work well for twofold information commodities. In the case of the lost-labour-power commodity, the use value does not derive from its material properties. What makes it useful for capitalists is not its external body, its physical representation – i.e., lost-time injury rates – but its class function: to financially shield individual capitalists. Here, the use value cannot be known because it is not a matter of a material determination. Rather than being determined by its physical body, the use value of the lost-labour-power commodity acquires its meaning from a historical structured totality – i.e., the replacement of a litigation-based mode of compensation by an information-intensive mode of compensation.

First, its use value derives from a mandatory contract between insurance boards and individual firms. Sold as a guarantee – i.e., a promise to pay for injured workers – this commodity protects firms from the direct costs of compensating lost labour power and lengthy and expensive disputes in court. Under a contractual agreement, insurance boards assume the financial liability of disbursing medical and wage-replacement benefits on behalf of the capitalist class. As a use value, this commodity shields firms not only from direct payments but from the unpleasant aspects of dealing with injured workers' disagreements about benefits, absence notes, medical rehabilitation, vocational rehabilitation, return to work, loss of earnings, pensions, etc. In some countries like Canada, this contractual agreement takes the form of a *de facto* class accord between wage labourers and capitalists where the former gives up the right to sue the latter.

Second, the use value of this commodity lies in its function as a medium of exchange of lost labour power in class societies rather than its function as a medium of measurement. Contrary to common sense, this commodity is not useful as a measurement of workplace health, as a technology of inductive inference, one that allows a conclusion to be reached on the total mass of lost labour power produced in capitalist societies. Although insurance boards do process information to construct risk as a medium of measurement of lost labour power in order to exchange and transform lost value into money value, investment value, medical value and wage-replacement value, this does not mean its usefulness derives from its capacity to act as a measurement of lost labour power. The recording and processing of injury information to construct risk as a medium of measurement of expected lost labour power is undoubtedly critical; however, it is critical because it is instrumental to the function of exchanging and spreading lost labour power in class societies. Predicting, exchanging and spreading lost labour power is the dominant function of this commodity. As already explained, this commodity is not consumed by capital as a product for final consumption in order to satisfy the need for identifying the number/types of injuries, number/types of diseases, the average number of working days lost, the injury rate, among other descriptors, to prevent the occurrence of work accidents, diseases and fatalities. It is consumed to predictably spread the cost of replacing the value of the means of repair, recovery and maintenance of labour power during the incapacity to work period. The usefulness of this commodity for individual capitalists lies in the function of spreading a payment of lost labour power based on every firm's contribution to and deviation from the total mass of expected lost labour power in a subset of firms within a branch of industry. The collective construction of risk as a medium of measurement enforces a disproportionate distribution of lost labour power. Divided into rating groups, firms are collectively held liable for the total mass of lost labour power produced in a subset of firms. Every firm's contribution, a prediction based on the historical lost labour power produced at the firm level, subset of firms and branch of industry, is transformed into a percentage of its wage bill in relation to the total mass of lost labour power and the total wages in an aggregate. This allow insurance boards to spread the expected burden of payments in disproportion to the effective amount of lost labour power produced at the firm level. The use value of this information commodity is to equalize the rates of compensation based on a prediction of the ebb and flow of lost labour power in a rating group within a branch of industry thus making the capitalist class collectively liable through the spreading of payments in disproportion to the performance of individual capitalists. In simpler words, the use value of the lost-labour-power commodity is to protect capitalists from the full cost of compensating lost labour power and the unpredictability of compensation payments. Individual profits are shielded by an information commodity that socializes compensation payments and reduces financial uncertainty.

Finally, a third but significant utility of this commodity is to limit the compensation of lost labour power to wage labourers' necessary needs, the physiological needs of reproducing the wage labourer as a natural subject and those needs that normally enter into the consumption of workers (see Chapter 3). Compensation benefits are restricted to replacing the value of the necessary means of repairing, recovering and maintaining labour power during the incapacity to work period. Insurance boards put a cap on compensation benefits by solely operationalizing lost labour power in a particular

way. This gives the capitalist class enormous leverage. When insurance
boards operationalize lost labour power as the value equivalent to the medical and financial resources to repair, recover and maintain injured workers
during their disability period, the need as an internal object is created in
order to produce an information commodity to exchange, spread and replace
the value of wage labourers' incapacity to work. A specific type of injury
information is thus recorded and processed in order to produce a commodity to fulfill the needs of exchanging and spreading the value of the means
of repair, recovery and maintenance of labour power. This occurs because
the act of operationalizing lost labour power conditions the act of recording
and processing information to produce the lost-labour-power commodity. As
Marx (1993) points out, consumption creates the aim for production, that is
to say, needs precede production. Once this information commodity is created in order to exchange and spread what insurance boards operationalize
as lost labour power, the commodity itself as an external object determines
the manner through which lost labour power will be effectively exchanged,
spread and replaced. The materiality of this commodity rules over consumption by limiting the replacement of lost labour power to a value equivalent
to medical and wage-replacement benefits. Here we have Marx's (1993) pro-
duction/consumption movement of co-determination. On the one hand,
consumption creates the aim for production, while, on the other hand,
production creates the commodity for consumption. Once the lost-labour-
power commodity is created to fulfill wage labourers' necessary needs it
tends to perform as demanded by its internal construction. It is therefore the
internal construction of this information commodity that limits compensation benefits to necessary needs in exclusion of social needs.

4.3   Exchange Value

The exchange value of a commodity can be understood as "[...] the quantitatively specific expression of its capacity for serving as medium of exchange"
(Marx, 1993, p. 199). It represents a quantitative relation, a proportion through
which one commodity can be exchanged (Marx, 1990). As an exchange value,
the lost-labour-power commodity can be quantitatively exchanged for a specific proportion or sum of money. The privilege to exchange this commodity
for money is highly regulated by the capitalist state. It is insurance boards
who have the monopoly right to produce and exchange the lost-labour-power
commodity among the many capitalists. As explained in Chapter 3, insurance
boards exchange the value of the lost-labour-power commodity into money
value in the first stage of the circuit of metamorphosis of lost labour power
(C – M – I – MW). The process of exchange '–' appears as the selling and buying

of a guarantee. While insurance boards appear as the sellers of a guarantee, individual capitalists appear as the buyers. It is at this moment when the lost-labour-power commodity is exchanged for money and thus transformed into money. Now, as an exchange value, a quantitative relation through which it can be exchanged, insurance boards sell this commodity at a specific amount of money. The specific amount of money is determined by the rate of compensation, the percentage of the wage bill that represents the contribution to and deviation from the total mass of expected lost labour power in an aggregate. It is thus at the rate of compensation that this commodity is exchanged for money. The exchange value of the lost-labour-power commodity is therefore the rate of compensation, a wage-relation formula. It manifests itself in a value relation with the wage bill; it is through the wage bill that the exchange value attains its quantitative point of reference.

Although the construction of the rate of compensation is a collective process, one that involves the recording and processing information in a subset of firms within a branch of industry, the process of exchange itself is always an individual activity between an insurance board and a capitalist. As explained in the previous chapter, insurance boards place firms within a rating group – i.e., a subset of firms within a branch of industry – in order to estimate each firm's contribution to and deviation from the total mass of expected lost labour power and settle on the rate of compensation. Once the rate of compensation is collectively constructed and individually determined, insurance boards sell the commodity at its exchange value, a quantitative relation that takes the form of a percentage that represents the lost value of labour power in terms of the total wages to be paid at the firm level. Individual capitalists buy the commodity at the rate of compensation and pay a specific price, the premium, the money expression of the rate of compensation or the exchange value. In this regard, the premium is nothing but the money value of the rate of compensation, without which it is not possible to know the money value to be exchanged. If the total wages of a firm are equal to $100,000,000 and the rate of compensation is equal 1.4%, the money value – i.e., the premium – to be paid for this commodity by a firm would be equal to $1,400,000. Now, despite the fact that capitalists are confronted with the premium rather than the rate of compensation, the exchange value of this commodity should not be confused with the premium. This is due to the fact that the premium is a representation in the money form of the rate of compensation rather than the other way around. While the rate of compensation establishes the quantitative proportion through which the lost-labour-power commodity will be exchanged, the premium only discloses the money value of the quantitative proportion established by the rate of compensation.

The rate of compensation or the exchange value of this commodity confronts individual capitalists not only as the premium but as the base premium and the experience premium. While the base premium expresses the money value of the wage bill that represents the individual firm's expected contribution to an aggregate, the experience premium expresses the money value of the wage bill that represents the individual firm's expected deviation from an aggregate. If the wage bill that represents the firm's contribution to an aggregate is, for example, 1%, the base premium of a firm whose total wages are equal to $100,000,000 will yield $1,000,000; if the wage bill that represents the firm's deviation from an aggregate is, for example, 0.2%, the experience premium of a firm whose total wages are equal to $100,000,000 will yield $200,000. In this case, the premium rate, that is, the sum of the base and the experience premium, will yield a total money value of $1,200,000.

Finally, the exchange value of this commodity not only confronts capital as the base and experience premium but as ground-rent, a monthly payment. As a means of production, a compulsory cost element required for the capitalist labour process, the lost-labour-power commodity is purchased by capital on a monthly basis. Capitalists regularly pay a ground-rent for this commodity. The exchange takes place even though the commodity might not be effectively consumed by individual capitalists. Regardless of the absence of work accidents, diseases and fatalities, for the non-necessity of compensating the lost value of labour power through medical and wage-replacement benefits, firms are compelled to regularly pay for this commodity. It is the rent form – i.e., the frequency of payments – that enables the exchange value of the commodity to be kept stable through time.

4.4   *Value*

Marx's value theory may be one of his most controversial contributions to his critique of political economy, particularly in its relation to price formation. However, as Baumol (1974) and Foley (1998) argue, Marx's value theory was never intended as a theory of pricing, as it aimed to explain the process of the production of value and the extraction of surplus value in various sectors of a capitalist economy. His main concern regarding capitalist societies was the production, distribution and consumption of value (Foley, 1982). For Marx, values are not approximations to prices, but rather an underlying reality where prices are a surface manifestation (Baumol, 1974; Lee, 1993). The fact that Marx's analysis proceeds on the assumption that commodities are exchanged at their values does not mean that values are proportional to prices. Nonetheless, this does not mean that prices are independent and delinked from values. From a Marxian perspective, the price of a commodity is the amount of money that

represents more or less the value embodied in a commodity; there is a dis-
crepancy between prices and the embodied value in a commodity (Foley, 1982,
1998). How should Marx's value theory be approached in regard to the lost-
labour-power commodity? As Fleetwood (2001) suggests, it is more helpful to
move away from a quantitative version of Marx' value theory and closer to a
qualitative one. Rather than analyzing and expounding the lost-labour-power
commodity in terms of its quantitative relationship between the expenditure
of labour power and its price – i.e., the premium rate – it is more relevant to
employ a qualitative approach that possesses explanatory power. Following
Fleetwood (2001), Marx's value theory is approached as a causal-explanatory
mode of theorisation that uncovers social structures, mechanisms and power
relations of the labouring activities involved in the value formation of the lost-
labour-power commodity. This approach is aimed at understanding the process of production and extraction of value in the creation of the lost-labour-
power commodity.

Marx (1990) explains that commodities express themselves in the marketplace through a dual character, two different forms that play contradictory
roles: a use value and a value. As a use value, a commodity is its utility. As a value,
a commodity is objectified labour power. As Marx puts it, "[...] the value of a
commodity represents human labour power pure and simple [...]" (p. 135). The
value of a commodity has nothing to do with the physical properties and qualities of a given commodity; it is abstract labour power, something immaterial.
By the sole act of expending labour power in producing a commodity, labour
power is crystallized and accumulated in a commodity as value, something
invisible. Marx (1990) characterizes the value of a commodity as a phantom-
like form. This phantom-like form is the common factor in an exchange relation. It is the quantitative quality of value – i.e., the amount of labour power –
that allows commodities to be swapped for one another. Specifically, it is the
magnitude of value, measured in days or hours – i.e., labour time – that quantitatively establishes the exchange. Value is measured by labour time. However,
it is not the amount of labour time effectively embodied in a commodity but
a social average. Marx corrected Ricardo's value theory by defining the magnitude of value as the amount of labour time socially necessary to produce a
commodity (Foley, 1998). As Marx (1990) put it, "Socially necessary labour-time
is the labour-time required to produce any [commodity] under the conditions
of production normal for a given society and with the average degree of skill
and intensity of labour prevalent in society" (p. 129). In sum, while the substance of value is abstract labour power, its magnitude is socially necessary
labour time; both substance and magnitude are key elements in a commodity
exchange relation.

What can we say about the lost-labour-power commodity in terms of value? The first thing that should strike us is that the lost-labour-power commodity, as abstract lost labour power, is the antithesis of the substance of value or labour power. Let us remember that the lost-labour-power commodity is a twofold information commodity: a material object and an immaterial substance. As an immaterial substance, this commodity is wage labourers' incapacity to work due to an accident, disease or fatality. It is the negation of labour power, a substance that lacks an inherent reality but acquires its properties in relation to another. As the negation of labour power, lost labour power needs the existence of labour power; labour power is a precondition of lost labour power. An event leading to temporary, permanent or total destruction of labour power must take place in order to produce this commodity. Once an event of the kind occurs, lost labour power gets crystallized as a material object. By the simple act of recording and processing wage-labour-related accidents, diseases and fatalities, lost labour power is objectified as a group of signs in the form of injury rates.

Does this mean that no value or labour power is required to produce this commodity? Certainly not. Lost labour power due to accidents, diseases and fatalities does not have the ability to objectify itself into a group of signs. Someone must perform the information-producing operations of recording and processing accidents, diseases and fatalities to come up with a group of signs that represent lost labour power. Actually, what insurance boards do is objectify lost labour power into the form of recorded and processed information. Insurance boards consume labour power for the labouring process of objectifying lost labour power into lost-time injury rates. The value component of this commodity comes directly from the information-producing operations exerted by insurance boards in order to construct lost labour power into a commodity. There is nothing natural or immediate in the value formation of the lost-labour-power commodity: it has a value because it is materially produced by insurance boards to enter into an exchange relation. This commodity is thus the product of both value or labour power and its lack, lost value or lost labour power. This is a unique contradiction. Unlike any other commodity, this commodity is the product of two opposite substances: labour power and lost labour power. Only the fusion of labour power and lost labour power gives birth to this information commodity. This trait is something unique for a commodity.

However, the most striking feature is that the labour power performed by insurance boards never gets objectified into the commodity thus never gets exchanged. Although insurance boards consume labour power – i.e., wage labour employed by insurance boards – to produce this commodity, the amount of labour power consumed does not play any part when compared to the total mass of lost labour power objectified in the commodity in the form of lost-time injury rates. The exchange takes place in relation to the portion of lost labour power objectified in the commodity rather than the labour power consumed by insurance boards to produce the commodity. The money value that capitalists pay to insurance boards is a percentage of the wage bill that represents the contribution to and deviation from the total mass of expected lost labour power in a subset of firms within a branch of industry. Capitalists pay an exchange value at a price – i.e., the premium – that has no proportion whatsoever with the amount of labour power consumed by insurance boards. In this case, there is not only a disproportion between the price – i.e., the premium – and the value embodied in a commodity. The value or labour power is not even an underlying reality in this commodity. Here, the price – i.e., the premium – is not a manifestation of value or labour power; on the contrary, it is a manifestation of its opposite: lost value or lost labour power. The price mechanism of insurance boards is based on lost value, where the rate of compensation and its money form – i.e., the premium rate – are amounts that represent more or less the lost value or lost labour power embodied in the commodity. In this regard, the exchange value of this commodity – i.e., the rate of compensation – is not a form of appearance or a mode of expression of value as Marx (1990) points out but rather a mode of expression of lost value. Lost labour power is the underlying reality of this commodity. This commodity is exchanged at its lost value rather than at its value, where its exchange value and its price are the manifestations of lost value. The exchange relation established by insurance boards is the only form of appearance of lost value inasmuch as lost value cannot naturally appear by itself.

Now, although the exchange value and the price of this commodity are manifestations of lost value rather than value, the magnitude of lost value is determined by time as is the case with the value of any other commodity. Time still plays a major role as the fundamental unit of exchange. However, what determines the magnitude of this commodity is not the labour time necessary for its production but the lost labour time necessary for the general production of commodities in a subset of firms within a branch of industry. Capitalists consume the lost-labour-power commodity as an input for the capitalist labour process of production, a process that involves the production and consumption of lost labour power. While the capitalist labouring process produces lost labour power in the form of injuries and diseases leading to disability, individual capitalists consume lost labour power as a market externality, a commodity in the form of a guarantee. As a compulsory insurance against lost labour power, this commodity is supplied at an amount equivalent to the cost of repairing, recovering and maintaining labour power during the disability period. Therefore, the amount of money exchanged for this commodity is conditioned by the magnitude of lost value, in other words, the quantity of lost labour time produced during the capitalist process of production. The number of working days lost, the permanent impairment rate, and the fatality rate, among other rates that measure the temporary, the permanent or the total extinction of labour time at an average degree of skill prevalent in the labouring process, reflect the role of time in establishing the quantitative proportion of the commodity's exchange value and price. The exchange value and the price of this commodity are not only an expression of lost value but of its magnitude: lost labour time. In addition, it is not just lost labour time but social lost labour time. This commodity is not exchanged at an exchange value and a price that represents the total mass of lost labour time at the firm level, but at an exchange value and price that represents the average of lost labour time in a subset of firms within a branch of industry. What is being exchanged is a social average, the average of lost labour time produced in an aggregate and effectively embodied in the commodity in the form of rates. From the vantage point of its magnitude, capitalists pay for this commodity a percentage of the wage bill that represents the contribution to and deviation from the total mass of expected lost labour time in a subset of firms within a branch of industry. Paraphrasing Marx (1990), we can define this commodity's magnitude as a proportion of the total mass of lost labour time that is socially necessary to produce any commodity under the hazardous conditions of production normal for a given branch of industry. It is the quantity of lost labour time socially necessary for the production of commodities in an aggregate that determines the magnitude of the exchange value of this commodity and its price. Its true reality is that of being the product of the destruction of labour power in general rather than individually; what is being exchanged is essentially socially necessary *lost* labour time. The price mechanism of insurance boards is based on the average lost labour time objectified in the commodity in the form of rates. This explains why the lost-labour-power commodity gets objectified in the form of lost-time injury rates rather than no injuries and no time-lost rates. It is the inner construction of the commodity as a medium of exchange of socially necessary lost labour time that conditions its external form. Thus, as a material object, a physical representation, this commodity takes the form of rates such as the average number of working days lost, the permanent impairment rate, and the fatality rate, among others, that allow insurance boards to quantitatively monetize the magnitude of temporary lost value, permanent lost value and the total extinction of lost value.

To be clear, as a substance, this commodity is abstract lost labour power, in other words, wage labourers' incapacity to work due to a work accident, disease or fatality. As a magnitude, it is concrete lost labour time, wage labourers' incapacity to work due to a work accident, disease or fatality during an amount of time within an aggregate. As a social magnitude, it is socially necessary lost labour time, that is, an average of lost labour time socially necessary to produce commodities under the hazardous conditions of production normal for a given aggregate. It is important to note that it is in regard to its social magnitude that this commodity performs the critical function of reducing different types of accidents, diseases and deaths to units of the same kind for exchange purposes at an average level. Let us have a closer look at this.

As a social magnitude, this commodity can be simply thought of as congealed socially necessary lost labour time. It is the embodiment of workers' socially necessary lost labour time due to their inability to perform their job with an average degree of skill and intensity due to a work injury, disease or death. As congealed socially necessary lost labour time, this commodity is mainly represented by rates such as the workers' treatment time – e.g., average number of working days lost – their incapacity to perform the job as an average worker – e.g., permanent impairment rate – or the perpetual incapacity to work due to a major injury or death – e.g., loss of earnings rate. In regard to Marx's (1990) claim that "As exchange values, all commodities are merely definite quantities of congealed labour-time" (p. 130), the exchange value of this commodity is its opposite: plainly congealed lost labour time. It is the embodiment of socially necessary lost labour time due to workers' inability to perform their job due to an injury, disease or death that quantitatively enables the exchange. Socially necessary lost labour time is the essence of this commodity. The proportion of the exchange value – i.e., the rate of compensation – is conditioned by the magnitude of lost value rather than the quality of lost value. This occurs because, as with any commodity, the exchange value is quantitative rather than qualitative. When taken in certain proportions, the lost labour time of different types of accidents, diseases and deaths are equal in exchange value. The lost value may be the outcome of an unusual accident, but through its magnitude – i.e., lost labour time – it is posited as equal to another accident. Since the social magnitude of the lost value of this commodity represents the quantity of socially necessary lost labour time, it follows that all risks of accidents, diseases and deaths when taken in certain proportions are equal in lost labour time. Therefore, within the same aggregate, equivalent quantities of lost labour time due to different risks yield exactly the same exchange value and price. Different types of risks have a relative form of lost value, where the lost value of an accident presupposes that some other accident, disease or death can confront it in an equivalent form, that is, as lost labour time. It is in the magnitude of the lost value relation of one accident risk to another that they have a relative form of lost value. This relative form is key for the commodity to emerge as the embodiment of socially necessary lost labour time within an aggregate that produces diverse types of accidents, diseases and deaths. Therefore, under equal lost labour time, the exchange value of dissimilar lost-time injury claims such as falls, cuts, electrical shocks, burns, strains, bruises and sprains are the same. Paraphrasing Marx (1990), as a magnitude of lost value, lost-time injury claims from different work accidents and diseases are identical as 'two peas'. When placed in a lost-value relation, lost-time injury claims of accidents and diseases are nothing but lost labour time. They differ only in quantity. The socially necessary lost labour time as the social magnitude of this commodity is equal to the average expenditure of individual lost labour time in an aggregate regardless of the type of accident, disease or death. As a magnitude and embodiment of socially necessary lost labour time, this commodity reduces the risk of accidents, diseases and deaths to units of the same kind: lost labour time. The lost-labour-power commodity collapses and equalizes the flood of accidents and diseases in a branch of industry into lost labour time in order to perform the exchange of lost labour time at an average level. Lost labour time is the atom of the commodity, the most basic and fundamental measure of lost value in any of its manifestations, be it an electrical shock, a burn, a strain, a fall or a cut. As a unit and medium of measurement, lost labour time is needed as the most elemental category, without which the social average of lost labour time due to work accidents, diseases and deaths within a branch of industry cannot be attained, objectified, exchanged and monetized.

This value examination of the commodity by no means discredits Marx's value theory. On the contrary, it is proof of the utility of approaching Marx's value theory as a theoretical framework for the understanding of the value structure of complex information commodities. As a causal-explanatory mode, Marx's value theory enables disclosure of the social relations involved in the value, exchange value and price formation of the lost-labour-power commodity, particularly the institutional structures, the scientific and technical means, and the power relations embedded in the construction of the commodity as a medium of exchange. In addition, this value analysis shows that Marx's value theory has the capacity to provide the basis for theories around those labour activities that produce commodities that aim at capturing value without producing and adding value to the total mass of surplus value in society – i.e., unproductive labour (see Finkelstein, 2018). Rather than contradicting the law of value, this analysis shows the concealment and inversion of value that takes place in the value formation of the lost-labour-power commodity. In this case, the lost-labour-power commodity not only exemplifies a commodity that captures value without objectifying an equivalent amount of value, but, even more, a commodity whose exchange value and price are the reverse manifestation of value. It is the commodity's aim that comprises an internal obstacle for the crystallization of value. The fact that its exchange value and its price are not a reflection of the value embodied in the commodity is due to the fact that this commodity is designed and constructed to exchange lost value. Its purpose poses an internal obstacle for the objectification of value. However, as this analysis shows, the proportion of the commodity's exchange value and its price is not a fortuitous combination of external circumstances. It can neither be explained solely in terms of competitive pressures, different socioeconomic environments or technological impediments to the mobility of labour, among other external factors. This examination discloses that the exchange value and price of this commodity, as an expression of the social magnitude of lost value – i.e., socially necessary lost labour time – is eminently the product of an internal relation within the commodity. This vantage point is critical to the understanding of how this commodity manifests in capitalist societies beyond ownership and control distinctions – i.e., public versus private – thus placing the problem on a level of generality that brings into focus the inner construction of the commodity and its articulated combination within the capitalist mode of production.

4.5   Value and Lost Value: The Transformation of Non-equivalents

The abovementioned value analysis of the commodity shows that insurance boards consume value – i.e., wage labour employed by insurance boards – in order to objectify lost value into lost-time injury rates. Also, it depicts that the portion of value consumed by insurance boards does not play any part in the process of exchange when compared to the total mass of lost value objectified in the commodity. The commodity is exchanged at its lost value rather than its value. Lost value is the underlying substance of the commodity. These are already interesting contradictions about the value formation of the commodity. However, another remarkable feature of this commodity is the fact that it acts as a medium of conversion of lost value into value, that is, as a medium of conversion of non-equivalents. Let us look at this matter more closely.

Value is consumed by insurance boards to objectify lost value into the commodity as a social magnitude. This value process is performed by insurance boards during the first stage of the circuit of metamorphosis of lost labour power. In the stage $(C - M)$, insurance boards construct the lost-labour-power commodity (C) as a guarantee to be exchanged in a business relationship.

While insurance boards receive an amount of money value (M) equivalent to the exchange value and price of the lost-labour-power commodity (C), capitalists outlay an amount of money value (M) equivalent to the exchange value and price of the commodity (C). The commodity (C) is thus transformed into money value (M) at equivalent proportions. This process of transformation appears at first sight as something trivial. However, further analysis finds something very peculiar. If we consider that both the commodity's exchange value and price are the form of appearance of lost value rather than value, as has been argued so far, this process involves the transformation of non-equivalent substances. By the act of exchanging the commodity for money, a process of converting non-equivalent substances takes place. Lost value is transformed into value, and congealed lost labour time in the form of the commodity (C) is transformed into congealed labour time in the form of money (M). The first act of the circuit of metamorphosis of lost labour power not only involves the transformation of lost labour power from the commodity form to the money form, but the transformation of lost value objectified in the commodity into value objectified in money. The transformation of lost value into value for exchange purposes constitutes one of insurance boards' greatest achievements. The entirety of their information-intensive operations of recording and processing wage-labour-related injuries, diseases and deaths serves the conversion of lost value into value to allocate compensation payments and compensation benefits. The conversion of non-equivalents performed by insurance boards is paramount to effectively monetizing work accidents leading to temporary, permanent partial or total lost labour power and thus to represent accident risks as economic equivalences.

Once the transformation of lost value into value has been successfully realized, the probability of injuries, diseases and fatalities leading to lost labour power can be effectively considered as value. As a mental relation, lost labour power can now be thought of as money, the universal equivalent. Money acquires the capacity not only to measure value but to act as the universal measure of lost value, therefore representing the amount of lost labour power objectified in the commodity. Money is now the form of appearance of the quantity of lost value that is immanent in the lost-labour-power commodity. The social implications of this are not innocuous. Due to the transformation of non-equivalents performed by insurance boards, capitalists are conditioned to think about the risks of accidents, diseases and fatalities in terms of money. Since the conversion of lost value into value enables them to situate work accidents, diseases and deaths in relation to money, capitalists cannot think about the probability of accidents as anything but their money value regardless of their type or human consequences. The chance of suffering a fall, a burn, a strain, or a cut enters the capitalist's mind as an amount of money that needs to be paid to insurance boards. Money as the universal measure of lost value enables different risks to be represented qualitatively as money in any of its forms – e.g., paper money, digital money, credit money – and quantitatively as a magnitude of money – e.g., $1,000,000. Money situates every risk of accident, disease and death in a value relation rather than in a lost value relation. While in a lost value relation, accident risks have a relative form of lost value, where the lost labour time of an accident presupposes that other accidents can confront it as lost labour time, in a value relation, risks have a relative form of value, where the amount of money of any accident presupposes that other accidents can confront it as money. It is not only that money makes different accident risks economically comparable, but that risk is expressed as money. Risks become reified as money. Placed as a mirror of money, risks are money and money is risks.

The reification of risk as money caused by the exchange and transformation of non-equivalents produces a dominant discourse of labour health, namely that accidents have to be compensated rather than eliminated from the worksite. By reducing accidents, diseases and fatalities to exchange values, accident risks are normalized and presented as something natural to the workplace, as common sense or statements of fact. It makes perfect sense to exchange accident risks for money in capitalist societies whose aim is production for exchange. It mirrors the social totality, accurately expressing the whole. Who would dare to challenge the exchange of accident risks for money value? That would amount to challenging the mode of production upon which capitalist societies stand. It is insurance boards' commodification process, through which lost labour power becomes a commodity, that produces the ideology that wage-labour-related injuries, diseases and fatalities are ordinary events that can be fairly compensated. The commodity relocates the problem from a health issue to an exchange one. It presents the dilemma as how lost labour power can be compensated rather than how it can be eliminated. In fact, the term 'compensation', as something given to balance something undesirable, makes it clear that the exchange rationale of the system is dominant. Risks of accidents are depoliticized, transformed into an exchange issue, one that aims at 'fairly' compensating them in the form of medical and wage-replacement benefits at their lost value. By establishing quantitative equality between accidents, diseases and deaths in the form of value, the exchange value and price of the commodity can be rationally set. Insurance boards produce a universalized mode of representation in which injuries, diseases and deaths are individuated and assigned in a system of economic equivalences to exchange them for money. Consonant with the capitalist mode of production, which transforms everything into exchange values, the commodity subsumes accidents, disease and deaths as lost labour time to enable the representation of lost value as a quantitative magnitude for exchange purposes. The commodity is not governed by moral imperatives but by the power of economic abstraction and the principle of exchange value.

5   The Commodification of Lost Labour Power

Lost labour power must pass through a process of production in order to become a commodity and be exchangeable. This process of production, the becoming of a commodity, is known as commodification (Mosco, 2009). In the case of an information commodity, the process of commodification is firmly grounded in information-intensive operations. As Mosco (2009) points out, the informational process of commodification involves recording, processing, calculating and combining different pieces of information to make something exchangeable. In this case, what is made exchangeable is lost labour power. Highly mediated by information, lost labour power is commodified to be exchanged for money.

As with any commodity, the lost-labour-power commodity is produced by insurance boards to serve as a use value (see Marx, 1990); however, it serves as a use value for capital not for wage labour. Insurance boards produce the lost-labour-power commodity as a compulsory means of production, a producer good required for the production of all commodities in capitalist societies. As aforementioned in the use value analysis of the commodity, its utility lies in its capacity to (a) shield capitalists against disputes in court, (b) socialize the cost of compensation payments, and (c) limit the cost of compensation payments to wage labourers' necessary needs to the exclusion of social needs.

To serve as the stated use values, the commodity is constructed by insurance boards as a medium of exchange and transformation to draw money from firms and reconvert that money into medical and wage-replacement benefits. As a medium of exchange, the commodity aims to exchange two different things: lost labour power for money. As a medium of transformation, the commodity aims to convert similar but non-equivalent things: lost value into value. To say the commodity is a medium of transformation is simply to put an emphasis on the lost value objectified in the commodity and converted into money value. This vantage point allows the commodity's function to be understood in terms of value. It simply places the value form at the forefront. Since the analysis that follows places a focus on value, henceforth the expression *medium of transformation* will be deployed to explain the construction of the commodity.

As a medium of transformation, the commodity's goal is to convert lost value into money value and initiate the circuit of metamorphosis of lost labour power (C – M – I – MW). The commodity is the start of the circuit. Its purpose is to transform the amount of lost value objectified in itself (C) into money value (M) in order to convert money value (M) into investment value (I) and at the later stage reconvert investment value (I) into medical and wage-replacement value (MW). The commodity aims to be transformed into money value; it lives and dies for money. Once the commodity is transformed into money value, the commodity vanishes. For this transformation to happen, the commodity needs to be constructed not only as a medium of transformation but as a medium of transformation of non-equivalents. This is because the transformation of the lost-labour-power commodity (C) into money value (M) involves the conversion of lost value into value, that is, the conversion of non-equivalents. Therefore, to serve as a use value for capital, this commodity has to be constructed as a medium of conversion of non-equivalents. This constitutes the key function of the commodity, without which the risk of accidents, diseases and fatalities cannot be monetized.

Insurance boards' information apparatuses are meticulously designed to effectively convert non-equivalents in conditions that are favourable to capital. Through an information-intensive process, lost labour power is commodified in order to function as a medium of conversion of lost value into value, lost labour time into labour time, and socially necessary lost labour time into socially necessary labour time. To do so, the production of the commodity must follow two fundamental requisites. First, insurance boards need to construct a commodity capable of transforming lost value into value at equivalent proportions. Why is this proportionality a requisite? Because it is key to balance the total mass of compensation benefits against the total mass of compensation payments. The commodity needs to ensure that the conversion of the total mass of lost value in a branch of industry into the total mass of money value – i.e., all the premiums – is in equilibrium. Second, insurance boards need to construct a commodity capable of spreading the total mass of money – i.e., premiums – in disproportion to the performance of the many capitalists. Why is this disproportionate spread also a requisite? Because it ensures that every capitalist is collectively sharing the burden of lost labour power in a subset of firms within a branch of industry regardless of the total mass of lost value produced at the firm level. This assures the collective character of the system, which is one of its main tenets.

Considering these requisites, the process of the commodification of lost labour power can be conceptualized as an informational-intensive process that produces a commodity capable of converting lost value into value at an equivalent proportion and spreads the cost of compensation payments in disproportion among many capitalists. Conceptually speaking, the commodification process involves the processes of objectification or reification, measurability, and monetary equivalence. The process of objectification or reification (see Lukács, 1999) of lost labour power is the transformation of lost labour power into a thing, an external object that can be disposed of. The properties and singularities of lost labour power, namely, the qualitative dimensions – e.g., a fall, a burn, a depression, a strain – become quantifiable in the form of lost-time injury rates. The process of objectification of lost labour power occurs in three successive moments: the working-day-lost moment, the reporting moment and the recording moment. The process of measurability of lost labour power aims at making it comparable among aggregates. It situates every firm's lost labour power in relation to the total mass of lost labour power produced by firms within the same branch of industry. It takes place during the processing moment, where different pieces of injury information are combined and calculated on the basis of certain rules and transformed into lost-time injury rates – e.g., average number of working days lost per aggregate, average number of working days lost per accident, fatality rate, permanent impairment rate, and loss of earnings. The process of monetary equivalence places lost labour power in an economic relation via the money form. This process takes place during the programing moment. It involves a series of orders or instructions that mathematically recombine lost-time injury rates into a medium of exchange, allowing it to transform lost value into money value – i.e., the premium. Based on the aforementioned processes, the commodification of lost labour power can be divided into five different temporal moments: (a) the working-day-lost moment, (b) the reporting moment, (c) the recording moment, (d) the processing moment and (e) the programing moment. Taken together, these particular moments in time comprise the commodification of lost labour power or the production of the lost-labour-power commodity.

5.1 The Working-Day-Lost Moment

The commodification process begins with an unfortunate event at the workplace that yields lost labour power. This event occurs in the form of an accident, disease or death leading to temporary, permanent partial or the total destruction of labour power. This commodity is a suffering-dependent one, since for it to come into existence the pain of an injury should be strong enough to disable a wage labourer from performing his job. Lost labour power is naturally produced by the inability of a wage labourer to get back to work due to an injury. However, it is not a result of any injury but from a compensable injury – deemed compensable by WCS s – experienced during the capitalist labouring process, that is, during the consumption of labour power. The formula is simple: lost labour power produced during the consumption of labour power counts as the very substance of the commodity. It should be noted that the lost labour power that springs from the inability to work of freelance workers, migrant workers, undocumented workers, and all those precarious workers who do not work under a regular wage contract for a capitalist does not get commodified. Under the compulsory laws related to WCS s, only lost labour power that originates during the consumption of labour power can be objectified into the commodity. In addition, not any amount of lost labour power stemmed during the consumption of labour power but a particular quantity. There is a minimum threshold, measured in lost labour time, for lost labour power to be objectified into the commodity. In general, modern WCS s consider one working day lost as the minimum quantity of lost labour power to furnish the commodity. An accident or disease whose lost labour time does not yield an amount equal to or greater than one working day does not feed the commodity with lost days. In other words, the wage labourer should not be able to return to work for at least one working day. The commodity equalizes the flood of accidents and diseases into working days lost to perform the exchange of lost labour power. Thus, one working day lost as a particular amount of lost labour time constitutes the atom of the commodity; it is the most basic and fundamental measure of lost value in any of its manifestations.

This time rule for the objectification of lost labour power into the commodity is set by the capitalist state and can vary along countries and jurisdictions. For example, the Canadian WCS of British Columbia imposes a waiting period of one day. What this window actually does is increase the minimum threshold, thus blocking the lost labour time produced below the threshold from being objectified into the commodity. The minimum threshold is not trivial. By increasing the minimum threshold, less lost labour time gets objectified into the commodity, the exchange value of the commodity – i.e., rate of compensation – is reduced, and the amount of compensation benefits to be awarded to injured workers shrinks. Fluctuations in injury rates, rates of compensation, and compensation benefits can sometimes be simply explained by changes or differences in the minimum threshold. For example, when comparing injury rates between Germany and Austria from 1890 to 1906, Murray and Nilsson (2007) correctly point out that Austria's rates were higher than Germany's due to their waiting period rather than any other variable. By controlling the waiting period, the authors correctly conclude that injury rates increased in the two countries by almost the same proportion from 1890–1906 (Murray and Nilsson, 2007). It is important to note that, whether the minimum threshold is one, two or three working days lost, the commodification of lost labour time begins with a working day lost rather than an accident or a disease *per se*. As a unit and medium of measurement, a working day lost is needed as a basic category, one without which lost labour time cannot be attained, objectified, monetized and exchanged. This explains why insurance boards zealously keep track of lost labour time in the form of the number of working days lost at a firm level, a subset of firms, a branch of industry or all branches of industry. It is a key measure for the commodification of lost labour power. This process never begins when an accident with no time-loss happens. It starts only when a tragic event yields at least one working day lost. In this regard, Heinrich (1950) correctly criticizes the use of accident information recorded for insurance matters in order to do prevention work (see Chapter 3). He was aware that by focusing on time-loss accidents, significant and valuable data were left behind. He was adamant about placing efforts on the study of accidents with no time-loss. Nevertheless, Heinrich never understood that insurance boards do not aim to record accidents with working days lost for prevention purposes but rather for exchange purposes. It is due to the need to commodify lost labour time that a specific time unit – i.e., a working day lost – at a minimum threshold – e.g., one, three or four working days lost – is imposed by wcs s as a standard measure for the process of commodification to begin.

5.2   *The Reporting Moment*

Reporting is the act whereby lost labour time at its smallest unit – i.e., a working day lost – is brought to life. Lost labour power as the immaterial substance of the commodity comes into existence through the reporting moment. In this regard, the loss of working days equal or above the minimum threshold can happen during the labouring process, but if they are not reported and accepted they do not come into being. Without the reporting and accepting of working days lost due to compensable injuries that result from the capitalist labouring process, lost labour power cannot exist, let alone be commodified. Unfortunately for wage labourers, working days lost do not have the ability to report themselves, and human agency is needed. The reporting mechanism takes the form of injury claims. However, the reporting moment is not an easy one. Since the establishment of wcs s, the claim procedure was singled out as one of the most abusive aspects of the insurance system (see Eghigian, 2000). Workers and unions frequently complain about the complex, ambiguous and biased nature of the claim procedure.

An injury claim is usually a one- or two-page form with blank spaces for the insertion of lost-time injury information. Once an injury is deemed compensable, compensation in the form of medical and wage-replacement benefits is disbursed. The injury claim form allows an insurance board to gather key lost-time injury information for the commodification of lost labour power. Injury claims are comprised of information such as (a) the name, age, sex, phone number and address of the injured worker, (b) the name, phone number, address, payroll contact and type of business of the firm, (c) the worker's occupation and status – e.g., full time, part time, temporary –, (d) the date/time of the incident and time missed from work, (e) a description of the incident and the injury, and (f) wage information – e.g., base salary, gross earnings, tips, gratuities, overtime. Among all the lost-time injury information reported, the critical information for commodifying lost labour power is (a) the date/time of the incident and time missed from work and (b) the wage information. This information is essential for insurance boards to record lost labour power in terms of its magnitude – i.e., lost labour time – and economic equivalences.

The submission of injury claims is the responsibility of the firm and the wage labourer. It can be done manually, by phone, or online. In some countries and jurisdictions, the injury claim procedure takes place at the arrival of the injured worker to the hospital or medical facility. Although an injury claim can be directly filled by a wage labourer or a third party – e.g., clerical workers at a medical facility – it must be confirmed by the firm and accepted as compensable by the insurance board. Capital and the capitalist state have the prerogative. Let us remember that this commodity as a guarantee is a means of production required during the labouring process, one that serves as a use value for capital not for wage labour. Thus, firms are given the upper hand over the reporting moment. In addition, the fact that insurance boards do not actively collect working days lost to commodify lost labour power is a sign of how the reporting moment is laden in favor of capital. These agencies only provide the general steps on how to fill out injury claims and apply for compensation benefits. This vacuum is not negligible. Due to their lack of direct involvement, lost labour power is usually not effectively gathered through the injury claim mechanism. This happens because injury claims can be intentionally incorrectly filled out or not even filled out at all. Misreporting and underreporting are common reporting practices within WCSs (see Azaroff et al., 2004; Broadway and Stull, 2008; Brown and Barab, 2007; Dew and Taupo, 2009; Galizzi et al., 2010; Geller, 1996; Lippel, 2003, 2007; MacEachen, 2000; Mansfield et al. 2012; Strunin and Boden, 2004; Zoller, 2003). From the very establishment of WCSs in 1884 in Germany, the reporting moment was an issue. As Guinnane and Streb (2015) correctly claim, the reporting of non-fatal accidents in Germany between 1885 and 1914 was not reliable due to misreporting and underreporting practices. This is due to the fact that concealing or misreporting non-fatal injuries is easier than concealing or misreporting a fatal accident. These scholars suggest that misreporting accidents in wrong categories and dissuading workers not to report non-fatal accidents were ordinary practices (Guinnane and Streb, 2015). Similar to the act of increasing the minimum threshold during the working-day-lost moment, the misreporting and underreporting practices result in less lost value objectified into the commodity, a decrease in the exchange value of the commodity, and a reduction in compensation benefits. As we shall see in Chapter 5, there exists a battery of tools at the disposal of capitalists to hamper, manipulate and distort the reporting moment.

Even though injuries with no lost time do get reported through injury claims and recorded by insurance boards, this type of information does not get processed and objectified into the commodity. Only reports of injuries with lost time – i.e., injuries that yield a number of working days lost equal to or above the minimum threshold – count for the commodification of lost labour power. The reporting moment exists predominantly to collect injuries with lost time in order to furnish the commodity. Moreover, the reporting moment exists to produce lost labour power, the immaterial substance of the commodity. Lost labour power as the reference of the commodity comes into existence through the reporting moment. This moment can be thought of as an act that resurrects working days lost into lost value. It enables to revive and put to use once more those working days that were lost during the labour process. However, this resurrection moment is performed in conditions that are favourable to capital rather than to wage labourers. Rather than bringing back working days lost for the day of final judgement, like the previous Liability System, working days are brought back under principles of exchange required to furnish the lost-labour-power commodity. No capitalist should be held accountable for putting workers' lives at danger while pursuing profit. The reporting moment carries the judgement that no one has been wrong or unjust. Under wcs s, the account of working days lost loses its biblical connotations; divine justice and moral imperatives are replaced by those of exchange.

5.3   The Recording Moment

The recording moment is the act of inscribing and registering the lost-time injury information reported via injury claims. All the information reported via injury claims – e.g., injured worker info, company info, incident info, working days lost info, wage info – gets printed, registered, classified, organized and stored. This process brings the object of lost labour power into a material being, an independent material object that can be circulated, modified, grouped and set aside. It is through the recording moment that the commodity, as a twofold information commodity, acquires its physical body, the representation of a reference. While the reporting moment produces the immaterial substance of the commodity – i.e., lost labour power – the recording moment produces the object of the immaterial substance, a physical representation – i.e., lost-time injury information.

Conceptually, the recording moment is the operation of objectifying lost labour power, the act of crystallizing lost labour power into a material object – i.e., lost-time injury information. A vast amount of labour power in the form of living labour – i.e., workers employed by insurance boards – and dead labour – i.e., machines, technology, data centers – is used during this moment. It is insurance boards that consume labour power for the operations of objectifying lost labour power into lost-time injury information. Under a protestant logic, one that gives primacy to the written word as the source of truth, insurance boards deploy their information and communication technologies to perform their record-related activities; record inscribing, record classification, record keeping and record maintenance. These agencies store gargantuan amounts of information. Just to have an idea, in 2016 in Chile, private insurance boards recorded 176,716 lost-time accidents totaling 3,463,633 working days lost (Superintendencia de Seguridad Social, 2017). If the amount of related information for each lost-time accident is considered, the extent to which insurance boards rely on information and communication technologies to keep such a massive amount of data is evident. Insurance boards are the safe keepers of lost-time injury information. In this regard, it is helpful to see insurance boards not only as agencies that objectify lost labour power but as a big memory bank storing the lost-time injury information submitted through injury claims. Billions of working-days-lost-related information grouped along economic sectors, firm size, medical costs, wages, time periods and type of incident, among many other variables, are safely stored by insurance boards for exchange purposes.

The accuracy of insurance boards' record-related activities is critical to satisfy one of the main requirements of the commodification process, namely, the conversion of lost value into money value at an equivalent proportion. Let us remember that lost labour power is commodified as a medium of transformation of non-equivalents at equivalent proportions. To assure corresponding equivalences, the commodity needs to crystallize the actually existing and concrete amount of lost value produced in an aggregate. The rigor on the objectification of lost labour power enables the commodity to transform effective lost value into money value at an equivalent proportion.

Achieving corresponding proportions allows the total mass of lost value in an aggregate to be balanced against the total mass of money to be paid by all the member firms within an aggregate. This assures at the end of the circuit of metamorphosis that the total mass of compensation benefits is in equilibrium with the total mass of compensation payments. In other words, corresponding equivalences allow injured workers to be proportionally compensated in order to satisfy their necessary needs. Every bit and piece of lost-time injury information collected through injury claims and recorded by insurance boards must be performed with a high level of accuracy. Precision is constitutive to the recording moment. The recording moment not only brings up a material object that represents lost labour power but an accurate quantitative representation.

There is no clear division between the reporting moment and the recording moment. Both moments tend to blend together, making it difficult in practice to set a clear distinction between the two. Due to technological advances, the reporting moment tends to appear as the recording moment. In some cases, the sole act of reporting creates an entry that becomes a record in itself. In addition, the academic literature tends to use the concepts of reporting and recording interchangeably, thus contributing further to the blurring of the two moments. Nonetheless, it is important to theoretically distinguish both moments since each of them are different and present their own set of dilemmas in regard to the commodification of lost labour power. A lost-time injury cannot be recorded, classified and stored unless being previously reported; however, it can certainly be reported while not yet being recorded, classified and stored. While reporting precedes recording, recording does not precede reporting. As moments, they are not the same, and therefore it is appropriate to theoretically analyze them apart.

5.4   *The Processing Moment*

The processing of information can be simply conceived as the act of changing both the form and content of previously gathered information to come up with an aggregate type of information. It results from combining and computing different pieces of information on the basis of certain rules. The processing moment of the commodity is comprised of the computing of the information recorded and stored by insurance boards during the recording moment. It includes the information provided by injury claims as well as medical information in both its economic – e.g., costs, expenditures, tariffs – and technical forms – e.g., level of temporal disability, permanent partial disability or total disability. Under the laws of wcss in some countries, it also includes vocational rehabilitation information – e.g., return-to-work, ability to work assessments. This process is mainly a bureaucratic one, a process connected with many preestablished and complicated rules. Based on the principles of statistics and probability and a set of operational rules, the processing moment transforms lost-time injury information into rates. By combining and calculating the total mass of working days lost, the total mass of wages, total medical expenditures, the total number of fatalities, and the total amount of impairment, among many other units of information, this process results in a new form and content of information, namely, lost-time injury rates. Lost-time injury rates include (a) injury rate, (b) disease rate, (c) average of working days lost per aggregate, (d) average of working days lost per accident, (e) fatality rate, (f) permanent impairment rate, (g) loss of earnings, and (h) wage rate, among others. In terms of form, the processing moment transforms disparate information into quantitative units of information. In terms of scope or reach, the processing moment transforms individual information into social information. Taking both the form and scope together, lost-time injury rates can be simply equated as social averages of lost-time injuries produced at a firm level, a subset of firms and a branch of industry. Its purpose is to function both as a medium of measurement of lost labour power and a medium of exchange of lost labour power, but as social averages. Thus, the general purpose of the processing moment is to furnish the commodity with statistical information instrumentally capable of performing the conversion of lost value into value at social averages to spread compensation payments in disproportion among the capitalist class. Before delving into this matter closely, let us consider some general aspects of the processing moment.

As already pointed out, the prior moment of recording brings the material object of lost labour power into being as lost-time injury information. The act of recording injury claims in the form of physical signs produces lost labour power as an external object. Conceptually, the recording moment is the objectification of lost labour power, where lost labour power gets crystallized as lost-time injury information. In this regard, the processing moment can be conceptualized as the refinement of the objectification of lost labour power, a process that removes unwanted elements, improves lost-time injury information and leaves it ready to function as a medium of conversion of non-equivalents. As a process of refinement, the processing moment refines lost-time injury information into lost-time injury rates. This refined and cultivated version comprises the physical object of lost labour power. To be precise, the object of lost labour power, its material reference, is constituted by lost-time injury rates, not lost-time injury information. This is so because it is only as lost-time injury rates that the commodity as a physical object can perform its role as a medium of transformation of lost value into value. However, the becoming of lost-time injury rates depends on the first stage of objectification of lost labour power as lost-time injury information. As a continuous movement, the recording and the processing moments are different instances in the process of objectifying lost labour power. The objectification begins with the recording moment and ends with the processing moment. However, as two distinctive moments, the recording moment is the raw objectification of lost labour power while the processing moment is the refinement of the physical object into a form and content capable of converting lost value into value at social averages.

The processing moment produces an enhanced and upgraded version of the external body of the commodity, namely, lost-time injury rates. This refined version is the outcome of computing recorded information based on the application of statistics. Produced on statistical principles and in relation to the mass of lost labour power at the firm level, a subset of firms and a branch of industry, the commodity's external body – i.e., lost-time injury rates – is a social average. It embodies the total social lost value produced at three different aggregate levels. Thus, as a magnitude, the commodity is socially necessary lost labour time, reflecting the total mass of lost labour time socially necessary to produce any commodity in a subset of firms within a branch of industry. Insurance boards' colossal databases play a major role in the refinement of the commodity as a social average or socially necessary lost labour time. Due to their monopoly control of record inscribing and record keeping operations that allow them to store the signals leading to differential lost labour power emitted at every workplace, insurance boards can effectively construct the commodity as social averages. Like Marx's (1991) differential rent concept, which depends on the varying fertility of the land, insurance boards construct the commodity in order to reflect the social averages of varying lost labour power within aggregates. By organizing, classifying and manipulating lost-time injury information of individual firms in relation to rating groups in a branch of industry, the fluctuation of differential lost labour time among individual firms is equalized and the commodity is refined as an expression of socially necessary lost labour time. The processing moment collapses the flux of lost labour time into social averages in order to refine the commodity as the objectification of socially necessary lost labour time. This allows the commodity to fulfill its second requisite, the spreading of the cost of compensation payments in disproportion regardless of the total mass of lost value produced at the firm level. By constructing the commodity as the embodiment of social averages or socially necessary lost labour time, a disproportionate distribution of compensation payments is structurally enforced. It is embedded in the inner construction of the commodity. Capitalists are collectively held accountable for the total mass of lost labour power produced in society by the sole act of commodifying lost labour power as social averages.

5.5   *The Programing Moment*

The previous processing moments leave us with social averages, a set of lost-time injury rates such as the (a) injury rate, (b) disease rate, (c) average number of working days lost per aggregate, (d) the fatality rate, (e) the permanent impairment rate, (f) the wage rate, etc. These rates are not enough to enable the commodity to perform its function as a medium of transformation. A series of orders must be given to the commodity. The programing moment comprises these sets of instructions or orders that guide the commodity toward its goal, namely the conversion of lost value into value at an equivalent proportion to spread compensation payments in disproportion among the many capitalists. It tells the commodity exactly what to do in order to function as a medium of transformation. It is a set of basic coded instructions inserted in the commodity as genes or behavioral responses that enable the commodity to perform as a medium of transformation of lost value into value for the provision against the possibility that an accident leading to lost labour power might happen. The commodity converts lost value into value not only at social averages but against the possibility that those social averages might actually be produced. Let us remember that the commodity is a guarantee against expected lost labour power or the chance that a capitalist's investment will lose value due to an accident, disease or fatality leading to working days lost. As with every insurance contract, in which the chance of loss is the subject matter, the commodity's subject matter is the chance of lost labour power. As a chance, the commodity is probabilistically constructed to predict the future. It is a forecast. It aims at transforming lost value into money value in case an accident or disease leading to lost labour power takes place. What the programing moment does is infuse the commodity with the ability to forecast the total mass of lost labour power within aggregates for the exchange of social averages. To do so, the commodity is given instructions to process lost-time injury rates in a prospective and probabilistic fashion. Lost-time injury rates of the past are combined and processed to come up with social averages to transform past socially lost labour power into future money value. The commodity never crystalizes itself as the embodiment of current lost labour power but as past lost labour power. It never reflects present lost labour power but a particular interval of an outdated time. Although this interval varies along WCS s, the time frame for the processing moment is set at around four to five years. This temporal incongruity makes social averages not just an expression of a large aggregate but of a historical aggregate. Thus, besides being a large database, a historical archive is actually required by insurance boards to construct a commodity that probabilistically transforms lost labour power into money value. As the keepers of long-term-lost-time injury records, insurance boards' historical archives comprise a necessary resource for commodifying the chance of lost labour power. Constructed based on the previous flux of recorded lost labour power, the commodity is always outdated lost-time injury rates that predict future payment costs, a forecast based on the historical lost labour power produced at all branches of industry. Now, why would the commodity as social averages be constructed as a four-year prediction rather than concrete and real-time existent social averages? This is because as a use value for capital, a guarantee against the lost value of labour power, the commodity protects individual firms against the unpredictability of compensation payments. It is not a use value for wage labourers but for capital. The fact that wage labourers receive medical and wage replacement benefits is incidental; it is a side effect, a by-product of the commodity. Just as a car gets freely repaired due to a vehicle insurance contract that financially protects the car owner, wage labourers get repaired and compensated by insurance boards at zero cost to an individual firm. As a probability, the lost-labour-power commodity exists for capital. By prospectively and probabilistically constructing social averages rather than retrospectively – i.e., at the end of a period – insurance boards place a limit on the conversion of lost value into value. This restricts both compensation payments – to the benefit of the capitalist class – and compensation benefits – to the detriment of wage labourers. Firms' financial certainty is achieved through the limiting of benefits. By acting as a kind of capitalist oracle of future socially lost labour time, insurance boards construct the commodity in a probabilistic fashion to reduce firms' financial uncertainty. However, from the point of view of workers, rather than a group of high priests foretelling the future, insurance boards appear as speculators of lost labour power.

    As a medium to convert past lost value into value for the provision against the probability of an event leading to lost labour power, insurance boards infuse the commodity with a series of instructions and operations that probabilistically enable the commodity to process social averages and predict the future. The commodity is commanded to process lost-time injury rates as risk, namely, expected lost labour power. As explained in Chapter 3, risk as expected lost labour power is the possibility that lost labour power will likely be produced by businesses as a market externality. Insurance boards exchange expected lost labour power rather than concrete lost labour power. The circuit of metamorphosis of lost labour power is performed by insurance boards to distribute lost labour power as risk not as certitude. Two sets of basic instructions can be distinguished: (a) the construction of the chance of social lost labour power as a medium of measurement, and (b) the construction of the chance of social lost labour power as a medium of exchange.

Chances must be measured to exist. Without its measurement, chance cannot be a concrete or useful notion. In addition, chances must be rationally measured to be legitimately and officially used. Let us remember that it was during the 19th century that insurance businesses went from something irrational to something rational due to the appearance of statistics and probability. This science, central to the discovery of regularities in apparent chance events such as work accidents, has been paramount to insurance boards since their inception. As explained in Chapter 2, statistics and probability comprise a precondition for a collective system that prospectively enforces the total mass of expected lost labour power produced in society to be shared among the many capitalists. Risk as a medium of measurement of the chance of social lost labour power is carefully constructed by insurance boards. Risk as a medium of measurement brings into existence the chance of social lost labour power. It does not bring into being social lost labour power, which was already brought into existence through the previous processing moment, but rather expected social lost labour power. It also brings into being the deviation of expected social lost labour power in an aggregate. To recapitulate Chapter 3, risk as a medium of measurement of chances brings into being each firm's contribution to the total mass of expected lost labour power in an aggregate as well as its deviation from the same aggregate. While the contribution to the mass of expected lost labour power in an aggregate yields a normative measure, usually called the group rate, deviation from the total mass of expected lost labour power in an aggregate yields a deviate measure usually dubbed the experience rate. This last measure can be executed prospectively or retrospectively. Both measurements – i.e., the group rate and the experience rate – are constructed to enable the commodity to probabilistically transform social lost value into money value and thus structurally enforce disproportionate payments. The disproportion is structurally enforced by way of constructing the commodity as social averages. The purpose of constructing risk as a medium of measurement is to furnish the commodity with quantitative units of information to enable the conversion of social lost value into money value as a precise forecast. Both the group rate and the experience rate can be seen as the result of a set of instructions given to the commodity. Without these two measures, the commodity cannot perform its function as a medium of transformation of past social lost value into present money value for the provision against the possibility of accidents leading to lost labour power.

Once the chances of social lost labour power are brought into existence, the commodity is commanded to transform those chances into a medium of exchange. The construction of the chances of social lost labour power into a medium of exchange, which actually is the same as the construction of risk as a medium of exchange, transforms the group rate and the experience rate into the rate of compensation, a wage-relation formula that represents an individual firm's probability of social lost labour power. This instruction enables the conversion of chances into a mathematical representation that is readily exchangeable for money. This operation basically entails the conversion of the group rate and the experience rate into a wage expression at the firm level. It involves three steps: the transformation of the group rate into a percentage of the firm's wage bill, the transformation of the experience rate into a percentage of the firm's wage bill, and the summing up of the two quantities (see Chapter 3). For example, a group rate equivalent to 1.3% of the wage bill and an experience rate equivalent to 0.4% would yield a rate of compensation of 1.7%. A rate of compensation of 1.7% means that the commodity, as a medium of exchange, would convert the chance of social lost value into money value at a proportion equivalent to 1.7% of a firm's wage bill. By constructing the commodity as a medium of exchange of expected social averages, individual capitalists are protected from the full cost of compensation payments as well as the unpredictability of those payments. This commodity socializes compensation payments and reduces financial uncertainty via its inner mechanics rather than external forces.

CHAPTER 5

The Fetishism of the Lost-Labour-Power Commodity

1   Introduction

The establishment of wcs s and their information-intensive process to commodify lost labour power not only set lost labour power apart from a juridical order into a system of exchange value but masked the social relations arising out of work injuries, leading to the allocation of compensation payments and benefits. As a group of numbers and rates, the lost-labour-power commodity is mute as to the type of incident, the type of injury as well as the personal information of injured workers that compose the total mass of lost value objectified in the commodity. In addition, the commodity conceals the social structures, mechanisms and power relations involved in the production and value formation of the commodity. Rather than the result of a series of social relations, the commodity appears as autonomous. As a fetish, the commodity asserts itself as a fact of society, namely, the total mass of lost value produced in society to be exchanged in the form of compensation payments and benefits among the capitalist class and the working class.

This chapter examines the fetish character of the lost-labour-power commodity, that is, the hidden social structures, mechanisms and power relations involved in the value formation of the commodity. By fetishism, I specifically mean the mistaken perception that transforms the exchange value of the lost-labour-power commodity into a reality to the degree that its value appears to be proportional to the total mass of lost value of work injuries – i.e., the economic costs of medical and wage-replacement benefits. Instead of mechanically understanding the value of the commodity arising from the occurrence of work injuries, the analysis that follows penetrates the social relations established by insurance boards' circuit of metamorphosis that disguise the mass of lost value not objectified in the commodity. It reveals the hidden social relations involved in the value fluctuation of the commodity. This is crucial because the effective mass of lost value not crystallized in the commodity manifests as a tension between the two classes in the form of cheaper premiums and unfulfilled medical and wage-replacement benefits. While cheaper premiums are celebrated by the capitalist class, partial benefits are not welcome by the working class. The central argument of this chapter is that although the underlying

reality of the commodity is lost value, as revealed in Chapter 4, its value formation is not merely injury driven. By expounding the procedural mechanisms,
the economic-structural dynamics and the power relations that the insurance
boards' circuit of metamorphosis establish, the pretense of the commodity's
value as being determined by work injuries is ruled out. The reporting procedure, the deeming process, the rate-setting mechanics, the level of underemployment, the business cycle, the underreporting practices, the appealing of
legitimate claims, and the early-return-to-work programs, among other social
relations, are singled out as examples of the conditioning power of procedurally, structurally and class-connected social relations. This analysis debunks
the injury-driven determination of the commodity's value, thus revealing the
fetishism of the lost-labour-power commodity.

2   Fetishism and Lost Labour Power

As Harvey (2010) notes, Marx's fetishism is a technical concept fundamental
to political economy. It is "[…] an essential tool for unraveling the mysteries of
capitalist political economy" (Harvey, 2010, p. 38). Marx's fetishism signals how
important aspects of the production of commodities get hidden in capitalist
economies. Basically, it points out a series of social relations that are disguised
during the process of the exchange of commodities. As Harvey (2010) illus-
trates, when you buy a head of lettuce not only you do not know anything
about the amount of value objectified in the commodity but anything about
the process of production or the labourers themselves. It is not possible to
know if the lettuce was produced by "[…] happy laborers, miserable laborers,
slave laborers, wage laborers or some self-employed peasant" (Harvey, 2010,
p.40). "The lettuces are mute, as it were, as to how they were produced and
who produced them" (Harvey, 2010, p. 40). In regard to the lost-labour-power
commodity, the same obliviousness is present at the moment of exchange. As a
guarantee against lost labour power, the commodity does not say a word about
its process of production. When the commodity confronts the capitalist, the
only thing it utters to the capitalist is that he is paying a quota of social lost
labour power at a wage-relation formula and a price that reflects the firm's contribution to the expected lost labour power in a subset of firms within a branch
of industry – i.e., base premium – and the firm's deviation from such aggregate – i.e., experience premium. By the sole act of buying the commodity at a
base and experience premium, the capitalist is made aware that he is paying
a proportion of social averages of lost labour power in an aggregate. However,
the commodity does not provide any details about the qualitative composition

of the mass of lost value objectified and monetized in the commodity, about its value formation nor its informational process of commodification. As a portion of a homogeneous mass of socially lost labour time, the commodity is mute as to the type of incident – e.g., fall, collision, cut, crash, overexertion – the type of injury – e.g., strain, fracture, abrasion, laceration, dislocation, depression, stress – as well as the personal information – e.g., age, sex, occupation, employment status – of all those injured workers that compose the total mass of socially lost labour time objectified in the commodity. In addition, the commodity not only hides the qualitative composition of the total mass of lost labour time but also the social structures, mechanisms and power relations of the information-producing operations involved in the value formation of the commodity such as the rate-setting mechanics, the underreporting practices, the appealing of legitimate claims and the level of underemployment, among others. Before delving into the fetish dilemma of the commodity, let us go back to the previous Liability System.

Under the Liability System individual capitalists were confronted by lost labour power in the form of a lawsuit rather than a commodity. Whereas the burden of proof was placed on the injured worker or on the capitalist, the Liability System would force the capitalist to directly compensate injured workers for their lost labour power in cases in which they were found guilty of negligence. This juridical order, based on the common law defense plainly revealed the social relations which produced it. In the form of a case before the court, lost labour power was examined in every detail and barely placed under the sight of society. The name, age, sex, occupation, employment status, and family dependants of the wage labourer were fully disclosed. The date/time of the incident, type of injury, working days lost, and incapacity to work were also made available. The working conditions, salary, labouring activities, and even the relationship with their fellow workers were revealed in order to assess if the foreman or any fellow worker could be found liable. Eyewitnesses, testimonies and evidence were required, and the injured worker was thoroughly questioned in court to determine if he was guilty of contributory negligence, in which case the capitalist would not be held accountable. In addition, not only was the singularity of an injury brought to light but the singularity of the human face. As Holdren (2020) describes, courts provided a thick description of work accidents and all their consequences. During the trial of a court system, the full scope of individual suffering and loss was disclosed including the grief and breakdown of families; moving stories were told, morally charged arguments were given, and every detail was brutally presented and examined in an attempt to persuade judges and juries (Holdren, 2020). Once the case was sanctioned by the court, lost labour power in the form of medical and wage-replacement benefits would be awarded or denied at the discretion of the judge. All the actors involved in the lawsuit knew that what was being awarded or denied by the court was a concrete and specific amount of damage compensation due to a work injury. The social relations between all the actors during the court appeal appeared at all events as their own personal relations; the Liability System was totally transparent as to the social relations that converged into a lost-labour-power episode. The capitalist was directly confronted by the relations of production behind an accident – e.g., real people, their social bonds, their miserable existence, their family, their wages – as well as the forces of production behind an accident – e.g., technology, machinery, division of labour and in general the technical and social conditions to extract surplus value. Lost labour power as a social relation made its naked appearance as what it was, a class issue, or a manifestation of how overwork, overcrowded workplaces, speed-ups, increasing intensity, technology and machinery had a detrimental impact on the health of wage labourers. Therefore, the capitalist class was not only confronted by concrete lost labour power in the form of a lawsuit rather than abstract lost labour power in the form of a commodity but by the horrors of capital itself, namely, the conflict between the revolutionized forces of production and the relations of production that galvanized in the form of mass accidents.

The establishment of wcss and their information-intensive mode of compensation brought with it its fetish character. The lost-labour-power commodity as a bearer of lost value and thus a means of exchange of lost value appears not only when exchange has acquired a sufficient extension in society to allow lost labour power to be produced for the purpose of being exchanged but when the previous juridical order has been successfully torn down. By commodifying lost labour power, wcss not only set lost labour power apart from a juridical principle of justice into exchange value principles but masked all the social relations embedded in lost labour power. Through statistically and probabilistically constructing the commodity based on the recording and processing of work accidents, diseases and fatalities in large aggregates, lost labour power was removed from its direct, concrete and particular social relations. Human suffering was anonymized, abstracted and reified in the form of rates and turned into an informational commodity to be exchanged as a guarantee against work injuries. Justice as recognition, as the sense of awareness of the singularity of an injury and its unique and personal consequences to real social beings was abandoned (Holdren, 2020).

In its physical form as lost-time injury rates, the commodity disguises the social relations that combine to produce lost labour power.

Whether in the quantitative form of an injury rate of 2%, which accounts for the number of injuries per 100 workers, or in the form of an average number of lost working days of 12, which measures the average treatment time due to an injury, or in the form of a rate of compensation of 1.3%, a percentage of the wage bill that represents the firm's expected contribution and deviation, the commodity does not provide specifics about the human suffering and social relations involved in the crystallization of the mass of lost value into the commodity. In the words of Holdren (2020), statistics provide a thin rather than a thick account of a work injury. The commodification of lost labour power involves what Holdren (2020) calls 'moral thinning', that is, the reduction of the particularities of work injuries to instrumental abstractions. As a group of signs in the form of numbers and rates, the commodity does not appear as direct social relations between injured workers, their social bonds, their working conditions and their tragedy, but rather as material relations between things. The social relations between people arising out of lost labour power due to a work accident, disease or fatality are concealed by an exchange relation between the lost-labour-power commodity and money. It is both the commodity form and the money form that mask the social character and the social relations of a work accident leading to lost labour power by making those relations appear as a relation between physical objects. Paraphrasing Marx (1990), the lost-labour-power commodity and money "[...] appear as autonomous figures endowed with life of their own, which enter into relations both with each other and with the human race" (Marx, 1990, p. 165).

Besides appearing as something autonomous, the commodity appears as an objective reality. The institutionalization of selling lost labour power as a commodity confronts society as a simple fact. As the total mass of lost labour power in all branches of industry, the commodity appears as a fact of society, an indisputable truth, not the product of social relations arising from the capitalist mode of production. It appears as what it is: the total mass of lost labour time socially necessary to produce any other commodity under the capitalist mode of production. As a fact of society, the commodity can legitimately enter into a social relation with money in order to effectively transform lost value into money value at an equivalent proportion in order to distribute compensation payments and benefits among class societies. The fetish character of the lost-labour-power commodity, namely, its ability to conceal social relations and to disguise itself as a socio-natural reality, has enormous social consequences. These are not only moral or principle implications – e.g., moral thinning, the abandonment of justice as recognition – but mainly political and economic ones.

3   The Fetishism of the Lost-Labour-Power Commodity

The fetishism of the lost-labour-power commodity is like any other commodity in regard to its capacity to hide the social relations involved in the production process. However, the dilemma in this case is a bit different. Going back to Harvey's (2010) lettuce, the problem with this commodity is not that it is not possible to know if it was produced by miserable labourers. We already know that this commodity is the crystallization of wage labourers' suffering in the form of lost-time injury rates due to an accident, disease or death leading to temporary, permanent partial or the total extinction of lost labour power. It is the crystallization of the miserable labouring conditions of the whole wage-labouring class in capitalist societies. In addition, information about wage labourers' miserable conditions is procedurally recorded to a certain extent. Insurance boards do record, classify and store injury information reported via injury claims. Insurance boards possess a historical archive to statistically and probabilistically construct the commodity based on long-term lost-time injury records from many branches of industry. Therefore, although the social relations arising out of work accidents are disguised by the commodity to a high degree, it could be argued that a lot of the information that reveals those social relations still exists – if not the singularity of human suffering and all the social consequences that are implied, then at least much more than average commodities in the marketplace. I argue that the crux of this commodity as a fetish is not that hazardous labouring conditions are concealed or that it is impossible to know anything about the amount of lost value objectified in the commodity. It is a fact that there are many things we can know about the qualitative composition of the mass of lost value embodied in the commodity by simply scrutinizing insurance boards' historical archives. I argue that the dilemma of this commodity concerns the concealment of the social relations involved in the production and exchange of the commodity as a value. Its fetishism revolves around the social structures, mechanisms and power relations involved in the value formation of the commodity. As they are kept out of sight, these social relations in turn conceal the fact that the value formation of the commodity, based on the conversion of lost value into money value, is not only the outcome of lost labour power due to work accidents, diseases and fatalities but something else.

For example, the commodity does not say a word about whether and how much injury claim reporting practices – e.g., underreporting, misreporting – and stringent acceptance procedures affect the amount of lost value embodied in the commodity and thus its money value. The commodity does not say a word about the money value impact of managed care, early-return-to-work practices and vocational rehabilitation interventions that put workers back to work with unresolved medical problems. In addition, the commodity is mute as to how much less lost value was objectified by making the appeal process more complex and technical thus cheapening the money value of the commodity. By concealing the social relations established by insurance boards during the act of production, the commodity masks the mass of lost value not objectified in the commodity. Surplus lost value or unpaid lost labour is not revealed; it is a category that does not even enter the mind. The total mass of lost labour time embodied in the commodity at an equivalent money value appears itself as what it is in disregard of social relations that structurally condition the value formation of the commodity.

As a fetish, the commodity not only asserts itself as the total mass of lost labour power effectively produced in society exclusively due to work accidents, diseases and fatalities, but as a money value directly proportional to the lost labour time produced in society exclusively due to work accidents, diseases and fatalities. Therefore, a decrease in the money value of the commodity inevitably appears as a decrease in the total mass of lost labour power. If premiums go down, it appears in the mind as if there were fewer work accidents, diseases and fatalities. However, nothing can be farther from reality. The commodity's value formation and fluctuations respond to a series of social relations concealed by the commodity itself. The value might go up or down in disregard of the total mass of lost labour power produced in society. The causes for the value fluctuations are structurally hidden due to the fact that there is no direct relationship between the physical body of the commodity, the social relations embodied in it and its value form.

Marx (1990) already noted that there is no connection between the physical body of any commodity, the social relations arising out of it, and its value relations. This is one of the main traits that fetishism reveals. "[...] [T]he commodity-form, and the value-relation of the products of labour within which it appears, have absolutely no connection with the physical nature of the commodity and the material [...] relations arising out of this" (Marx, 1990, p. 165). As Harvey explains, "[o]ur sensuous experience of the commodity as use-value has nothing to do with its value" (p. 39).

In the case of the lost-labour-power commodity, this cannot be truer due to the fact that this commodity is basically the embodiment of lost value (see Chapter 4). The value formation of this commodity is mainly the product of lost value rather than value. Although insurance boards consume labour power or value to produce this commodity, the amount of value consumed by insurance boards does not get objectified in the commodity. Value does not play any part when compared to the lost value objectified in the commodity.

This commodity's money value is the product of lost value objectified in the form of lost-time injury rates. However, its money value is not derived because a fall, a strain or a burn has value. In fact, they have no value at all. The very fact that any work accident, disease or fatality has a money value is because it can be socially exchanged under a set of rules that statistically and probabilistically converts lost labour time into money value. To be clear, a fall with nine working days lost embodied in the commodity has a money value not because the fall is the crystallization of value itself but because it will be monetized or converted into money value by insurance boards. By producing a universalized mode of representation in which injuries, diseases and deaths are individuated and assigned in a system of economic equivalences, insurance boards are enabled to assign money value and monetize work injuries. The money value of the commodity has no direct relationship with the value needed to produce the commodity but with an artificial system of economic equivalences established by insurance boards. With respect to the lost-labour-power commodity, Marx's assertion proves to be correct; there is no direct connection between the commodities' physical body, as a group of lost-time injury rates, and its value-relation of the product of labour within which it appears.

This disconnection becomes even more acute if we consider the social basis of the construction of these indirect economic equivalences. In this regard, lost labour power becomes a commodity only because it is the product of injuries with lost-time experienced during the capitalist labouring process of many private firms who work independently of each other. The total mass of lost labour power of all these individual firms forms the aggregate lost labour power of society through which statistically and probabilistically the commodity is produced. Since individual firms, as the individual producers of lost labour power in the form of accidents, diseases and fatalities, do not come into contact with one another, the amount of lost labour power due to their hazardous labouring conditions is made visible only within the moment of exchange. It is only at the moment of exchange at a price – i.e., the premium – that the money value of the commodity is made visible to every individual firm. As Guinnane and Streb (2015) note, during the early years of insurance boards, the system had to be explained over and over to those firms that had few accidents but saw their costs going up due to an increase in the number of accidents at firms in the same rating group. Thus, the commodity's money value, as part of the total mass of lost labour time socially necessary to produce any other commodity under the capitalist mode of production, manifests only through the social relations that the act of exchange establishes between all the firms. It is only by being exchanged by insurance boards that every firm's portion of lost labour power acquires a socially uniform objectivity as money value, which is different from their sensuously objectivity as distinct types of accidents or diseases. Capitalists not only do not know the money value of the commodity until the moment of exchange, they also do not know the social relations involved in the formation of the social value of the commodity. Money value conceals the social relations, mechanisms and power relations involved in the construction of the commodity as a money value. In practice, individual firms surrender to the discipline of insurance boards' information-intensive process to commodify lost labour power and exchange it among firms to distribute the money value of lost labour power in the form of compensation payments and benefits.

4   The Value Fluctuation of the Commodity

To understand the money value fluctuation of the commodity, it is necessary to penetrate the fetishism of the commodity, that is, the set of hidden social relations that directly and indirectly condition the value formation of the commodity. As already explained, these social relations tend to be hidden because the commodity's money value is (a) the product of lost value objectified in the commodity rather than value, and (b) manifests only through the social relations that insurance boards' circuit of metamorphosis establishes between all firms within a branch of industry.

First, the lost-labour-power commodity has a money value due to insurance boards' information-intensive process of commodification. The value of the commodity comes as a result of insurance boards' informational process of commodification that converts lost labour time into money value. Without injury information going through the reporting, recording, processing, and programing moments of the commodification process, it is not possible to construct the commodity as a medium of measurement and a medium of exchange to transform lost value into value. The commodity, as a means to statistically and probabilistically convert past socially lost labour time into labour time for the provision against the chance of an event leading to lost labour power, relies on a gargantuan amount of injury information. The information dependence of insurance boards to establish the commodity's price – i.e., premiums – is due to the fact that the money value of the commodity is not the result of labour power or value but of socially lost value attained via an insurance board's informational commodification process. Due to this fact, many social relations related to the commodity's value fluctuation are found directly within insurance boards' information commodification process, which involves the (a) the working-day-lost moment, (b) the reporting moment, (c) the recording moment, (d) the processing moment and (e) the programing moment. I call these relations the procedurally hidden social relations that directly condition the value of the commodity.

Second, it is important to note that the set of hidden social relations that condition the commodity's value are not limited to insurance boards' informational process of commodification. Some social relations, such as a decrease in the wage-labour force or an economic crisis, are located far beyond insurance boards' jurisdiction. Indirectly, these social relations have a huge impact on the value of the commodity. In some cases, this is an even bigger impact than those social relations located within the sphere of action of insurance boards. This happens because these structural social relations are intimately intertwined with the economic dynamics established by insurance boards' circuit of metamorphosis of lost labour power. I call these relations the structurally hidden social relations that indirectly condition the value of the commodity.

The analysis that follows disproves the semblance of the merely injury-driven determination of the magnitude of value of the commodity, but by no means abolishes that conditioning social relation. Work accidents leading to lost labour power do impact the commodity's value; however, this impact is no greater than other social relations that insurance boards' circuit of metamorphosis establishes as well as its interplay with specific capitalist relations. These social relations can chiefly be found procedurally within insurance boards and structurally within the capitalist mode of production. In the next lines, the procedural and structural social relations that condition the commodity's value are singled out, conceptualized and examined as a way of revealing the fetish character of the commodity. Very different combinations among these conditioning social relations are possible. While under given conditions some relations remain constant, others may vary in an upward direction, while others may do so in a downward direction, thus increasing, decreasing or balancing the commodity's value. The number of possible combinations is augmented by the fact that not only the direction of a social relation conditions the commodity's value but the magnitude of the direction itself. Since an examination of every social relation and its combinations is out of the scope of this critique, only the chief social relations and their utmost combinations are considered as a way of disclosing the commodity's fetishism. Here, the commodity's value is examined as a homogeneous social quantity, an absolute quantity, or as the total mass of lost value produced in society in a given period of time. The commodity's value as a relative quantity, as a fraction of the socially lost value produced in a subset of firms and a branch of industry, will be addressed in the section pertaining to the relative value or price fluctuation of the commodity.

4.1 Procedurally Hidden Social Relations

4.1.1 Value Fluctuation Due to a Movement of Working Days Lost

The money value of the commodity is conditioned by the mass of lost value it can effectively objectify. The more lost value the commodity embodies in itself due to an increase in work accidents, diseases and fatalities, the more money value the commodity can withdraw from the capitalist class in the form of compensation payments. As already pointed out, the commodity's value appears as an equivalent of the total mass of lost value produced in society due to work accidents, diseases and fatalities. This form of appearance stamps in the mind the misleading idea that the commodity's value is directly proportional to the amount of lost labour power in society. However, this is not accurate. As discussed in Chapter 3, lost labour power extends only to medical and wage-replacement benefits due to lost-time injuries. Insurance boards are designed to spread compensation payments for work injuries that result in working days lost.

For example, the experience premium or the money value that represents the individual firm's deviation from the total mass of expected lost labour power in an aggregate is constructed based on the information provided by lost-time injury claims rather than no-lost-time injury claims. As Tompa et al. (2012a) point out, insurance boards calculate lost-time injuries to estimate the firms' individual costs – i.e., the experience premium; no-lost-time injuries are not processed by insurance boards to come up with costs for the firm. The commodity, as a medium of measurement and a medium of exchange of each firm's deviation from the total mass of expected lost labour power in a subset of firms within a branch of industry, is furnished exclusively by lost-time injury rates. The reason for this procedure is that no-lost-time injury claims, also known as healthcare only, do not pay for benefits for lost time or working days lost (Tompa et al., 2016). Only lost-time injury claims, whether they are for short-term disability, long-term disability or permanent disability, have an impact on wage-losses. Thus, under the pressure of insurance boards' premium-setting mechanics, companies have an incentive to reduce lost-time injury rates rather than no-lost-time injury rates (see Tompa et al., 2012a). This explains firms' selective response regarding injury severity, the shifting of claims from the lost-time to the no-lost-time category, and the blatant suppression of lost-time injury claims (Tompa et al., 2012b).

In addition, the dominance of lost-time injury rates within the system is also due to a set of reporting and recording barriers. While the granting of time off or restricted duty due to a lost-time injury includes medical diagnoses and a series of bureaucratic steps that trigger inclusion in insurance boards' database, no-lost-time injuries do not trigger inclusion in insurance boards' database (Azaroff et al., 2004). Injured workers can be given medical treatment without having those costs funneled to insurance boards. This occurs because the majority of WCS s – the Chilean WCS is a notable exception – rely on the public health care system for medical benefits. Thus, the costs of no-lost-time injuries might not get reported, recorded, processed and charged to insurance boards because of administrative issues – e.g., the injured worker does not know his injury is work-related – or medical diagnosis issues – e.g., the physician was not given the information necessary to classify the injury as work-related. The costs of no-lost-time injuries or healthcare-only injuries have a greater probability of being cost-shifted to the public health system. No-lost-time injury claims get easily lost. This tends to happen because WCS s were initially designed to function as a part of a wider insurance system that would cover no-lost-time injuries. Contemporary WCS s are inserted within a social security system that includes other insurance funds. The focus of insurance boards on lost-time injuries corresponds to historical, systemic, economic and procedural relations.

The dominance of lost-time injuries has a direct impact on the commodity's value. However, the value formation of the commodity is not only conditioned by the frequency of lost-time injuries but also by the severity of lost-time injuries, commonly measured by the number of working days lost. It is neither the mass of no-lost-time injuries nor the mass of lost-time injuries but the severity of lost-time injuries or the mass of working days lost that causes the value of the commodity to move up or down. In this regard, the insurance boards' preferred indicator, the plainly named "injury rate", which is the number of lost-time injuries per 100 workers in a given period, has no direct influence on the value formation of the commodity. It is possible for the number of lost-time injuries per 100 workers to fall constantly and for this fall to be accompanied by a constant growth in the average number of working days lost. In this scenario, the commodity's value increases its money value even though a fall in the average number of lost-time injuries takes place. This movement in opposite directions between the average number of working days lost and the average number of lost-time injuries is not something extraordinary. In fact, it is very ordinary. In Chile, during 2007–2016, the average number of lost-time injuries due to accidents fell 5.6%, while the average number of working days lost grew 40%; similarly, the average number of lost-time injuries due to diseases fell 6.25%, while the average number of working days lost grew by 92% (Superintendencia de Seguridad Social, 2017). During one decade in Chile, the value of the commodity, as a homogeneous social quantity, went up even though the average number of lost-time injuries due to accidents and diseases went down. In disregard of the total mass of lost-time injuries, an upward movement in the number of working days lost pushes up the total amount of lost value crystallized in the commodity and in turn its money value. It follows from this that an increase or decrease in the mass of working days lost causes an increase or decrease in the value of the commodity, respectively.

In addition, the value of one working day lost also impacts the value of the commodity. If the total mass of working days lost constant, then an increase in the value of one working day lost has a positive impact on the commodity's value. Now, what exactly is the value of one working day lost? The value of one working day lost is simply (a) the social average of the total costs of medical expenses in an aggregate plus (b) the social average of the total costs of wage-replacement benefits in an aggregate divided by (c) the total number of working days lost in an aggregate. The value of one working day lost does change over time. While the medical-benefits portion changes due to a movement of medical costs, the wage-replacement portion changes due to a movement of wages. In Chile, the wage-replacement portion of the value of one working day lost increased from $12.393 Chilean pesos (USD 19 approx.) in 2007 to $18.733 pesos (USD 29 approx.) in 2016 (Superintendencia de Seguridad Social, 2017). This increase was mainly due to an increase in wages in Chile (Superintendencia de Seguridad Social, 2017). The value of the commodity can therefore increase through a rise in the value of one working day lost rather than a growth in the total mass of working days lost. If working days lost of more value are embodied in the commodity rather than working days lost of less value, with the total mass of working days lost being the same, the commodity increases its value. It follows that, regardless of the mass of lost-time injuries, an increase in the value of working days lost causes an increase in the commodity's value, with the number of working days lost being held constant. Although a few combinations among the mass and value of working days lost are possible to explain the commodity's value, it is important to note that the mass and value of working days lost and the commodity's value vary in the same direction regardless of the number of lost-time injuries. An upward movement of the mass and value of working days lost enables the commodity to withdraw more money value from the capitalist class in the form of compensation payments.

4.1.2   Value Fluctuation Due to a Movement of Reported Injury Claims

One of the biggest fetishes of the commodity is that it effectively embodies lost value or lost labour power. In reality, the commodity does not embody lost labour power but reported lost labour power through injury claims. As explained in Chapter 4, lost labour power as the immaterial substance of the commodity only comes into existence through the reporting moment. If lost-time injuries are not reported, working days lost do not get crystallized in the commodity. Claims or reports are not synonymous with injuries (Shannon and Lowe, 2002; Tompa et al., 2012a). It is a fundamental flaw to assume that reported injury claims reflect the frequency and severity – i.e., working days lost – of lost-time injuries. Many injuries do not result in reported claims. There exists an important reporting bias within WCS s that prompts some researchers to identify injuries that are less likely to be affected by it (see Guinane and Streb, 2015; Mansfield et al., 2012; Tompa et al., 2012a; Tompa et al., 2012b). For example, to avoid this bias some studies focus on fatality rates, which are unlikely to be unreported. However, as Mansfield et al. (2012) note, unfortunately not all researchers attempt to distinguish between reduced lost-time injuries based on fewer reports and reduced lost-time injuries based on fewer accidents, diseases and fatalities. The majority of quantitative studies are unable to distinguish between reports and real injuries because their data source comes from insurance boards (Mansfield et al., 2012). The dilemma behind this is that the reliance on reported injury claims makes it difficult, if not impossible, to distinguish between a movement of working days lost and a movement of reported working days lost. While a fall in the mass of working days lost implies an improvement in health and safety performance, a better educated workforce and more advanced technology, as suggested by Ussif (2004), a fall in reported working days lost does not imply any of the above. Nevertheless, the reporting moment does have a direct impact on the value of the commodity.

Reporting injuries condition the value of the commodity by enabling more or less working days lost to be objectified in the commodity. The reporting moment can be thought of as a valve that controls the mass of working days lost to be embodied in the commodity. While a wider valve or flexible reporting procedure increases the flow of working days lost into the commodity, a narrower valve or a stringent reporting procedure reduces the flow of working days lost into the commodity. Similar to the mass and value of working days lost that varies in the same direction of the commodity's value, the rate of reported injury claims also varies in the same direction. A growth in the mass of reported injury claims increases the value of the commodity; a fall in the mass of reported injury claims diminishes the value of the commodity. In this way it is possible, given a fall in reported injury claims, for the value of the commodity to fall and for this fall to be accompanied by a constant growth in the mass of working days lost. A fall in the value of the commodity under the conditions given – i.e., a fall in reported injury claims – is not the result of better health and safety performance but of procedural mechanics related to the reporting moment from the process of commodification. In this case, the reporting hypothesis used to explain a drop in the number of working days lost and a depressed commodity value is applicable.

A fall in the mass of reported injury claims offsets a growth in the mass of working days lost. In fact, these two social relations are proportionally related. A decrease of, let us say, 100 reported injury claims equivalent to 1,000 working days lost, cancels out an increase of 1,000 working days lost. If we consider that the value of one working day lost remains the same in a given period, no matter the type of accidents or the range of wages, then the offset between a fall of 100 reported injury claims and 1,000 working days can occur at its value. It can be said that if the value of working days lost remains constant and the value of reported injury claims is equivalent to the value of the mass of working days lost, a fall of the same magnitude, let us say, 10% of the mass of reported injury claims, effectively cancels out a growth of 10% of the mass of working days lost. Thus, in disregard of an upward movement of working days lost, the value of the commodity might remain the same if an equivalent downward movement of the mass of reported injury claims takes place.

This is one possible combination among many others among these intertwined social relations. For example, given a constant value of one working day lost, if the magnitude of a fall in reported injury claims is higher than the growth of the mass of working days lost, the commodity's value does not remain the same and instead drops. In another combination, if the magnitude of a fall in reported injury claims is lower than the growth of the mass of working days lost, but the value of one working day lost diminishes at a magnitude that offsets the difference between the mass of working days lost and the mass of reported injury claims, the commodity's value also drops. Thus, the value of the commodity is conditioned not only by the direction of the movements but by the magnitude of these movements. As a bearer of lost value, the commodity' value is highly sensitive to the crisscross of the directions and magnitudes of the mass of working days lost, the value of working days lost, and the mass of reported injury claims.

4.1.3   Value Fluctuation Due to a Movement of Deeming Injury Claims

The establishment of WCSs and their information-intensive process to commodify lost value was intended to replace a juridical system in order to compensate wage labourers' lost value due to a work-related accident regardless of fault. In theory, insurance boards are compelled to compensate every disability or any lost time arising from an injury resulting from employment. Thus, wage labourers are, in theory, entitled to be compensated for every and all lost-time injuries within the labouring process; however, in practice this rarely happens. The literature reveals that many injuries are not covered or fully covered (see

Tompa et al., 2006). Since compensation benefits are awarded based on the presence and extent of incapacity due to a work-related injury, the issue of work-relatedness and its definition plays an important role in discriminating lost-time injuries. Paraphrasing George Orwell (2008), 'all lost-time injuries are equal, but some lost-time injuries are more equal than others'. While some lost-time injuries get fully compensated, others get partially or not compensated at all. Since WCSs' establishment in Germany in 1884, the determination of compensation and the extent of a worker's entitlement to compensation has been contested terrain (see Eghigian, 2000). In Germany in 1901, there were 298,983 appellable accident pension decisions and 66,091 litigations among them (Eghigian, 2000, Table 3, p. 69). A bureaucratic system for disbursing compensation benefits regardless of fault naturally imposes a set of procedural filters that in practice make lost-time injuries very different from one another.

The deeming or assessment of injury claims is not a fair or easy process. First, an injury must be recognized as compensable within the approved list. Insurance boards have an open-ended classification of disabilities to guide the acceptance of injury claims. It is usually insurance boards rather than the capitalist state that are given the authority to define injuries as compensable or non-compensable. However, there is some overlap. Reasons et al. (1981) remind us that senior insurance board personnel in medical, rehabilitation, legal, and statistics departments also sit on a variety of public policy-making bodies. Second, a lost-time injury and its work-relatedness must be assessed by a physician and accepted by the insurance board. In the majority of countries and jurisdictions, the assessment is made in public hospitals and clinics, while in others, like the Chilean WCS, it is exclusively done by physicians employed by insurance boards. Also, under a set of particular conditions – e.g., legal disputes, hearings – independent medical examiners can participate in the assessment process. In general, requirements for proving work-relatedness are stringent. As Barnetson (2010) argues, insurance boards adopt a biomedical model of causation that implies that injuries and illnesses must have a biological source. Although so-called psychosocial risks have opened the door for social sources as evidence of work-relatedness – e.g., high demand, low control, effort/reward imbalance – this psychosocial model is not dominant and is currently highly contested by corporations. Third, the extent of compensation benefits, particularly the wage-replacement portion, is set based on the degree of incapacity and a series of calculations that insurance boards perform. While temporary wage-loss benefits can range from around 70% to 90% of net income, excluding paid holidays, overtime and incentive bonuses, permanent wage-loss benefits are calculated according to an exhaustive chart – e.g., permanent disability evaluation chart – that matches specific injuries to specific percentages of impairments. In cases where the wage labourer cannot return to work, insurance boards perform a loss of earnings assessment by comparing wage labourers' pre-injury job earnings with those available in the market. The variability in determining the extent of compensation benefits among insurance boards from different countries and jurisdictions is very high. Nevertheless, it is insurance boards that control the deeming process that determines the presence and extent of incapacity that arise from lost-time injuries. Thus, compensation benefits are not disbursed on the basis of wage labourers' temporary, permanent or total lost value, but on what insurers deem as the effective lost value suffered by wage labourers, whether it is temporary, permanent or total.

Insurance boards' deeming process is highly variable, fluid and porous. In Chile in 2016, the three nationwide insurance boards rejected a total of 22% of injury claims (Superintendencia de Seguridad Social, 2017). In this case, it is interesting to note the high variability among insurers. One insurer rejected a total of 15% of injury claims, a second rejected a total of 23% of injury claims, and a third a total of 24% of injury claims (Superintendencia de Seguridad Social, 2017). As explained by the government report, this high variability among insurers is due, among other factors, to the different criteria deployed by insurance boards to deem an injury as work-related (Superintendencia de Seguridad Social, 2017). Besides the technical requirements for proving work-relatedness, political, economic and social factors have a strong impact on the deeming process. For example, a change to corporate-friendly senior insurance board personnel or the appointment of a conservative state regulator might make the process tighter. Stringency has always been an issue for employers. From the very inception of WCS s, capitalists were interested in seeing insurance boards conduct their deeming process as strictly as possible (Eghigian, 2000). Why is this so? Because the deeming process has an impact on the value of the commodity. A more tight or narrow deeming process reduces the value of the commodity, while a looser process increases the value of the commodity. By re-defining and re-classifying disabilities, reducing the list of compensable injuries, increasing the requirements for proving work-relatedness, and diminishing the target for the earnings replacement rate, less lost value is crystallized in the commodity, thus cheapening the value of the commodity. Here, we are in front of an opposite relation. The deeming process and the value of the commodity vary in opposite directions. A variation in the mass of injury claim rejections, its increase or diminution, causes the value of the commodity to move in an opposite direction. While a growth in the mass of injury claim rejections decreases the value of the commodity, a fall in the mass of injury claim rejections increases the commodity's value. It follows from this that a movement in the mass of injury claim rejections causes an opposite movement in the lost value embodied in the commodity.

It is interesting to note that in Chile, in the period 2012–2016, while the mass of reported injury claims increased by around 14%, the mass of injury claim rejections also increased by around 6%, thus containing the value of the commodity (see Superintendencia de Seguridad Social, 2017). There is a complex interplay between these social relations. An upward movement of injury claim rejections offsets both an upward movement of working days lost and an upward movement in the mass of reported injury claims. Where the mass of injury claim rejections increases, there is a corresponding decrease in the value of the commodity independently of an increase in working days lost and reported injury claims. A stringent deeming process cancels the upward movement of working days lost and reported injury claims at any magnitude; however, this is not the case when the mass of injury claim rejections moves in a downward direction. When the direction of the mass of injury claim rejections decreases, the value of the commodity might go up or down depending on the direction and magnitude of the movement of working days lost and reported injury claims. With diminishing injury claim rejections and a simultaneous increase in working days lost and reported injury claims, the value of the commodity goes up, whereas with diminishing injury claim rejections and a simultaneous decrease in working days lost and reported injury claims, the value of the commodity goes down.

Finally, in regard to its magnitude, it is impossible to say if an upward/downward movement in the mass of injury claim rejections causes a proportional downward/upward movement in the value of the commodity. Since the mass of injury claims rejections is based on the number of injuries rather than the number of working days lost, it is not possible to know solely based on the magnitude of the injury claim rejection the extent to which the value of the commodity fluctuates. For example, an increase of 10% in the mass of injury claim rejections of work diseases whose working days lost average 51 days is not the same as an increase of 10% in the mass of injury claim rejections of work accidents whose working days lost average 19.6 days (see Superintendencia de Seguridad Social, 2017). Although the same magnitude of injury claim rejections takes place for both diseases and accidents, the impact on the value of the commodity is higher when disease-injury rejections increase rather than accident-injury rejections because the former hampers more days lost being embodied in the commodity. It is necessary to know the average number of working days lost from the mass of injury claim rejections to measure its precise impact on the value of the commodity. Many combinations are possible if the number of working days lost associated with the mass of injury rejections is considered. For example, given a constant average of five working days lost, an increase of 30% of injury claim rejections at an average of five working days lost decreases the value of the commodity by 30%, while an increase of 10% of injury claim rejections at an average of 20 working days lost decreases the value of the commodity by 40%. In this second example, an increase of 30% of injury claim rejections proportionally reduces the value of the commodity by 30% while an increase of 10% of injury claim rejections disproportionally reduces the value of the commodity by 40%. This occurs because the former injury-claim-rejection rate represents fewer working days lost than the latter. Therefore, the magnitude of the mass of injury claim rejections does not inversely correlate to an equivalent magnitude of the commodity's value. They simply vary in opposite directions. It can then be said that the mass of injury claim rejections varies in opposite directions to the value of the commodity at a proportion to the number of working days lost it represents, independently of an increase in working days lost and reported injury claims when it goes up and dependently of an increase/decrease in working days lost and reported injury claims when it goes down.

4.1.4   Value Fluctuation Due to a Movement of Rate-Setting Mechanics
To serve as a means of exchange, the lost-labour-power commodity needs to acquire the form of an exchange value, a specific quantitative proportion through which it can be effectively exchanged for money value. As described in Chapter 4, the exchange value of the commodity is the rate of compensation, a wage-relation formula that represents the contribution to and deviation from the total mass of expected lost labour power in an aggregate. To come up with the rate of compensation or the exchange value, insurance boards engage in a long informational process of commodification that involves a series of five temporal moments. These moments are the steps necessary to produce the commodity as an exchange value. In particular, it is the fifth moment of the commodification process, the programing moment, that is the key stage that enables the commodity to serve as a means of exchange. During this moment, the commodity is given a set of coded instructions that guide it toward its goal. Two basic instructions can be distinguished: to function as a medium of measurement and to function as a medium of exchange. These instructions allow the commodity to be traded as an exchange value and thus serve as a means of exchange, namely, the exchange of lost labour power for money or in value terms, the conversion of lost value into value.

    Although the end result – i.e., the rate of compensation – is similar to almost every insurance board, the mechanics of how rates are set vary dramatically among countries and jurisdictions, particularly the experience-rate portion of the rate of compensation (Tompa et al., 2012a). These mechanics involve a series of rules such as the concentration of classes in aggregates, the rating factor, the type of adjustment (retrospective/prospective), cost caps, cost relief, and cost adjustment periods, among others. The rate-setting procedure has a profound impact on the value of the commodity. This occurs because the commodity's value, as already explained, does not come from insurance boards' consumption of labour power but from insurance boards' informational process of commodifying lost labour power, which involves the setting of rates to come up with the rate of compensation or the exchange value of the commodity. These inner workings are largely responsible for individuating and assigning firms in a system of economic equivalences based on their contribution to the mass of lost labour power in an aggregate and their deviation as well as monetizing these equivalences or transforming them into money value.

In general, these rate-setting mechanics can be differentiated based on their financial sensitivity or financial reactivity. Highly reactive or aggressive rate-setting mechanics cause a decrease in the value of the commodity by encouraging individual firms to pursue economic incentives; on the other hand, unreactive or yielding rate-setting mechanics do not have any impact on the value of the commodity. Here, we are witnessing a qualitative relationship rather than a quantitative one. It is a movement of the quality of rate-setting mechanics rather than its quantity that conditions the value of the commodity.

A qualitative variation of rate-setting mechanics towards financial reactivity causes the value of the commodity to fall while a qualitative variation of rate-setting mechanics away from financial reactivity causes the value of the commodity to remain the same or to grow, depending on the magnitude of the movement of other social relations. The literature and research on rate-setting mechanics is clear on revealing the relationship between these inner workings and the value of the commodity. The appearance in the last decades of the 20th century of the experience rating, that is, the mechanics through which firms are measured and charged in relation to their deviation from the total mass of lost labour power in an aggregate, tends to reduce the value of the commodity by creating incentives for undesirable behaviours such as claim suppression, disputing claims and pressuring injured workers to return to work early (see Hyatt and Kralj, 1995; Kralj, 1994; Thomason and Pozzebon, 2002). Due to these behaviours, less lost value is embodied in the commodity, thus causing a fall in its value. A study that examines the introduction of experience rating in British Columbia, for example, shows a reduction in the mass of reported lost-time injury claims and short-term disability claims, thus cheapening the commodity (Campolieti et al., 2006). This phenomenon occurs because experience rating increases individual firms' responsibility for their claim costs (see Tompa et al.,

2012a). In addition to moving toward the direction of financial reactivity, a higher magnitude of this movement causes a bigger fall in the value of the commodity. Based on panel data on all firms over a 10-year period from an experience rating program in Ontario, Canada, Tompa et al. (2012a) demonstrate that an increase in the magnitude of experience rating, measured by the rating factor, reduces the commodity value by decreasing the mass of reported lost-time injury claims, increasing the mass of injury claim rejections and increasing the mass of cost relief claims. This positive and significant correlation among the rating factors and the abovementioned social relations occurs because, under a higher degree of experience premium, employers are financially encouraged to obstruct injury claims, reopen claims and appeal claims with the aim of reducing the economic burden on firms (Tompa et al., 2012a). These findings suggest that a higher degree of experience rating does reduce the value of the commodity through means other than preventing work-related accidents, diseases and fatalities (see Tompa et al., 2012a). In addition to the magnitude, the adjustment approach to experience rating also conditions the value of the commodity. In a comparative analysis of different adjustment approaches to rate-setting among insurance boards in two Canadians jurisdictions: British Columbia and Ontario, Tompa et al. (2016) found that a retrospective approach is more financially reactive than a prospective approach. While a prospective approach adjusts the experience rate at the beginning of a period based on historical lost labour power at the firm level relative to the total mass of lost labour power in an aggregate, a retrospective approach adjusts the experience rate at the end of the period based on their performance relative to their deviance from the mass of lost labour power in an aggregate. Essentially, the study shows that in a retrospective experience rating program the rate of reported injury claims and lost-time injury claims are significantly lower than in a prospective experience rating program. In addition, the short-term disability rate and the rate of working days lost are also lower, although only modestly so. However, as Tompa et al. (2016) warn, while the reduction on rates and related costs appears as desirable, these results may not be indicative of better prevention but rather of claim management practices. What an aggressive experience rating program does is reduce the value of the commodity. By decreasing the mass of reported lost-time injury claims and the mass of working days lost, a retrospective experience rating program causes a decrease in the value of the commodity. Less lost labour power is objectified in the commodity due to a number of social relations triggered by a more aggressive way of setting rates.

The rate-setting mechanics interrelates with some of the already-analyzed social relations. A causal relationship is observed when rates are set in a more aggressive way. An increase of rate-setting mechanics towards financial reactivity is usually the cause, not the consequence, if the corresponding diminution in the value of the commodity is due to a drop in reported injury claims and a growth in injury claim rejections. However, an increase in rate-setting mechanics towards financial reactivity might not be the cause if the corresponding increase in the value of the commodity is due to a growth in reported injury claims and a fall in injury claim rejections. This is not an autonomous relation independent from other social relations; its impact on the value of the commodity depends on the direction and magnitudes of other social relations such as the mass of working days lost, the mass of reported injury claims, and the mass of injury claim rejections. There are many possible combinations. It is possible, given aggressive rate-setting mechanics, for the value of the commodity to drop and for this drop to be accompanied by an increase in the mass of working days lost and a fall in reported injury claims that exceeds the growth of working days lost. It is also possible, given aggressive rate-setting mechanics, for the value of the commodity to grow and for this growth to be accompanied by an increase in the mass of working days lost that offsets a fall in reported injury claims. Finally, it is possible, given aggressive rate-setting mechanics, for the value of the commodity to increase and for this growth to be accompanied by an increase in the mass of working days lost that cancels out growth in injury claim rejections. In sum, a movement of rate-setting mechanics causes the value of the commodity to move in a direction and at a magnitude in which the interplay of other social relations conditions the commodity to do so. Nonetheless, as a structural procedural framework, a movement of rate-setting mechanics does have an impact on the value of the commodity and should be regarded as a key social relation in the conditioning of the commodity's value.

4.2   *Structurally Hidden Social Relations*

4.2.1   Value Fluctuation Due to a Movement of the Wage-Labour Market
Researchers on workplace health tend to forget that insurance boards do not deliver medical and financial benefits to workers but to wage labourers. This occurs because WCS s' discourse recognizes the worker as its recipient, but it fails to recognize the historical alienation of the worker or its wage-dependent manifestation. Wage labour, as the product of class division and the establishment of an economy for exchange, is central to the appearance and functioning of WCS s. Let us remember that these systems were in part a response to a historical build-up of wage labourers and the social instability they caused. Compensation for injured wage labourers during employment was developed to tame their discontent due to their inability to earn a living during the disability period. The term adopted in this critique, lost-labour-power commodity,

implies this connection. The sale, purchase, consumption and destruction of labour power are constitutive of the lost-labour-power commodity. In the same vein, there is an unbreakable connection between wage labour and the value of the commodity. Unemployment, underemployment, demographic changes, war, economic crises and any other process that brings a change to the total mass of wage labourers employed causes the value of the commodity to fall or grow.

The value of commodity, as the total mass of lost value produced in society, is directly and proportionally conditioned by the total mass of wage labourers employed. If all procedurally hidden social relations remain the same – i.e., the number of working days lost, the mass of reported injury claims, the mass of injury claim rejections, the reactivity of rate-setting mechanics – the value of the commodity varies in the same direction as the mass of wage labourers employed. For example, given an average number of working days lost of 20 days, a rate of 10% of reported injury rates, a rate of 20% of injury claims rejections, and constant rate-setting mechanics, an increase of 10% of the mass of wage labourers employed increases the value of the commodity by 10%. On the other hand, a decrease of 10% of the mass of wage labourers employed decreases the value of the commodity by 10%. This happens because more or less lost value is crystallized in the commodity due to an upward movement of the mass of wage labourers employed.

Now, this does not affect the price of the commodity – i.e., the premium – to be paid by capitalists. As we shall see later, the premium as a social average remains the same even though an upward or downward movement of wage labourers takes place given that all the procedurally hidden social relations remain the same. Nonetheless, the total lost value and money value of the commodity as an absolute value, not as a relative value, varies in the same direction and magnitude as the mass of wage labourers employed. This cause-effect relationship can be seen in Germany during 1886–1910, a period in which wage labourers were incrementally brought under insurance boards' coverage (see Hobbs, 1939). While in 1886 the number of wage labourers insured was 3,822,000 and the total expenditures amounted to 10,000,000 Marks, in 1890 the number of wage labourers insured was 13,680,000 and the total expenditures amounted 39,000,000 Marks, while in 1910 the number of wage labourers insured was 27,554,000 and the total expenditures amounted 228,000,000 Marks (see Eghigian, 2000, Table 1, p. 27). Here, the number of wage labourers under coverage acts as a proxy for the number of wage labourers employed, while the total expenditures acts as a proxy for the value of the commodity. An increase in the wage labourers under coverage causes an increase in the total expenditures, which is equivalent to an increase in the value of the commodity. Although this relationship was significantly altered from 1914 to 1980, mainly due to the interplay of other social relations such as the two world wars, hyperinflation, and policy making, with all the other social relations remaining the same, the value of the commodity varies in the same direction as the mass of wage labourers employed. It follows from this that a growth in formal employment – i.e., wage-labour employment – causes a growth in the value of the commodity, while a fall in formal employment causes a fall in the value of the commodity if all other procedurally hidden social relations remain constant. Today, there is some evidence of how a movement of formal employment causes a variation in injury rates and a consequent variation of the value of the commodity. In the period 1979–93 in the United States, Hartwig et al. (1997) found that the level of employment is positively associated with reported injury claims. Similarly, in Quebec, Canada, Fortin et al. (1996) found a negative association between unemployment and reported injury claims between 1976–86. In these studies, injury rates act as a proxy for the value of the commodity, where higher/lower injury rates equal more/fewer lost value objectified in the commodity and thus a growth/fall in the value of the commodity. In both studies, an increase in employment results in an increase in injuries, which is equivalent to an increase in the value of the commodity. Although not broadly, employment levels have been recognized by some scholars as an explanatory variable for the movement of injury rates (see Azaroff et al., 2004).

Beside the conditioning power of employment, the value of the commodity varies due to the exclusions and contractual agreements of the total mass of wage labourers. Although wcs s' legislation mandates the coverage of all wage labourers, there exist contractual agreements that impede the commodity from absorbing all wage labourers' lost labour power. Precarious wage labourers – i.e., short-term, part-time, temporary, on-call – who depend on continually obtaining new positions are generally discouraged from reporting lost-time injury claims (Azaroff et al., 2004). Their reticence is due to their need to not damage their future job prospects. Also, in some countries and jurisdictions, precarious workers are not even eligible for compensation benefits (Azaroff et al., 2004; Barnetson, 2010). In addition, under some type of contracts, precarious wage labourers might not be eligible for compensation due to subtle technicalities such as the form of the wage – e.g., income, stipend or scholarship. For example, in Canada, graduate students under a teaching-assistantship contract are eligible for compensation benefits, but if they are on a research-assistantship contract they are not. Although in both cases the employer is the university, and graduate students are expected to use the university's facilities to perform their job, under a research-assistant contract, graduate students are not eligible for compensation benefits. An increase in the number of independent contractors also conditions the value of the commodity. Self-employment, which has grown exponentially, not only distorts injury rates as Cox and Lippel (2008) correctly claim but causes a fall in the commodity's value. The outsourcing of jobs to self-employed workers reduces the number of working days lost that are embodied in the commodity due to the wage-labour criteria for compensation. This can have a huge impact on the value of the commodity if those jobs outsourced to temporary work agencies are risky jobs, a form of economic incentive studied by MacEachen (Tompa, 2012c). Also, the movement of dynamics within the informal economy – i.e., domestic labour, artistic and cultural performers, and other groups of workers – causes a variation in the value of the commodity not only because the majority of cases remain ineligible but because many of these jobs do not provide an administrative structure for wage labourers to report injuries (see Azaroff et al., 2004). Finally, the mass of immigrants in society substantially reduces the reporting of injury claims and leads to a consequent fall in the value of the commodity. This occurs not only because in some countries legislation prohibits public health and compensation benefits but because they avoid reporting injuries due to the fear of being deported for abusing the system (Azaroff et al., 2004). These underclasses, who suffer severe work injuries and diseases due to the risky jobs in which they are employed, have little chance of being compensated. As Azaroff et al. (2004) note, the greatest fall in injury claims during the 1990s in the United States was seen by precisely those businesses – e.g., hotels, restaurants, grocery stores – staffed by immigrants (see Fletcher, 2001). In practice, being an immigrant implies an unwillingness to report injuries.

Contrary to the movement of formal employment, the movement of underemployment – i.e., precarious, self-employed, under-the-table, and immigrant workers – causes the commodity's value to vary in an opposite direction. With all other social relations remaining constant, an increase in the mass of underemployment causes a drop in the value of the commodity. Thus, the combination of the movement of formal employment and underemployment cancel each other when their magnitudes are equivalent in value terms. With increasing formal employment and a simultaneous growth in underemployment at the same value magnitude and all procedurally hidden social relations remaining constant, the value of the commodity may continue unaltered. However, if the magnitudes are uneven, the value of the commodity might react on the basis of the difference. Given a growth in formal employment, it is possible for the value of the commodity to rise if the growth in underemployment is smaller than its counterpart; given a growth in formal employment, it is possible for the value of the commodity to fall if the growth in underemployment is bigger than its counterpart. In today's economic and political landscape – e.g., outsourcing, offshoring, flexible labour, deregulation, cuts in social spending, lack of unionization – (see Harvey 1990, 2005; Klein, 2007; Webster, 1995) it may well be the case of an offset of the growth of formal employment by the growth of underemployment and a consequent reduction in value of the commodity. More combinations are possible if the procedurally hidden social relations at their directions and magnitudes are taken into consideration. However, the mentioned basic combinations at different magnitudes are the necessary ones to understand the impact of the wage-labour market on the commodity's value. In sum, grounded in the wage-labour relation, the value of the commodity is always reflective of the employment conditions of society.

4.2.2   Value Fluctuation Due to a Movement of the Economic Activity

To say the value of the commodity is conditioned by a movement of the wage-labour market is to imply that it is also conditioned by a movement of economic activity more broadly. Since the wage-labour market is intimately intertwined with the ups and downs of the economy, particularly in a capitalist economy whose aim is production for exchange, it is concomitant that the commodity's value varies in relation to the economy. The relation between the economy and the commodity is an indirect one, which is not easy to grasp, specify or quantify. Like the tides of the sea, the movement of the economy has such a broad impact on capitalist societies that its multiple distinguishing factors are extremely difficult to isolate. Nevertheless, economic literature has identified two major movements of the economy that impact on reported injury claims and consequently on the value of the commodity: business cycle fluctuations and long-term growth. As Moore and Tompa (2011) report, most studies demonstrate a pro-cyclical relationship between reported injury claims and the business cycle. This means that during up cycles, when employment is high, the rate of reported injury claims increases, while during down cycles, when employment is low, the rate of reported injury claims decreases. The number of reported injury claims tends to increase/decrease at the same rate as aggregate business activity grows or falls. In regard to the business cycle, Kossoris (1938) found a reduction in reported injury claim frequency for lost-time injuries lasting one week or less during the United States' Great Depression. In Ontario, Canada, during 1975–93, Brooker et al. (1997) found that reported lost-time injury claims increased in boom times and fell in recessions. In the United Kingdom, Davies et al. (2009) found that minor injuries increased in business activity upturns and decreased in downturns. In a recent study in Ontario, Moore and Tompa (2011) found a positive and significant relation between reported injury claims and Ontario's major economic dip around 2001.

The precise reasons why this happens are not clear. As an indirect social relation, business cycles cannot directly vary the amount of lost value crystallized in the commodity. Other social relations must come into play. Robinson (1988) suggests three hypotheses. First, during upturns more work injuries tend to happen due to an increase in the hiring of less experienced workers. This hypothesis suggests an increase in the total number of working days lost and a consequent rise in the value of the commodity. Second, during upturns workplace safety deteriorates due to an increase in the pace of production. This hypothesis also suggests an increase in working days lost and a consequent rise in the commodity's value. And third, during downturns and their consequent increase of management power and decrease of union power, reported injury claims decrease. This third hypothesis suggests something different, a decrease of reported injury claims and a consequent fall in the value of the commodity during downturns. So, it is possible for an economic boom to take place and be accompanied by an increase in the mass of working days lost and a consequent rise in the value of the commodity; or to be accompanied by an increase in reported injury claims and a consequent rise in the value of the commodity; or to be accompanied by both social relations, an increase of the mass of working days lost and an increase of reported injury claims with a consequent rise in the value of the commodity. It might also be possible, given an increase in working days lost and a decrease in reported injury claims at the same magnitude, for the value of the commodity to remain constant during a boom. In this case, a fall in reported injury claims cancels an increase in working days lost at the same magnitude. The value of the commodity may continue unaltered during a boom due to an offset between a rise in working days lost and a fall in reported injury claims. It might also be possible, given an increase in working days lost, a decrease in reported injury claims and an increase in injury claim rejections, for the value of the commodity to fall during a boom. In this case, a fall in reported injury claims and a rise in injury claim rejections exceeds in value terms an increase in working days lost, thus causing the value of the commodity to fall. The number of possible combinations is large, particularly if the different directions and magnitudes of the procedurally hidden social relations are taken into consideration. If we include the previous structurally hidden social relation, the wage-labour market, things can become even more complex. Given a significant growth in underemployment during an economic boom, it might be possible for the commodity's value to drop even though the number of working days lost increases, the mass of reported injury claims increases, and the mass of injury claim rejections drops. In this case, a significant growth in underemployment and a consequent reduction of the mass of wage labourers under coverage would cancel and exceed all the other social relations in play. The important thing to note here is that the conditioning power of the business cycle on the value of the commodity is highly mediated by the interplay of other social relations. The business cycle by itself does not have explanatory power. It follows from this that an upward movement of the business cycle causes a rise in the value of the commodity dependently of the direction and magnitude of other social relations, while, on the other hand, a downward movement of the business cycle causes a fall in the value of the commodity dependently of the direction and magnitude of other social relations.

Finally, what happens to the value of the commodity during a major financial downturn? History shows that other social relations such as the capitalist state enter the field in an attempt to cheapen the value of the commodity and aid the capitalist class. During Germany's 1923–24 hyperinflationary period – i.e., the acute depreciation of the Mark – the system imploded because the commodity's value was directly conditioned by a wage-relation formula, which at the time could not keep up with the rate of inflation. Through policy making, the capitalist state reduced compensation benefits, both medical and financial, thus diminishing the real value of the commodity (see Eghigian, 2000). In this case, the value of the commodity was directly lessened by the capitalist state, canceling the movements of any other social relations at play in any direction and magnitude.

Regarding long-term growth, the value of the commodity varies in an opposite direction. In contrast to the pro-cyclical relationship between injury claims and the business cycle, studies show that during long-term growth, injury claims take a downward direction (see Azaroff et al., 2004; Moore and Tompa, 2011). Long-term growth is usually accompanied by a constant fall in reported lost-time injuries. In the United States during 1992–2000, reported injury claims dropped substantially even though the period coincided with an upsurge in the business cycle (Azaroff et al., 2004). It is interesting to note that long-term growth cancels out the impact of the business cycle on reported injuries and the commodity's value. A study in Ontario, Canada shows that during the 1991–2008 period, reported injury claims were driven by strong negative long-term growth (Moore and Tompa, 2011). In this study, strong negative long-term growth appears as the largest contributor to the variance of the total injury claim rate, surpassing the business cycle and seasonal trends (see Moore and Tompa, 2011). Again, long-term growth, whether it is positive or negative, tends to ameliorate the impact of the business cycle. Similar to the business cycle, long-term growth does not explain why injury claims fall. It is the coming into play of other social relations that explains the variance of injury claims during long-term growth. Ussif (2004) suggests that the fall of injuries during long-term growth as a result of the effects of advanced technology, improved safety measures, legislative reforms and a better educated workforce. In a similar fashion, Conway and Svenson (1998) claim that advances in technology and the automation of high-hazard jobs played a role in the decline of injuries. This hypothesis implies a fall in the total number of working days lost and a consequent fall in the value of the commodity. Shuford and Wolf (2006) argue that the drop in injuries is due to unreporting practices attributable to global competition. This hypothesis implies a decrease in reported injury claims and a consequent fall in the value of the commodity. Moore and Tompa (2011) conjecture a third factor to explain the impact of long-term growth: the outsourcing and offshoring of risky jobs due to global competition. This third hypothesis insinuates a growth of underemployment and a consequent fall in the value of the commodity. Therefore, it is possible for a positive long-term growth period to be accompanied by a decrease in working days lost and a consequent fall in the value of the commodity, or to be accompanied by a decrease in reported injury claims and a consequent fall in the value of the commodity, or to be accompanied by an increase in underemployment and a consequent fall in the value of the commodity. Similar to the business cycle, there are many possible combinations. It follows that positive long-term growth causes a fall in the value of the commodity, dependently of the direction and magnitude of other social relations, while, on the other hand, negative long-term growth causes a rise in the value of the commodity, dependently of the direction and magnitude of other social relations. Although the value fluctuation of the commodity due to a movement of economic activity is highly mediated by a complex interplay of many other social relations, including the intervention of the capitalist state on behalf of the capitalist class, the ups and downs of the economy are key factors for the understanding of the value fluctuation of the commodity. Inserted within a capitalist economy, the value of the commodity is always reflective of the economic conditions of society.

4.2.3   Value Fluctuation Due to a Movement of Cost-Shifting
WCS s are part of a set of insurance funds in capitalist societies referred to as social security. These insurance funds involve benefits and services to disabled, sick, unemployed and elderly individuals. Rather than relying on taxpayers, similar to welfare benefits, social security is funded by individuals who contribute to a collective fund. As part of social security, WCS s do not stand alone but function in tandem with other insurance funds, such as pension funds, common health funds and unemployment funds. From their inception, WCS s were

designed to work together with these other insurance programs. This can be noted in relation to the number of weeks needed for the German WCS to begin providing benefits. While the Sickness Insurance Fund provided benefits until the thirteenth week, the WCS provided benefits from the thirteenth week and thereafter (see Hobbs, 1939). The two systems were interconnected. However, from the beginning, the boundaries among these insurance programs were not clear. This happened because, among other reasons, some claims were not mutually exclusive. Benefits could be collected from more than one branch at the same time. In Germany, if a disability amounted to more than two-thirds of a wage labourer's capacity to earn a living, he could collect benefits both from the WCS and the Invalid and Old-Age Fund (see Eghigian, 2000). In addition, under some circumstances some benefits could be entirely borne by one insurance branch at the expense of the other. These insurance funds, especially WCS s, are extremely porous in their ability to provide their mandated benefits. Compensation benefits and costs tend to drain along the system. This phenomenon, in which compensation costs pass to another insurance branch, to welfare programs or to society at large, is referred in the literature as cost-shifting. This is a common dilemma in those countries where the WCS is not the only system that provides benefits to wage labourers unable to work (see Campolieti et al., 2006; Fortin and Lanoie, 1992; Koning, 2009). The shifting of benefits and their associated costs to other insurance branches, publicly funded programmes or society in general has a direct impact on the value of the commodity.

Cost-shifting varies in the opposite direction to the value of the commodity. An increase in cost-shifting causes the value of the commodity to drop, while a decrease in cost-shifting causes the value of the commodity to grow. By shifting compensation benefits and costs to other providers, less lost value is crystallized in the commodity, and thus the value of the commodity falls. Clayton (2002) notes that by making use of private disability plans, around one-fifth of employers in Ontario, Canada can effectively shift costs from the province's insurance board. Campolieti et al. (2006) describe how changes to workers' compensation and social assistance programs increase cost-shifting to Canadian pension plan disability programmes. In Chile, a study reveals that more than 38.6% of work-related diseases are treated by private health plans rather than insurance boards (Bitran Asociados, 2011). In these cases, the value of the commodity drops due to the simple reason that benefits and costs associated with legitimate work-related accidents and diseases are being borne by other providers. As a bearer of lost value, the commodity drops in its money value due to the movement of cost-shifting away from insurance boards.

However, it could perfectly well be the case that an increase in cost-shifting causes an increase in the value of the commodity. If an increase in cost-shifting toward insurance boards and away from other providers takes place, the value of the commodity grows rather than drops. In this regard, Fortin and Lanoie (1992) found that lower unemployment insurance benefits increase the frequency and duration of work-related injuries. In the same vein, Koning (2009) shows how the number of reported injuries increases dramatically when compensation benefits serve as a substitute for unemployment insurance. In these examples, the value of the commodity increases due to more lost value being crystallized in the commodity due to a higher number of reported injury claims and working days lost. Thus, it can be said that an increase and decrease in cost-shifting varies in the opposite direction to the value of the commodity only when the direction of the movement is away from insurance boards and toward a third-party provider. If the direction of the movement is, on the contrary, toward insurance boards and away from third-party providers, the exact opposite takes place, that is, an increase in the value of the commodity. Thus, the from/to direction of a cost-shifting movement makes a difference in the commodity's value fluctuation.

Finally, in regard to the interplay of other social relations, the conditioning force of cost-shifting is strongly mediated by the interplay of other social relations. Similar to the movement of the economic activity – i.e., business cycle fluctuations and long-term growth – the impact of cost-shifting depends on the movements of the procedurally hidden social relations. An upward movement of cost-shifting away or toward insurance boards causes a drop or an increase in the value of the commodity, respectively, dependent on the direction and magnitude of working days lost, reported injury claims, and injury claim rejections, while on the other hand a downward movement of cost-shifting away or toward insurance boards causes an increase or a drop in the value of the commodity, respectively, dependent upon the direction and magnitude of the aforementioned procedurally hidden social relations. Very different combinations are possible if other social relations are considered. In fact, the value of the commodity might even remain the same during a movement of cost-shifting if the interplay of other social relations balances each other in their directions and magnitudes. Nevertheless, the shifting of costs from/to insurance boards and publicly funded and private providers is a relevant structurally hidden social relation for an understanding of the commodity's value.

5   The Relative Value and Price Fluctuation of the Commodity

As a fetish, the value formation of the commodity is not exclusively the outcome of the total mass of lost labour power produced in society but a series
of social relations that include the mass of working days lost, the mass of
reported injury claims, the mass of rejected injury claims, the type and adjustment of rate-setting mechanics, employment and underemployment levels,
ups/downs of the business cycle, positive/negative long-term growth and
from/to cost-shifting dynamics. These hidden procedural and structural social
relations play an important role in the conditioning of the commodity's value.
However, these social relations, which account for the commodity's value as
an absolute quantity, do not account for the fluctuation in the commodity's
value as a relative quantity, as a fraction of the socially lost labour time in a
subset of firms and a branch of industry. The commodity is exchanged as a
guarantee at a value and a price that represents social averages of lost labour
power. For this commodity, capitalists pay a price that represents the contribution to and deviation from the total mass of expected lost labour power in a
subset of firms within a branch of industry. In other words, capitalists do not
pay a proportional fraction of the total mass of lost labour power produced in
society, but a relative fraction depending on the performance of the subset of
firms they belong to – i.e., group rate – and their own performance – i.e., experience rate. Given this relative form of value that accounts for the individual
price of the commodity, it is entirely possible for the value of the commodity
as an absolute quantity to grow and for this growth to be accompanied by a fall
in the value of the commodity as a relative value. The opposite is also true. It
is possible for the value of the commodity as an absolute quantity to fall and
for this fall to be accompanied by a growth in the value of the commodity as
a relative value. In addition to this inorganic movement, we might also have
an organic movement of lost value in society, where both the absolute and
the relative value of the commodity move in the same direction and magnitude. Under this scenario, a growth or fall in the value of the commodity as
an absolute quantity is accompanied by a growth or fall in the value of the
commodity as a relative value, respectively. This organic movement does not
require further explanation. It is comprehensible that given a growth or fall
in the value of the commodity as an absolute quantity for an individual firm
to see a growth or fall in the relative value of the commodity, respectively. But
how can an inorganic movement be explained? How can an individual firm
see the relative value of the commodity moving in an opposite direction to the
absolute value of the commodity? This inorganic movement has three possible
explanations. First, the branch of industry an individual capitalist belongs to

may see its total mass of lost value moving at a different direction or magnitude to the total mass of lost value produced in all branches of industry. For example, while the sum of all branches of industry in society experience an increase in the total mass of lost value, a particular branch, let us say manufacturing, experiences a decrease in the total mass of lost value. Under this scenario, all firms belonging to the manufacturing sector would see a fall in the relative value or the price of the commodity while a general increase in the absolute value of the commodity takes place. Second, the subset of firms an individual capitalist belongs to may see its total mass of lost value moving at a different direction or magnitude to the total mass of lost value produced in a particular branch of industry or all branches of industry. For example, while a particular branch, let us say forestry products, experiences an increase in the total mass of lost value, a particular subset of firms, let us say pulp and paper mills, experience a decrease in the total mass of lost value. Under this scenario, all the pulp and paper mill firms would see a fall in the relative value or the price of the commodity at the same time as an increase in the absolute value of the commodity occurs. Third, an individual firm may experience its total mass of lost value moving at a different direction or magnitude to the total mass of lost value produced in a subset of firms, a particular branch of industry or all branches of industry. In this case, the individual firm would see a fall in the relative value or the price of the commodity while there is a general increase in the total mass of lost value in all branches of industry, in a particular branch of industry or even in the subset of firms it belongs to – i.e., group rate. Summing up, it is therefore possible, given an increase in the total mass of lost value in all branches of industry, for the relative value of the commodity to fall and for this fall to be accompanied by a fall in a particular branch of industry it belongs to; it is possible, given an increase in the total mass of lost value in the branch of industry it belongs to, for the relative value of the commodity to fall and for this fall to be accompanied by a fall in the subset of firms it belongs to; and, finally, it is possible, given an increase in the total mass of lost value in the subset of firms it belongs to, for the relative value of the commodity to fall and for this fall to be accompanied by a fall at the firm level. This inorganic movement, where the absolute value of the commodity might be at odds with the relative value of the commodity, is an essential feature of the commodification of lost labour power. It is conceivable for all firms to be collectively compensating the total mass of lost labour power produced in society at an equivalent proportion while at the time an individual firm might be contributing to the collective share in disproportion to its own performance. For the commodity, an individual firm might be paying a price – i.e., a premium – that is over or under the lost value produced at the firm level. Therefore, the relative value of

the commodity or the individual value of the commodity manifests in disproportion to the absolute value of the commodity or the total mass of lost value
produced in society. This gap between the relative and the absolute value of
the commodity produces a series of social relations that condition the relative value and the price of the commodity. These social relations that aim at
the relative value and price of the commodity constitute what I call the class-
hidden social relations. These are essentially power relations, in other words,
social relations rooted in differential power among the two classes, capitalists
and wage labourers. Here, the fetish of the commodity in its relative value formation and price extends from the procedural and structural social relations
to the class-hidden social relations. These class-hidden social relations play a
key role in the conditioning of the relative value and price of the commodity.

5.1   Class-Hidden Social Relations

Before singling out and examining the class-hidden social relations in their
conditioning of the relative value and the price of the commodity, it is necessary to understand the systemic roots of these power relations. First, let us
remember that the commodity is produced by insurance boards to satisfy the
needs of firms rather than their own needs as a means of production, an element required for the production of commodities (see Chapter 4). Capitalists
are compelled to purchase the lost-labour-power commodity as they are any
other productive instrument. But as an element of production, one that is supplied to the labour process like any other means of production, individual firms
aim at purchasing it at its cheapest cost. Here, we have Marx's (1990) internal
contradiction between use value and exchange value hidden within the commodity. Firms aim to maximize the use value and minimize the exchange value
of the commodity. They seek for (a) protection against disputes in court, (b) the
socialisation of compensation payments, and (c) the limiting of compensation payments to wage labourers' necessary needs at the lowest possible rate
of compensation – i.e., the exchange value of the commodity. Since the rate of
compensation is a collective process, one that represents each firm's contribution to and deviation from the total mass of expected lost labour power in an
aggregate, this internal contradiction of the commodity manifests externally
as the conflict between the absolute and relative form of value of the commodity. This external opposition, namely, the conversion of lost value into money
value at an equivalent proportion to the total mass of lost labour power and
the spreading of compensation payments in disproportion at the firm level,
triggers a series of social relations to reduce the rate of compensation and
cheapen its money form, the premium. This occurs because, on the one hand,
insurance boards impose the obligation of sharing the burden of the absolute

value of the commodity and, on the other, enforce a disproportionate distribution of lost value relative to the performance of each individual firm in relation to aggregates. These two mutual undermining forces in the construction of the exchange value of the commodity – i.e., the rate of compensation – result in a series of class-hidden social relations that aim to reduce the internal tension between the use value and exchange value of the commodity. This manifests as a constant pressure on the exchange value and the price of the commodity.

Second, insurance boards produce the commodity as part of the circuit of metamorphosis of lost labour power, that is, the transformation of lost labour power into money value, investment value, medical value, and wage-replacement value (see Chapter 3). Let us also remember that this circuit not only involves insurance boards and capitalists but wage labourers as well. In this regard, the purpose of the circuit of metamorphosis is twofold: on the one hand, it distributes the total mass of lost value in the form of compensation payments among the capitalist class, and, on the other, it disburses compensation benefits in the form of medical and wage-replacement benefits to injured workers. As already analyzed, this circuit entails an inner contradiction, a tension between lost labour power in the form of the premium and in the form of medical and wage-replacement value. While lost labour power in the form of the premium pulls capitalists in the direction of decreasing it, lost labour power in the form of medical and wage-replacement benefits pulls wage labourers in the direction of increasing it. Thus, the premium stands in opposition to medical and wage-replacement benefits. As a contradictory unity, premiums and medical and wage-replacement benefits can be thought of as a social wage, one that is collectively and indirectly paid by capitalists to insurance boards (see Chapter 6). Similar to the traditional wage, this social wage – i.e., premiums and benefits – moves in opposite directions in terms of class interests and is therefore inversely reciprocal. This inner contradiction of the circuit of metamorphosis of lost labour power expresses itself as a number of class-hidden social relations that put pressure on the exchange value and the price of the commodity.

These two internal contradictions, that is, the use value/exchange value opposition of the commodity and the class conflict of the circuit of metamorphosis, result in a series of class-hidden social relations pressing in opposite directions. These social relations erupt in order to reduce both the inner contradictions of the commodity and of the circuit of metamorphosis. As a partial movement, this resolution is periodically and partially achieved through class-hidden social relations. With the purpose of decreasing the relative value and the price of the commodity, individual capitalists engage in informational class struggle in order to disrupt the value formation of the commodity. This informational class warfare manifests as a constant disruption of the different moments of the informational commodification of lost labour power: (a) the working-day-lost moment, (b) the reporting moment, (c) the recording moment, (d) the processing moment and (e) the programing moment. Capitalists' information hostility includes misinforming workers about injury claim procedures, dissuading and threatening workers to keep them from reporting accidents, misreporting accidents or reporting them in the wrong categories, appealing workers' legitimate claims, promoting safety incentive programs, and establishing early-return-to-work programs, among other social relations. Similar to financial information in the stock market, capitalists intend to introduce materially false and misleading information into the lost-labour-power commodity market. These actions can be equated as commodity fraud, as lost value manipulation, conspiracy to commit accident information fraud, and spoofing insurance boards' information-intensive systems with false statistics, underreports and misreports.

For their part, with the purpose of re-establishing the conversion of lost labour power into money and their reconversion in medical and wage-replacement at their value, wage labourers fight back by providing information about injury-claim procedures, assisting in the reporting of injury claims, producing independent reports to contest official reports, organizing labour forums to discuss concerns and elaborate on strategies, and developing partnerships with research centres and universities to produce scientific knowledge on their areas of concern. Depending upon the balance of class power, the relative value and price of the commodity may increase or shrink to satisfy either capital or wage labourers' sectional interests. Now, although some economic literature on health and safety recognizes the contradictions between safety and profitability that arise due to power relations and adversarial behaviour (see Hart, 2010; LaDou, 2006; Mansfield et al. 2012), no one to my knowledge has recognized them as the result of inner structural contradictions and distinguishable power relations that arise as a way to reduce this tension. This constant flux in the relative value and price of the commodity is the result of the class-hidden social relations or capitalists and wage labourers pressing in opposite directions, a movement that periodically erupts due to the internal contradictions of the commodity and the circuit of metamorphosis of lost labour power.

The analysis that follows singles out, conceptualizes and examines the power relations that condition the commodity's relative value and price. It by no means invalidates the conditioning power of the procedural and structural social relations already analyzed. In fact, it extends the nuance of the commodity's value formation to the power relations that insurance boards' circuit of metamorphosis between different classes establishes. In the next lines, the commodity's value fluctuation is examined as a fraction of the socially lost value produced within an aggregate to be paid by an individual capitalist at a specific price. Here, the commodity's value is addressed as a relative quantity. It exclusively pertains to the relative value and price fluctuation of the commodity, in other words, to the rate of compensation and the money form – i.e., the premium – that confront individual capitalists as a guarantee against lost labour power. Different combinations among these power relations are examined. While under given conditions some relations remain constant, others may vary in an upward direction or downward direction, thus expanding or contracting the commodity's relative value and price. As mentioned, the interplay of class-hidden social relations in their conditioning of the value and price of the commodity vary, mainly due to the balance of class forces in society. While a contraction in the relative value and price of the commodity is indicative of capitalists having the upper hand, an expansion of the relative value and price of the commodity is indicative of wage labourers' power. From this vantage point, it can be said that the relative value and price of the commodity is a measure of class struggle or capitalists and wage labourers pressing in opposite directions.

Since the analysis of each and every power relation is beyond the scope of this critique, only the most common class-hidden power relations are examined. In addition, only those attributable to the capitalist class are addressed. True to my positionality as a Marxist scholar, a positionality that aims to advance the sectional interests of wage labourers, I openly decline to analyze wage labourers' use of power. While I feel morally comfortable examining capitalists' common techniques and machinations in their attempt to contract the value and price of the commodity for their own economic benefit, I do not feel the same when examining and providing details on how wage labourers use their power to expand the value and price of the commodity for their health benefits. This is so because there is a moral gap between these two opposite movements. While the capitalists' movement aims to decrease the cost of the commodity, the wage labourers' movement is aimed at the satisfaction of necessary needs. Following my social conscience, I refuse to disclose wage labourers' class-hidden relations and provide evidence for the so-called 'moral hazard' or the practice of cheating the system, a condemnation unsurprisingly applied only to wage labourers (experience of author). Although there is some truth about the notion of workers simulating illnesses and symptoms or deceitfully reporting common accidents as work related, this has been greatly exaggerated by insurance boards, capitalists and the capitalist state. In my ten years of work experience at an insurance board, I heard of only one case of symptom simulation and no more than ten cases of falsely reporting common accidents as work-related accidents (experience of author). What follows focuses only on the fluctuation of the relative value and price of the commodity attributable to capital or more precisely to what Marx (1990) calls 'capital personified', that is, its unconscious movement through employers, insurance boards, private providers and the capitalist state.

5.1.1   Relative Value and Price Fluctuation Due to a Movement of
          Misreporting and Underreporting Injury Claims

As already examined, the commodity does not embody lost labour power but reported lost labour power through injury claims. The commodity crystallizes lost labour power only if it has been reported to an insurance board via an injury claim. Due to the fact that lost labour power does not have the ability to report itself, this procedurally hidden social relation creates a bias in favour of capital. While the action of reporting furnishes the commodity with lost value, thereby increasing the value of the commodity, the inaction of non-reporting does exactly the opposite; it disallows the infusion of lost value, thus decreasing the value of the commodity. If we consider that it is in the interest of the capitalists to purchase the commodity at its cheapest exchange value, the reporting sensitivity of the commodity generously favours the capitalist class. This constitutes the procedurally hidden reporting bias of the informational commodification of lost labour power. However, besides this procedurally hidden reporting bias there is also a class-hidden reporting bias. This second bias is the consequence of the unequal power relations that surround the pushing of injury claims. Although both wage labourers and capitalists can report injuries, it is capital that has the upper hand. Individual firms enjoy a greater amount of power in the reporting moment of the informational commodification of lost labour power (see Chapter 4).

In abusing their power, individual firms engage in a series of misreporting and underreporting practices that result in the contraction of the relative value and price of the commodity. These class-hidden practices are not novel, as they were born with the emergence of WCSs (see Guinnane and Streb, 2015). Misreporting and underreporting injury claims, especially non-fatal ones, were common activities in Germany in the 19th century. These practices are still ordinary, but they have grown in complexity and sophistication in todays' workplace. Underreporting and misreporting practices take many different forms. We have for instance the pressure imposed on workers not to report (see Broadway and Stull, 2008; Brown and Barab, 2007; Galizzi et al., 2010; Geller, 1996; Lippel, 2003, 2007; MacEachen, 2000; Strunin and Boden, 2004; Zoller, 2003). For example, there is the 'if you get injured you get fired' atmosphere (Broadway and Stull, 2008), encouraging workers not to report to avoid repercussions in their annual performance evaluations (Walker, 2010), dissuading reporting in order to decrease premiums and increase personal bonuses (Galizzi et al., 2010), and workers' hesitation to report to avoid being framed and stigmatized as lazy or a complainer (Zoller, 2003) or simply due to peer pressure (Geller, 1996). Under this form, under-reporting is linked to factors associated with wage labourers' vulnerability and differential class power, that is, the economic, social and symbolic gap between wage labourers and the capitalist class or its representatives – i.e., top management. Here, class power manifests as a failure to report due to a fear of discipline; being stigmatized as lazy, careless or a complainer; putting career opportunities in danger; and the firm's economic goals of having no reported injuries, among others.

In addition to indirect class pressure, underreporting can take the form of direct deceit such as funneling injured workers through non-official health institutions (see Azaroff et al., 2004; Zoller, 2003). This strategy is exerted to avoid recording work injuries in claims for insurance boards. Company health-care personnel and over-the-counter preparations are used at the worksite to treat minor injuries in-house (see Dew and Taupo, 2009; Emmett, 2002; Mansfield et al. 2012). Dew and Taupo (2009) describe how physicians in a meat packing facility in New Zealand administer cortisone on a regular basis to wage labourers to treat shoulder, wrist, back and leg pain. In the mining sector of Chile, this underreporting practice is normal. By funneling injured workers to their own *in situ* medical or first-aid facilities, Chilean mining companies effectively underreport a large number of minor injuries, which results in fewer working days lost (experience of author). It is interesting to note that from 2007 to 2016, the number of reported injuries per 100 work-ers of the mining sector remained the lowest among every branch of indus-try at between 2.3% and 1.4% (Superintendencia de Seguridad Social, 2017). However, during the same period, the mining sector was the leading branch among all branches of industry in terms of working days lost, accounting for a range between 25.3 and 38.1 working days lost (Superintendencia de Seguridad Social, 2017). How is it possible for the mining sector to be the branch of indus-try with the fewest injuries and at the same the highest average number of working days lost over a decade? Here, we have the already explained opposite movement between lost-time injuries and working days lost. The mining sec-tor reflects this contradiction, where a constant fall in lost-time injuries per 100 workers during a decade is accompanied by a constant growth in the average number of working days lost per injury. This can certainly be explained by an increase in long-term injuries with more working days lost accompanied by a strong decrease in short-term injuries with fewer working days lost. But can this anomaly be sustained over a decade? It is likely that this contradiction reflects nothing more than the sustained practice of channeling minor injuries away from official health institutions, an underreporting practice that is systemic in the Chilean mining sector (experience of author). In regard to the differences between fatality rates, illness rates and injury rates, Azaroff et al., (2004) suggest the study of their divergence as a way to understand changes in injury-reporting practices.

Finally, misreporting injury claims is another practice performed by top management in order to contract the relative value and price of the commodity. The most ordinary form of misreporting claims is the non-recognition of an injury as work-related thus categorizing it as a common injury (see Zoller, 2003). This class-hidden practice allows cost-shifting from WCSs to public/privately funded health programs. Compensation costs are effectively passed to other health providers or society at large. The numbers are not negligible. Although it is not possible to know if all the cases are due to misreporting practices, a study in Chile claims that around 38.6% of work-related diseases are annually passed as common diseases to private health programs (Bitran asociados, 2011). During my tenure as the president of the Joint Health Safety Committee at an insurance board, I had to strongly push back against misreporting practices. As one example, the corporate affairs manager attempted to re-classify a worker's severe neck pain as a common injury in the guise that the injury occurred outside of office hours during the firm's annual party. I firmly rejected that re-classification. Under Chilean laws related to WCSs, work injuries include injuries that occur during any firm's events including annual celebrations. Another time, the human resources manager attempted to re-classify a work injury as a to/from work injury in order to avoid a surge in the premium. This might sound odd to a Canadian scholar from British Columbia, where injuries that occur while a worker is travelling to/from work are not covered at all unless they exceptionally take place on a captive road – i.e., controlled or maintained by the employer (personal communication with L. Bennett, March 20, 2019). However, under Chilean laws, to/from work injuries are fully compensable, but they do not enter into the rate and premium-setting mechanics. What the human resources manager was trying to do was not to hamper the disbursement of medical and wage-replacement benefits but rather prevent a surge in the premium, the price of the commodity. This misreporting practice is a more sophisticated one and is aimed at categorizing a work injury into a type that has no impact on the premium-setting mechanics. Misreporting is a complex practice to expose since it requires comprehensive knowledge of local WCS' laws. Top management are eager to re-classify work injuries and diseases in favour of capital and at the expense of workers' health needs (experience of author).

The practice of underreporting and misreporting aims mainly at diminishing the number of injury claims. This is so because fewer claims translate into lower premiums. As already discussed, a fall in the mass of reported injury claims decreases the value of the commodity by simply reducing the crystallization of working days lost in the commodity. Now, it is important to note that underreporting and misreporting practices do not aim to reduce the absolute value furnished in the commodity. Firms do not care about how much lost value is crystallized in the commodity as a whole. They also do not care about the total mass of lost value in their branch of industry or the subset of firms they belong to. Firms only care about reducing the relative value and the price of the commodity, which they encounter as the premium rate. The fact that less absolute lost value is crystallized in the commodity due to their misreporting and underreporting practices is not their concern. Some firms may know that the absolute value of the commodity does contract due to these practices; however, it is not their intention, only a consequence of their intention. Whether or not it is or not their purpose, the end result is that underreporting and misreporting practices do contract both the absolute value and the relative value of the commodity and its money form, the premium.

As the absolute value has already been discussed under the heading of the value fluctuation due to reported injury claims, it is time to go over the relative value and price contraction of the commodity due to individual firms' injury-reporting malpractices. For simplicity purposes, henceforth, the term 'premium' is used to refer both to the relative value and price of the commodity. Let us remember that individual capitalists do not pay a fixed proportional fraction of the total mass of lost labour power produced in society but a relative price depending on the performance of the subset of firms they belong to – i.e., base premium – and their own performance – i.e., experience premium. Capitalists are never confronted by the absolute value of the commodity but its relative form, the premium rate, which in its two segments, the base premium and experience premium, accounts for the firms' expected contribution and deviation from that subset of firms, respectively. The practice of underreporting and misreporting does impact the two segments of the premium, both the experience premium and the base premium; however, individual firms' goal is to decrease the experience premium, that is, the deviation from the total mass of expected lost value in the subset of firms they belong to. They try hard to decrease the magnitude of the deviation, usually described as the degree of experience rating. Firms aim at a negative value in the following formula: lost value at the firm level – average lost value at a subset of firms. If their lost value at the firm level is smaller than the average lost value in an aggregate, their experience premium will shrink to a negative value; if their lost value at the firm level is greater than the average lost value in an aggregate, their experience premium will increase to a positive value. It follows from this that a variation in the movement of underreporting and misreporting injury claims, whether a growth or fall, does not simply cause the experience premium to move in an opposite direction. In other words, the growth of underreporting and mis-reporting injury claims does not mechanically result in a smaller experience premium; vice versa, a fall in underreporting and misreporting injury claims does not result in a higher experience premium. For this to happen, a third ele-ment, the base premium, must enter the scene at a direction and magnitude that enables this opposite movement to take place. The impact of underre-porting and misreporting practices on the experience premium depends on the movement of the base premium. This occurs because these three relations are proportionally related. Thus, the magnitude of the experience premium varies with the extent to which it deviates from the base premium or its normal social level of intensity. When this deviation is positive or the total mass of lost value at the firm level is greater than the total mass of lost value in an aggre-gate, a given working day lost no longer creates an absolute value but a positive relative one. This added working day lost builds on the experience premium as a surcharge. On the other side, when this deviation is negative or the total mass of lost value at the firm level is smaller than the total mass of lost value in an aggregate, a removed working day lost no longer creates an absolute value but a negative relative one. This taken-away working day lost builds on the experience premium as a discount or rebate. Within this scenario, there are three possible combinations: (a) a growth in underreporting and misreporting injury claims causes the experience premium to fall only if it is accompanied by a movement in the base premium in the same direction at a magnitude that exceeds the total mass of lost value at the firm level, (b) a fall in underreporting and misreporting injury claims causes the experience premium to grow only if it is accompanied by a movement in the base premium in the same direction at a magnitude that falls behind the total mass of lost value at the firm level, and (c) a fall/growth in underreporting and misreporting injury claims keeps the experience premium unchanged only if it is accompanied by a movement in the base premium in a direction at a magnitude that balances the total mass of lost value at the firm level. In this last combination, in disregard of an upward/ downward movement of underreporting and misreporting injury claims, the experience premium remains the same if an equivalent upward/downward movement of the base premium takes place.

Take this example: an increase of, let us say, 100 underreporting and mis-reporting injury claims equivalent to 1,000 working days lost decreases the experience premium only if it is accompanied by a base premium, the average of which is kept or moves beyond 1,000 working days – let us say it is kept at 2,000 working days. In this case, a firm whose total lost value initially accounts for an equivalent of 2,000 working days and an experience premium of $0 due to a base premium equivalent to 2,000 working days lost would see its experi-ence premium fall to an equivalent of the difference of 1,000–2,000 working days lost, that is, -1,000 working days lost. Here, the firm's experience premium drops because a growth of 100 underreporting and misreporting injury claims equivalent to 1,000 working days is accompanied by a movement in the base premium that exceeds the 1,000 working days. If the base premium moves in a direction and magnitude that falls behind 1,000 working days lost, let us say, 900 working days lost, the firm would not see a drop in its experience pre-mium; on the contrary, the firm would see an increase in its experience pre-mium at an equivalent of 100 working days lost. These combinations show that the movement of misreporting and underreporting injury claims varies in the opposite direction to the experience premium only when it is accompa-nied by a movement of the base premium in the same upward direction at a magnitude that exceeds the total mass of lost value at the firm level or in the same downward direction at a magnitude that falls behind the total mass of lost value at the firm level. The contraction of the experience premium due to a movement of misreporting and underreporting practices is highly mediated by the base premium.

5.1.2   Relative Value and Price Fluctuation Due to a Movement of
         Appealing Legitimate Claims

Once an injury claim is reported and deemed compensable by an insurance board, the informational process of commodification continues its course through the recording moment, the act of properly inscribing and register-ing lost-time injuries. The recording moment classifies, organizes and stores lost-time injury information for further combination during the processing moment or the act of transforming lost-time injury information into lost-time injury rates through a series of preestablished and complicated rules (see Chapter 4). Some may think that once an injury claim is accepted by an insur-ance board the path that follows and leads to the conversion of lost value into money value is a smooth one. Unfortunately for wage labourers, that is not the case. Capital is still given a chance to halt the conversion of lost value into money value and avoid a premium surge.

By appealing legitimate claims, capitalists can diminish the number of injury claims and potentially circumvent an increase in the experience premium despite injury claims being already accepted. As Cox and Lippel (2008) note, "Some employers may systematically challenge claims as a part of a 'claims management' strategy aimed at keeping the costs of premiums down" (p. 19). This is due to the prerogative enjoyed by employers within the commodification process. Although wage labourers can directly push injury claims, individual firms are entitled to confirm reported injuries as work related. In this regard, it is important to note that countries and jurisdictions have diverse legislation on the matter; some are more stringent, and others are looser. Thus, the variability in the chances of effectively contesting injury claims is high. Nonetheless, appealing claims is a bet that firms are usually eager to take. In contrast to misreporting and underreporting practices that target the reporting moment of the commodification process, this practice targets the recording moment of the commodification process. Its goal is to undo that what has already been successfully reported and to impede the inscription of a work injury as such. This practice aims to block the process that brings the object of lost labour power into an independent material object, a piece of information, particularly, lost-time injury information (see Chapter 4). By disrupting the objectification of lost labour power as a material record, capitalists make sure lost labour power will not be processed and transformed into higher premiums by insurance boards' information-intensive systems.

Appealing claims is strongly rooted in differential class power. Capitalists and workers differ in their likelihood to pursue contested claims. While firms can economically endure years in legal battles, this is not the case for wage labourers who depend on a wage to survive. Firms have far more resources to contest injury claims (see Ison 1986, 1993). As a personal example, in 2011, during my tenure as the worker's representative and president of the Joint Health Safety Committee of an insurance board, I dropped my legal case against the firm due to a lack of resources to pursue a long legal fight. Ison (1993) notes that employers can put pressure on physicians for confidential medical information in order to contest an injured worker's claim. Lippel (2003, 2007) reports on video and surveillance techniques used by private investigators hired by employers to covertly collect evidence to challenge injury claims. Strunin and Boden (2004) argue that workers have reported being filmed, photographed and monitored by claim representatives. Intrusive techniques can go as far as placing hidden cameras in hospital rooms – a blatant violation of a patient's privacy – in order to contest an injury claim (experience of author). There are reports of entrapment techniques such as planting money by an injured worker's vehicle and taking a picture when the worker bends down to pick it up

(Lippel, 2003). This intrusive behaviour performed by firms is the personification of capital, the quest of reducing insurance premium costs in order to expand the rate of profit.

Appealing claims is not a moral but an economic movement and is nothing more than a sustained effort to contain or contract the experience premium. There is plenty of research focusing on the economic relationship between appealing claims and premiums (see Hyatt and Kralj, 1995; Mansfield et al., 2012; Thomason, 2005; Tompa et al., 2016; Weiler, 1983). Using claims data from a WCS in Ontario, Canada, Hyatt and Kralj (1995) found that experience-rated firms are more likely to appeal insurance boards' decisions rather than non-experience-rated firms. Around 80% of appeals in Ontario are from experience-rated firms. This was also higher for larger firms than for smaller ones who have a lower degree of experience rating. In regard to the degree of experience rating, the economic literature on health and safety suggests that a higher degree decreases injury claims at the aggregate and employer level (see Tompa et al., 2016). As Tompa et al. (2016) note, some claims reductions may be associated with improved health and safety and some with appealing claims; however, it is not easy to disentangle them. Although the experience rating is intended to economically encourage firms to improve safety at the workplace, a growing body of research reveals that this approach has had the opposite effect due to employers' focus on claim management rather than risk prevention (Mansfield et al., 2012). As a result of appealing claims, wage labourers can spend months to years in legal conflicts to obtain their legitimate benefits. In addition, the incremental costs associated with appealing claims – e.g., lawyers, paralegal detectives, workers' representatives – have created a new industry of employer claims management consultants (Ison, 1986).

A variation in the movement of appealing injury claims, either an increase or diminution, causes the experience premium to move in an opposite direction. However, similar to misreporting and underreporting practices, the movement of appealing claims does not mechanically vary in the opposite direction of the experience premium. It does this only if it is accompanied by a movement in the base premium in the same upward direction at a magnitude that exceeds the total lost value of appealing legitimate claims or in the same downward direction at a magnitude that falls behind the total lost value of appealing legitimate claims. Also, an increase/decrease of the total mass of appealing injury claims under a movement of the base premium in a direction and magnitude that balances the mass of lost value at the firm level leaves the experience premium unchanged. Only when the base premium increases over the total mass of lost value at the firm level due to an increase in appealing legitimate claims could the capitalist compensate himself with a smaller experience premium. Now, if a variation in the same direction among the movement of appealing legitimate claims and the movement of misreporting and underreporting injury claims takes place simultaneously, the same holds true. Unless this twin movement is not accompanied by a movement in the base premium in a direction and magnitude that enables the contraction or expansion of the experience premium, this twin movement will not cause the experience premium to move in an opposite direction. Of course, this twin upward movement increases the chances of a capitalist compensating himself with a cheap experience premium. However, it is still a bet, a gamble against the base premium, in other words, a gamble that is conclusively solved by the movement of the total mass of lost value at the aggregate level.

5.1.3   Relative Value and Price Fluctuation Due to a Movement of Managed Care

While underreporting/misreporting and appealing injury claims are power relations that aim to diminish the number of injury claims in order to contract the experience premium, the practice of managed care aims to decrease the number of working days lost to keep the commodity from being exchanged at the lost value of a work injury. Contrary to common sense, the goal of managed care is not the restoration of health but the restoration of labour power via the minimization of working days lost. Managed care is an ex-post way to contract the experience premium of the commodity. It is an after-the-event power relation, one that capital turns to when the previous power relations – i.e., underreporting/misreporting and appealing injury claims – were not successful in blocking the reporting and recording of a work injury. Under the euphemism of secondary prevention – i.e. minimizing the impact of an injury once it happens – this relation can be regarded as a damage-control strategy. How exactly does it aid capital? The commodity's value formation involves a process of converting non-equivalents: lost value into value (see Chapter 4). The purpose of insurance boards' information-intensive operations of recording and processing work injuries is to transform lost value into money value. In terms of the commodity's value formation, lost value and value are directly reciprocal. While greater lost value translates into greater value, less lost value translates into less value. In this regard, the class-hidden social relation of managed care focuses on diminishing the amount of lost value to be crystallized in the commodity to avoid a premium surge. Contrary to underreporting/misreporting and appealing practices that aim to block the total mass of lost value produced by a work injury, managed care aims to decrease the number of working days lost, a portion of the total mass of lost value produced by a work injury.

The practice of managed care targets the recording moment of the commodification of lost labour power. It focuses on disrupting the quantitative accuracy of this process. In particular, it aims at distorting the magnitude and the basic unit of the commodity: the working day lost. Let us keep in mind that, while as a substance this commodity is lost labour power, as a magnitude it is socially necessary lost labour time, and as a basic unit it is a working day lost (see Chapter 4). Lost time plays a major role in the commodity's value formation process. What managed care does is distort the total mass of lost labour time objectified in the commodity at its basic unit, the working day lost. By decreasing the number of working days lost or cheapening the money value of a working day lost, capitalists expect to turn the commodity's magnitude into something smaller.

Managed care takes many different forms. There exists a huge repertoire of subtle and not-so-subtle techniques to decrease working days lost. One of the shapes it takes is as express medical services – i.e., quick medical assistance – to directly reduce the amount of treatment time. In collusion with individual firms, managed-care companies encourage physicians to see more patients, devote less time for diagnosis, provide fewer services, and in general reduce treatment times by providing medical services more 'efficiently' (see Azaroff et al., 2004). Express medical services can lead to administrative barriers in ordering testing, procedures and referring patients to specialists that are better prepared to diagnose occupational problems. Managed care can also take the form of case managers' control. Under direct corporate pressure, a physician's decision might subtly change in favor of a firm's interests, especially when a patient is accompanied by a case manager (see Lax, 1996; Sommers et al., 2001). As Brown and Barab (2007) note, by accompanying injured workers to the examination room, case managers can influence the wording and information recorded in the incident report. In Chile, big corporations are usually awarded case managers whose job includes lobbying the medical system in order to diminish the number of working days lost. Their lobbying can be as harsh as putting pressure on physicians to amputate an injured worker's finger rather than perform a complex surgery that could lead to more treatment time and working days lost (experience of author). I still remember my shock and rage when a case manager friend of mine showed me, under strict confidentiality, the official letter of a big corporation demanding the amputation of an injured worker's finger (experience of author). Another managed care strategy is to bureaucratically distort the quantity and value of working days lost through a series of administrative procedures. This technique is the most insidious one since it is very difficult to detect. An example of this is the bureaucratic practice of some medical facilities in Chile of reclassifying treatment days as 'postponements' or 'deferrals' to prevent treatment days from being considered as working days lost (experience of author). Due to its subtleness, reclassifying medical data is extremely difficult to denounce since it is executed under administrative and technical procedures. In the same vein, as Mansfield et al., (2012) describe, bureaucratic managed care strategies include fee schedules limiting hospital and physician costs, limiting physician choice, and reduced benefits, among others.

The overall outcome of managed care is a low quality of patient care, less time per appointment, patient-physician interaction dissatisfaction, negative impacts on recovery and of course poorer health (see Dembe and Boden, 2000; Hellinger, 1998; Mechanic, 2001). However, for capital, the overall outcome is something less painful: injury-costs savings. D'Andrea and Meyer (2004) estimate that in the 1990s, managed care resulted in reductions of between 20% and 30% per claim in medical and indemnity costs in Washington State, Florida and New Hampshire. The resulting effect of managed care is a commodity whose value is in disproportion to the effective lost value produced by a work injury. What managed care does is decrease the price of the commodity below the lost value effectively produced by an injury. So, while the commodity is exchanged at its value, that is, the effective amount of lost value crystallized in the commodity, it is not exchanged at the lost value of a work injury, in other words, the total mass of lost value produced by a wage-labour-related accident, disease or fatality. The commodity is therefore sold at its value but in disproportion to the injury's lost value. This movement results in the partial satisfaction of wage labourers' necessary needs, what unions and workers' organizations correctly call below the level of full compensation (see Chapter 3). Under managed care, the satisfaction of physiological and necessary needs is never met.

Managed care varies in an opposite direction to the number of working days lost. An increase in managed care decreases the number of working days lost objectified in the commodity; a decrease in managed care increases the number of working days lost objectified in the commodity. However, managed care does not vary in an opposite direction to the lost value of a work injury. As a damage-control strategy that focuses on cheapening the commodity, an increase in managed care does not necessarily decrease the lost value of a work injury; usually, it does exactly the opposite. There is ample evidence that managed care has a negative impact on the recovery and health of a patient, thus increasing the lost value of an injury (see D'Andrea and Meyer, 2004; Dembe and Boden, 2000; Hellinger, 1998; Mechanic, 2001). So, while managed care varies in an opposite direction to the number of working days lost, it varies in the same direction to the lost value of an injury.

Regarding the experience premium, managed care moves in its opposite direction if it is accompanied by a movement in the base premium in the same upward direction at a magnitude that exceeds the total mass of lost value at the firm level or in the same downward direction at a magnitude that falls behind the total mass of lost value at the firm level. An increase in the movement of managed care under a growth in the base premium at a magnitude that exceeds the total mass of lost value at the firm level causes the experience premium to fall. A decrease in the movement of managed care under a drop in the base premium at a magnitude that falls behind the total mass of lost value at the firm level causes the experience premium to grow. An increase/decrease in the movement of managed care accompanied by a movement in the base premium in a direction and magnitude that balances the total mass of lost value at the firm level leaves the experience premium unchanged.

5.1.4   Relative Value and Price Fluctuation Due to a Movement of Early-
        Return-to-Work Practices
We should remember that, from their birth, wcs s made the recovery of labour power their overriding goal beyond the recovery of health (see Chapter 3). As Eghigian (2000) states, "Insurers needed institutions that offered not simply the restoration of health, but the restoration of earning and productive capacity" (p. 135). The cessation of symptoms offered by hospitals, clinics and sanatoriums alone was not enough. While intimately related, these two purposes are not the same. In fact, under an environment marked by economic exchange such as the one imposed by insurance boards, these two goals tend to enter into stark contradictions. While the recovery of lost labour power presses wage labourers to return back to work and cut wage-replacement benefits, the recovery of health presses capitalists to maintain wage-replacement benefits. Within a wcs, lost-labour-power restoration and health restoration press each other in opposite directions. Unfortunately for wage labourers, the recovery of labour power was historically given the upper hand in the equation.

In 1890, German insurance boards were granted the right to manage their own medical facilities to ensure the restoration of labour power (Eghigian, 2000). The shift of treatment from the restoration of health to the restoration of labour power resulted in the birth of occupational rehabilitation, a form of training designed to put injured workers back to work as early as possible (see Eghigian, 2000). Initially, the actual means of production – i.e., the very tools and instruments of industrial and agricultural production – were introduced into the treatment process. Putting disabled workers to work as a part of a therapeutic regime resulted in one of the most pervasive ideologies of wcs s: work as a goal and a remedy. As Eghigian

(2000) notes, rather than simply being the goal of treatment, work became the treatment itself. The ideology of work as a goal/remedy can be understood in terms of Marx's (1978a) base/superstructure metaphor. Based on this metaphor, work as the purpose of treatment has its roots in insurance boards' economic process of exchange. The act of commodifying lost labour power on the basis of treatment time, specifically working days lost, shapes how medical benefits and their outcome are conceptualized. In this case, measured in employment terms rather than by reference to health, working days lost as a unit of measure implies that returning back to work is the desired behaviour. The same happens with work as a remedy. The activity of occupational rehabilitation based on a series of body motions that resemble the use of the means of production indicates that the labouring process is a therapeutic activity. Work as a goal/remedy is not a question of consciousness but is anchored in the day-to-day economic operations and activities of insurance boards. Here, the movement of consciousness is not the main driver of this ideology; it is a by-product of the power relations that insurance boards' process of exchange between capitalists and wage labourers establish. However, this does not mean the many capitalists remain silent on the issue. Employers strongly support this ideology, embracing it as a way to get injured workers back on the job and off wage-replacement benefits. Drawing from Marx's (1978b) ruling class metaphor, one that recognizes ideologies as a set of ideas that advance the interests of the dominant class at the expense of the subservient one, it can be added that the mystification of work as a goal/remedy is also part of a movement of class consciousness that aims to obscure the interests of wage labourers. In subordination to the logic of capital accumulation, this consciousness movement naturalizes, legitimizes and universalizes the belief of work as a goal/remedy, making it one of the core ideologies of wcs s.

Early-return-to-work practices are nothing but the by-product of insurance boards' focus on the recovery of labour power and the aforementioned ideological formation. They are generally enforced by capitalists to get injured workers off wage-replacement benefits and thus cheapen the premium. Analogous to managed care, early-return-to-work practices focus on decreasing the number of working days lost during the recovery period. They target the recording moment of the commodification of lost labour power by disrupting the quantitative accuracy during the recovery period. As part of the so-called secondary prevention, this class-hidden social relation also aims at minimizing the impact of an injury by lessening work absences. It results in a commodity whose relative value and price falls behind the total mass of lost value of a work injury. While managed care consists mainly of a series of medical-related activities, early-return-to-work practices consist of a series of bureaucratic and organizational activities.

The most common form of early-return-to-work practice is simply to put pressure on injured workers to return to work, even when they are not medically ready to do so. Here, the aim is simply to minimize the duration of the recovery period in order to decrease the number of working days lost to be crystallized in the commodity. This requires a willful act on the part of the employer. However, not every capitalist wants to bear the burden of pushing injured workers back to job. Rather than doing it themselves, some employers may hire third-party case managers to "facilitate" early return to work (see McInerney, 2010). Here, a third party under the guise of technical expertise does the dirty job of pushing workers back to the workplace. The classic early-return-to-work practices are light-duty and modified-work programs. These forms of early return to work are the most popular within the insurance business. In tandem with the ideology of work as a remedy, the purpose is to bring injured workers back on light duties as part of a therapeutic regime in order to gain confidence, train their working abilities, restore their productive capacity and successfully reintegrate into them the labour force. However, the truth is that the worker is brought back under light duties to reduce lost time (see Ison, 1993). Under the laws related to WCS s, when an injured worker is at modified work he is no longer eligible for wage-replacement benefits. Modified work, light duty work, or any kind of wage labour activity counts as work, and as such it implies the restoration of labour power and as a consequence the end of wage-replacement benefits. Some employers might even pressure doctors to certify that the worker is ready for light work when there is actually no modified work available (see Ison 1986; Lippel, 1999; Pransky et al., 1999). Some may just fire the injured worker once the period of modified work ends and a good number of working days lost have been successfully averted (see Ison 2009; Purse, 1998). Early-return-to-work practices tend to mushroom when the proper legislation is put in place. For example, legislation requiring wage labourers to accept any work offer or rewarding employers who bring injured workers back quickly tends to increase the movement of early-return-to-work practices (see Martin, 2001; Ruser, 1999). In general, stricter return-to-work policies – e.g., shorter limits on benefits, forced acceptance of a work offer – tend to increase the movement of early-return-to-work practices.

As a strategy aimed at minimizing the economic impact of an injury, the movement of early-return-to-work practices varies in the opposite direction to the number of working days lost. While an upward movement of early-return-to-work practices causes the number of working days lost to fall, a downward movement causes the number of working days lost to grow. Research on health and safety has found that when working days lost fall, light-duty and modified-work cases grow steadily (see Fletcher, 2001; Ruser, 1999). While this positive correlation does not explain the magnitude of the decrease of the total mass of working days lost, it certainly demonstrates that in many cases a drop in working days lost is the result of a complementary upward movement of early-return-to-work practices. Is there any relationship between light-duty programs and the severity of lost-time injuries? Tompa et al.'s (2013) findings suggest that incentive through accommodation effectively dominates in less serious lost-time injuries. Here, we have an increase of light-duty cases accompanied by a fall in the number of working days lost due to short-term disabilities but unaccompanied by a fall in the number of working days lost due to long-term and permanent disabilities. As Tompa et al. (2013) explain, this happens because short-term disabilities are more readily accommodated and thus transformed into no-lost-time claims rather than long-term and permanent disabilities. Therefore, it can be said that the movement of early-return-to-work practices chiefly varies in the opposite direction to the number of working days lost produced by short-term lost-time injuries while maintaining the direction of long-term and permanent lost-time injuries unaltered.

With respect to the experience premium, early-return-to-work practices move in its opposite direction if the movement of the base premium allows it to do so. A growth in early-return-to-work practices accompanied by a movement of the base premium at a magnitude that exceeds the total mass of lost value at the firm level causes the experience premium to fall. A fall in early-return-to-work practices accompanied by a movement of the base premium at a magnitude that falls behind the total mass of lost value at the firm level causes the experience premium to grow. If the base premium moves in a direction and magnitude that cancels the increase/decrease of early-return-to-work practices and thus balances the total mass of lost value at the firm level, the experience premium remains unaltered. Finally, similar to managed care, early-return-to-work practices vary in the same direction to the lost value of a work injury. This occurs because early-return-to-work practices push workers back to the job with unresolved medical conditions, thus increasing the lost value of a work injury. While an increase in early-return-to-work practices results in a growth in the lost value of a work injury, a decrease in early-return-to-work practices results in a fall in the lost value of a work injury.

5.1.5   Relative Value and Price Fluctuation Due to a Movement of Vocational Rehabilitation Interventions

One of the initial goals of WCSs was to reduce the burden of poor relief boards due to the new faces of poverty that had emerged, namely, the disabled, the chronically ill, the widowed and the unemployed (see Chapter 2). Insurance boards began to absorb the costs of the temporarily disabled, the permanently disabled and the widows and/or dependents. In addition to medical disability, insurance boards had to deal with market disability or the inability of disabled workers to go back to their pre-injury job or find a new one in the labour market. The inability to find a job was mainly because capitalists were reluctant to hire disabled workers (Eghigian, 2000; Gerstenberger, 1985), who were seen as less productive and prone to accidents. In 1890, German insurance boards discussed the idea of establishing a network of labour exchanges for disabled workers to deal with the lack of job opportunities for those with a permanent disability (Eghigian, 2000). The rejection to such plans came about through the pressure of capitalists who thought the economic benefits did not outweigh the costs. Although the tentative plan was never established, this early attempt shows that the difficulty of disabled workers to find a job was an issue that came about with the establishment of WCS s. However, this dilemma was never to be solved by WCS s, partly because this problem was deeply rooted in capitalist societies. Profit making through exploitation, what Marx (1990) technically describes as the extraction of unpaid labour – i.e., surplus value – from wage labourers, naturally results in the rejection of disabled or unexploitable labour power. Embedded as they are in the immanent laws of capital, the costs of not finding a job cannot be eliminated in a market where labour power is freely exchanged and exploited.

With the arrival of the experience premium in the last decades of the 20th century, individual firms began to experience first hand not only the economic burden of disabled workers being unable to return to work but being unable to return to a post-injury job with pay equal to the pre-injury one. The loss of earnings assessment performed by insurance boards, which compares the difference between the disabled worker's pre-injury job and available and suitable post-injury job opportunities, put capital in the position of needing to exhaust all the means necessary in assuring disabled workers get back to a job as good as the pre-injury one. Beginning in the 21th century, some WCS s began to implement vocational programs to help employers avoid a loss of earnings pension due to jobs that paid much less compared to the earnings of their pre-injury job. Although countries and jurisdictions define and operationalize "much less" in very different ways – e.g., in British Columbia, Canada, 80% or less of the pre-injury earnings is considered much less – the end result is preventing a loss of earnings pension. The class-hidden social relation that follows focuses on return to work in order to avoid a loss of earnings pension.

Vocational rehabilitation is a class-hidden social relation that is aimed at (a) avoiding a loss of earnings pension by putting the worker back in a similar-paying job to their pre-injury job or (b) manipulating the loss of earn-ings assessment to minimize the difference between the disabled worker's earnings of the pre-injury job and the earnings of those jobs deemed available and suitable. As a process, vocational rehabilitation can be broken down into four phases: evaluation, planning, treatment and placement (Robinson and Paquette, 2013). The procedures applied comprise identifying evaluee-specific variables expected to inhibit/facilitate vocational potential, assessing data to arrive at a conclusion on an evaluee's vocational potential, and applying voca-tional rehabilitation methods such as psychometric measurement, transferable skills analysis, wage-earning capacity and work-life participation (Robinson and Paquette, 2013). Workers are referred to vocational rehabilitation by insur-ance boards following many return-to-work attempts (MacEachen et al., 2013; Sears et al., 2014a). Similar to early-return-to-work practices, this social rela-tion is the by-product of insurance boards' historical focus on the recovery of labour power. It is also a bureaucratic practice, part of secondary prevention that seeks to minimize the cost of an injury. However, it is a desperate measure. In contrast to early-return-to-work practices, this social relation does not focus on decreasing the number of working days lost during the recovery period but rather on the avoidance or minimization of a loss of earnings pension. It tar-gets the processing moment of the commodification of lost labour power, that is, the series of operational rules that combine and calculate the total mass of impairment and the total mass of loss of earnings, among other units of infor-mation. Now, of course, this strategy also decreases the number of working days lost, but its goal goes beyond diminishing the number of working days lost. It is not a damage-control strategy but a last-resort strategy to employ when everything else has failed, the final and frantic effort to avoid the crystal-lization of permanent lost income in the commodity in the form of a pension.

In terms of economic savings, vocational rehabilitation has a well-known and reported reputation. In terms of workers' health, it is usually associated with medical problems, poor functional ability, multiple retraining attempts and workers' dissatisfaction (Sears et al., 2014b; Wagner et al., 2011). It is dis-turbing to note that workers who return to work after vocational rehabilitation almost always report some type of health restriction (see MacEachen et al., 2011, 2012; Wagner et al., 2011; Young, 2010). Young (2010) found that 69% of the study group participants reported physiological function impairment, 6% reported experiencing no impairment at all, and 33% identified their physi-ological functioning as determining their work continuation. Inappropriate referrals for training due to vocational rehabilitation's cost efficiency goals tend to worsen workers' health conditions. Injured workers are usually sent to voca-tional rehabilitation at maximum medical recovery, that is, while experiencing severe chronic pain and shortly after undergoing surgery (MacEachen et al., 2011). In addition, since vocational rehabilitation interventions are supplied by outsourced providers, critical health issues are often not addressed. Vocational rehabilitation providers are often reluctant to communicate workers' poor health and unresolved medical issues to insurance boards because they want to maintain their contracts (MacEachen et al., 2012).

Another major deficiency of vocational rehabilitation is the stress on the 'ability' to return to work rather than effectively returning to work. Drawing from this 'ability paradigm', workers are deemed employable when in reality they are not ready to return to work (MacEachen et al., 2012). The focus on workers' abilities not only results in deeming disabled workers employable but also employable at higher-paying jobs, thereby minimizing the differ-ence between the pre-injury earnings and the suitable post-injury earnings. By overrepresenting disabled workers' ability to work, the loss of earnings assessment is distorted in the interest of capital, resulting in a cheaper loss of earnings pension. This ability notion disregards consideration for unresolved medical problems resulting in workers being sent back to work with chronic pain, depression, poor health and medical problems (MacEachen et al., 2012). Injured workers often feel that they are pushed to return to the desk during vocational rehabilitation (Wagner et al., 2011). Unsurprisingly, what still seems to be one of the main challenges is vocational rehabilitation's main declared outcome: employment. Vocational rehabilitation interventions have little to no effect on the employment rate (Sears et a., 2014a). Although explana-tions revolve around socioeconomic factors such as low employment rates, economic recession and cuts in public spending (Sears et al., 2014a), the fact is that the main goal of this class-hidden social relation is not employment but the loss of pension earnings. It is not that vocational rehabilitation under insurance boards' performance-based system has the potential for under-ser-vicing and lowering the standards of a good vocational rehabilitation outcome, as Matthews et al. (2015) incorrectly point out, but that vocational rehabilita-tion under insurance boards' performance-based system serves another goal, namely, eliminating/reducing the loss of earnings pension.

Vocational rehabilitation interventions vary in the opposite direction to the loss of earnings pension. By putting a disabled worker back in a paid job that is similar to his pre-injury job, vocational rehabilitation can avert a loss of pension earnings; by applying vocational rehabilitation methods and assess-ing disabled workers' ability to work above their real potential, vocational rehabilitation can effectively manipulate the loss of earnings assessment and thus minimize the loss of pension earnings. While in the first scenario the loss of pension earnings is completely prevented, in the second it is only minimized. It follows from this that a movement in the mass of vocational rehabilitation interventions causes an opposite movement in the loss of pension earnings. While a growth in vocational rehabilitation causes the loss of pension earnings to fall, a drop in vocational rehabilitation causes the loss of pension earnings to grow.

Contrary to early-return-to-work practices that dominate in short-term disabilities, vocational rehabilitation interventions dominate in permanent disabilities. Workers are referred to vocational rehabilitation after multiple return-to-work attempts. An increase in vocational rehabilitation is accompanied both by a fall in the loss of pension earnings and a fall in the working days lost due to permanent disabilities but unaccompanied by a movement in the working days lost due to short-term and long-term disabilities. On the other hand, a decrease in vocational rehabilitation is accompanied both by a growth in the loss of pension earnings and a growth in the working days lost due to permanent disabilities but unaccompanied by a movement in the working days lost due to short-term and long-term disabilities. Therefore, a movement of vocational rehabilitation varies in the opposite direction to the loss of pension earnings and to the number of working days lost produced by permanent disabilities while maintaining unaltered the number of working days lost produced by short-term and long-term disabilities.

Akin to managed care and early-return-to-work practices, vocational rehabilitation varies in the same direction to the lost value of a work injury. A growth/fall in vocational rehabilitation results in a growth/fall in the lost value of a work injury, respectively. As already explained, this happens because vocational rehabilitation has a negative impact on workers' health recovery due to its tendency to place workers back at work with unresolved health problems (see MacEachen et al., 2011, 2012; Wagner et al., 2011; Young, 2010). In regard to the experience premium, as is the case with all the above-mentioned class-hidden relations, this relation's movement and the magnitude of its impact on the experience premium is conditioned by the direction and magnitude of the base premium. A growth in vocational rehabilitation accompanied by a drop in the loss of earnings pension and a drop in the number of working days lost due to permanent disabilities will cause the experience premium to drop only if it is accompanied by a movement of the base premium at a magnitude that exceeds the total mass of lost value at the firm level. A fall in vocational rehabilitation accompanied by a growth in the loss of earnings pension and a growth in the number of working days lost due to permanent disabilities will cause the experience premium to increase only if it is accompanied by a movement of the base premium at a magnitude that falls behind the total mass of lost value at the firm level. Therefore, a movement of vocational rehabilitation varies in the opposite direction to the experience premium only when it is accompanied by a movement of the base premium in the same upward direction at a magnitude that exceeds the total mass of lost value at the firm level or in the same downward direction at a magnitude that falls behind the total mass of lost value at the firm level.

CHAPTER 6

Lessons from the Social Totality

1   Introduction

The last four chapters provide diverse vantage points to understand the category of lost-time injury rates. Chapter 2 examines lost-time injury rates from the vantage point of its origins, going back to 1884 in order to grasp the necessary preconditions that enable the category to appear and function as it does in capitalist societies. Chapter 3 addresses lost-time injury rates from the vantage point of insurance boards in their information-intensive process of recording and processing work injuries to measure, monetize and exchange lost value within the circuit of metamorphosis of lost labour power. Chapter 4 looks at lost-time injury rates from the vantage point of its commodity form and the commodification process, thereby as a means of production, a use value, an exchange value, and a value. Lastly, Chapter 5 analyzes the category from the vantage point of its fetish character, thus revealing the social structures, mechanisms and power relations involved in the value formation of the commodity.

The chapter that follows aims to connect all the dots and reconstruct lost-time injury rates as a cluster of internal ties between the specific conditions set by definitive historical events and the specific relations of the capitalist mode of production. It focuses on the internal structure of lost-time injury rates and its coherence with the historically capitalist mode of production. It brings to the forefront the inner traits of the category – e.g., commodity form, value, exchange value, use value – in connection with institutional power – e.g., insurance boards, the state – and dominant social processes in their convoluted interplay with specific capitalist relations. The misleading abstraction of lost-time injury rates as a proxy for work injuries or a series of inductive indicators is replaced by its true definition as a wider social relation or system of social relations. In simple words, the purpose of this chapter is to formulate the concept of lost-time injury rates and reveal its truth or the many relations through which it expresses the social totality. It attempts to present the category as a historical system of social relations, one that is relative and historically specific to the capitalist mode of production.

With the intention of revealing the truth of lost-time injury rates in opposition to their partial distorted appearance, the exposition of each section follows an essence/appearance format. By didactically pointing out to how the category deceptively appears to the uncritical eye, each passage aims at effectively expounding lost-time injury rates as a determinate historical social relation in contrast to their taken-for-granted abstraction as inductive indicators. Partially grasped as a medium of measurement of workplace health, lost-time injury rates are revealed as a class relation of exchange and disproportionate distribution of lost labour power in capitalist societies. Narrowly abstracted as administrative data or the by-product of WCS s' information-intensive process, lost-time injury rates are re-abstracted as belonging to capital and its specific capitalist relations. Appearing partially as premiums or the money value to be paid by individual capitalists, the value of lost labour power is distinguished and restored as phenomenal forms of lost value in transit during the circuit of metamorphosis of lost labour power. Wrongly viewed as a bearer of lost value, namely, an injury-driven magnitude, the lost-labour-power commodity is presented as a value quantity that arises from a series of procedurally, structurally and class-hidden social relations. Challenging their taken-for-granted capacity to deliver accurate health information, lost-time injury rates are laid out as an exemplary case of work injury misinformation or as the market failure to faithfully communicate risk levels and enable optimal preventive responses. In the same vein, lost-time injury rates are conceptualized as an epistemological ideology, that is, a falsification of reality that sustains class relations of domination via naturalizing, rationalizing and universalizing work injuries. Finally, the chapter ends with a coda or concluding passage that displays the broader role of an information-intensive mode of compensation in its conditioning power to prevent social change via the solidification of the capitalist/ wage labourer bond.

2 Understanding Lost-Time Injury Rates as a Historical Socioeconomic Formation

2.1 Lost-Time Injury Rates as a Class Relation of Exchange and Distribution

Lost-time injury rates in capitalist societies, where information-intensive modes of compensation prevail, appear as a collection of inductive indicators that measure the existence and degree of health. This critique extinguishes this sensory appearance arising from a set of statistico-empirical concepts produced by WCS s' information-intensive operations. It demonstrates that lost-time injury rates, as the material shell of the lost-labour-power commodity, are not a medium of measurement. Here, the misrecognition is due to the confusion between the material property of the lost-labour-power commodity – i.e., lost-time injury rates – and its primary functional determination, namely, the exchange and distribution of lost labour power within insurance boards' circuit of metamorphosis. The form of appearance of lost-time injury rates as inductive indicators conceals the definitive exchange function of the commodity. The commodity is consumed by firms to exchange and collectively distribute the cost of replacing the lost value of labour power among the many capitalists.

Now, it is important to note that whereas lost-time injury rates do function as a medium of measurement, this does not mean they *are* a medium of measurement. This is because the elements in any process are not defined by their specific characteristics and functions but by the place they occupy and the functions they fulfill in any process as a whole. Lost-time injury rates do function as a medium of measurement within the insurance boards' commodification process but only to function as a medium of exchange at a later stage. Their function as quantitative units to measure every firm's share of the total mass of expected lost labour power in an aggregate – i.e., group rate – and their deviation from the aggregate – i.e., experience rate – is purposely performed to determine the rate of compensation at which lost labour power will be exchanged in the form of money between capitalists and insurance boards. Lost labour power cannot be exchanged for money without first being measured and situated in relation to money. Its function as a medium of measurement within insurance boards' processes is auxiliary to its function as a medium of exchange. This secondary position within the circuit of metamorphosis of lost labour power determines the secondary function of lost-time injury rates as a medium of measurement. Thus, lost-time injury rates cannot be regarded as a medium of measurement due to the fact that their performance as such is ancillary to the exchange and distribution of lost labour power that insurance boards' circuit of metamorphosis establishes.

Should lost-time injury rates then be regarded as a medium of exchange? At a first glance this seems appropriate since its purpose is the exchange of lost labour power in the form of compensation payments and compensation benefits. However, as a medium of exchange, lost-time injury rates still fall short as a definition. This is due to the fact that in addition to their primary and secondary function – i.e., exchange and measurement, respectively – lost-time injury rates acquire a particular character, type, and form, and furthermore they are involved in a process of conversion of lost value into value leading to the socialisation of compensation payments. Let us look at this closely.

As a peculiar character, lost-time injury rates are class information reflecting the class structure of capitalist societies. Hierarchically and bureaucratically produced by insurance boards, these rates are the embodiment of the power and domination of the capitalist class over the working class. As a particular type of information, they embody work injuries that render working days lost leading to temporary disability, permanent partial disability, permanent total disability and deaths. They are primarily conceived to provide compensation for wage losses to injured workers who cannot get back to work. As a specific form, lost-time injury rates take the commodity form as a means of production for individual firms. They are a producer good, a cost element required for the capitalist labour process, a compulsory guarantee that protects firms from the direct costs of compensating lost labour power and disputes in court. Finally, lost-time injury rates are involved in the conversion of lost value into money value at an equivalent proportion but in disproportion to the total mass of lost labour power produced at the firm level. Located at the beginning of the circuit of metamorphosis, lost-time injury rates enable the conversion of lost value into value in a manner that structurally enforces the socialisation of compensation payments among the many capitalists. These traits – i.e., the character, type, form and the socialisation process – bring into focus the class distinctions that pervade lost-time injury rates.

From this vantage point, abstracting lost-time injury rates in terms of their primary function – i.e., medium of exchange – is insufficient to understand the category. How should it be abstracted and conceptualized? In order to make sense of the category, I propose to abstract it as a wider social relation or a system of relations, as the sum of all the above-mentioned procedural, economic and political connections, which are in fact attributes of what lost-time injury rates really are. In addition, I suggest conceptualizing lost-time injury rates as a wider social relation born from what is specific to people due to their division into classes. Approaching it from the lens of class, drawn from the vantage point of the class division of capitalist societies – i.e., capitalists versus wage labourers – brings to light the hidden class aspect key to understanding the category in question, specifically, the irreconcilability of class contradictions. Thus, based on the exposition of the main connections and ties of lost-time injury rates and their place among the two classes of capitalist societies, I conceptualize lost-time injury rates as a class relation of exchange and disproportionate distribution of lost labour power. This labeling puts at the forefront what I consider the economic-historical function of the category, namely, the exchange and socialisation of lost labour power among firms in capitalist societies. It centers around the equalization of the rates of compensation based on a prediction of the flux and reflux of lost labour power in different aggregates within capitalist branches of industry.

2.2   *Lost-Time Injury Rates Belong to Capital*

Lost-time injury rates in capitalist economies not only appear as a collection of inductive indicators but as the statistical and probabilistic means established by WCS s to scientifically measure the existence and degree of health at work. WCS s appear as the architects of lost-time injury rates. This critique abolishes this form of appearance. It demonstrates that lost-time injury rates, as a class relation of proportional exchange and disproportionate distribution of lost labour power, does not belong to WCS s but to the historical capitalist mode of production. This form of appearance, born from an indeterminate ahistorical process of abstraction, separates the category from its true subject, namely, the capitalist mode of production. This misrecognition is in part due to the work of mainstream scholars who since the early twentieth century have collected and correlated lost-time injury rates as fact-finding input for the understanding of workplace health. By narrowly abstracting the category as administrative data, lost-time injury rates have been stripped away from their real subject, which is a historical socio-economic formation. Conventional literature unintentionally makes the category into something general to societies, thus hiding its origin and functioning as part of capitalist societies and its articulation with the specific relations of the capitalist mode of production. In the text that follows, the indeterminate general abstractions that make up the category are replaced by determinate historical abstractions to make visible its real subject: capital.

Lost-time injury rates pertain to capital. They require the existence of a capitalist legal-political superstructure and economic base as a condition for their appearance. Both their existence and functioning are firmly grounded in specific capitalist relations that are common to all capitalist societies. First, as the material representation of lost labour power, lost-time injury rates cannot appear until labour power has come into being, that is to say, when the buying and selling of lost labour power has been socially met. The transformation of the labouring process into an activity aimed at production for exchange through the buying and selling of labour power as a commodity is a precondition for the appearance of lost-time injury rates. Lost-time injury rates appear once the worker is the free proprietor of his own labour power and the capitalists find labour power available in the market as a commodity. The existence of a high supply of those who only own their labour power – i.e., wage labourers – is constitutive of lost-time injury rates. At the same time, the category is rooted in the social relations that create the capitalist relation of labour power or wage labour. The expropriation from land, the separation from the means of subsistence and the privatization of the means of production, among other social relations that turned immediate producers into wage labourers, are constitutive of lost-time injury rates. These social relations existed before and independently of the information-producing operations established by wcs s to construct lost-time injury rates to commodify lost labour power. Without the encompassing social relations leading to the creation of a system of wage labour for the buying and selling of labour power, lost-time injury rates cannot come into being. Thus, labour power and the social relations that give rise to its existence are necessary for the appearance of the category.

Second, lost-time injury rates appear not only when labour power arises but when it is used up during the capitalist labouring process. A colossal build-up in the destruction of labour power during the production of commodities to be sold in the market is foundational for the emergence of the category. This is due to the fact that lost-time injury rates are nothing but the body of lost labour power, a quantitative representation resulting from recording and pro-cessing wage-labour-related injuries leading to temporary, permanent partial or permanent total lost labour power. As a group of material signs, lost-time injury rates determine the manner of measuring and exchanging lost labour power. Lost-time injury rates come into existence not only when labour power is available for sale, purchase and consumption but when its wide-spread destruction has been socially met. Thus, as the reference or the sub-stance of lost-time injury rates, lost labour power is integral to the category. In this regard, it can be said that while the capitalist mode of production is not liable for work accidents, it is historically liable for wage-labour-related acci-dents leading to lost labour power. Why is this so? It is because what passes into lost-time injury rates as lost labour power is not the indeterminate and general destruction of labour but the particular destruction of wage labour, a historically determined form of labour that bears the mark of the capitalist social structure. Mainstream scholars misrecognize this fact due to confusing labour as the essence of lost labour power rather than wage labour. However, as described in Chapter 2, wcs s provide medical and wage-loss replacement benefits only to wage labourers. Compensation benefits were developed to tame property-less wage labourers' discontent due to their inability to earn a living during the disability period. Following an instrumental-reform per-spective, that is, a reform that aims at ensuring social stability, compen-sation systems were introduced to integrate wage labourers and avoid a deeper social crisis (see Eghigian, 2000; Hobbs, 1939; Holdren, 2020, Jenks, 1965; Kleeberg, 2003; Meredith, 1913; Moses, 2018). In general, self-employed workers in the informal economy and precariously-employed workers – e.g., domestic labour, cultural performers – are excluded from compensation ben-efits (The wcs from British Columbia, Canada, is a notable exception). They are not part of the total mass of lost labour power in capitalist societies. Lost-time injury rates, as the physical representation of lost labour power, are only reflective of the total mass of wage labourers formally employed rather than the total mass of workers. Therefore, it can be asserted that lost labour power, as the inverse form of the manifestation of labour power, a manifestation of that relation of production – i.e., wage labour – essential to the capitalist mode of production, is totally indivisible from capital. Wage-labour-related accidents and their resulting lost labour power belong to the capitalist mode of production. In the same vein, lost-time injury rates, as the physical representation of the inversion of labour power, also pertain to capital due to its reliance on a wage-relation bond and wage-relation formula to compensate the amount of lost labour power produced in capitalist economies.

Third, the functioning of lost-time injury rates as a class relation of exchange and distribution of lost labour power is ingrained in money, one of the chief capitalist relations. It is money that makes wage-labour-related accidents, diseases and fatalities economically measurable, monetizable and exchangeable. Work injuries are brought under economic equivalences and made exchangeable for a guarantee against lost labour power by the money form. As a medium of measurement, money quantifies and monetizes the average number of working days lost in an aggregate, thus making every firm's lost labour power comparable in relation to money value. Burns, strains, falls, electrical shocks and cuts are qualitatively represented as the same thing – i.e., money – and quantitatively represented as the magnitude needed to compensate wage labourers – i.e., x quantity of money. Money situates lost labour power in a value relation in order to be assessed and compared among different aggregates. Grouped together in a branch of industry and a subset of firms, money enables the measurement and monetization of individual firms' expected economic contribution to the total mass of lost labour power in an aggregate – i.e., group rate – and its deviation from such aggregate – i.e., experience rate. Placed in a money relation, lost labour power or lost value is nothing but money. As a medium of exchange, money enables the circulation of the lost-labour-power commodity at a price – i.e., the premium – based on a wage-relation. By summing up the total medical and wage-replacement costs in an aggregate and at the firm level, dividing it by all the wages of the member firms in an aggregate and all the wages at the firm level, multiplying the number by a risk factor, and calculating the firm's deviation from the aggregate, the group rate and the experience rate are transformed into the rate of compensation – i.e., a percentage of the wage bill of an individual firm – and its money form, the premium. The premium, as the price of the guarantee, sets the exact magnitude of money to be exchanged among insurance boards and capitalists. Money becomes not only the main denomination of lost labour power but the enabler of the exchange. Lost labour power in its many forms is now ready to be circulated. As a commodity, lost labour power is sold by insurance boards to capitalists in the form of a guarantee. Money flows from individual capitalists to insurance boards. In its money form, lost labour power is invested by insurance boards in non-speculative and speculative assets. Money flows from insurance boards to an investment fund – e.g., bank deposits, government bonds, municipal bonds, corporate securities. As a portion of the insurance fund, lost labour power is redeemed in the form of money by insurance boards to pay for injured workers' medical and wage-replacement benefits. Money flows from the insurance fund to medical providers and directly to injured workers in the form of wage-loss replacement. The circuit of metamorphosis of lost labour power, where lost labour power changes its form three times, cannot take place without the money form. Money is the mediator of insurance boards' circuit of metamorphosis where lost-time injury rates play a pivotal role in the informational process of commodifying lost labour power for exchange. Without the money form, both as a medium of measurement and exchange, lost-time injury rates cannot function as a class relation of exchange and distribution of lost labour power.

Finally, the capitalist state, whose purpose is to run the capitalist economy through the assistance of private companies, is key for the functioning of lost-time injury rates in their goal to exchange and spread lost value among the two classes of society. State intervention is needed to (a) enforce a non-fault insurance system based on commodifying lost labour power via lost-time injury rates, (b) legislate around rate-setting mechanics such as rating groups, experience rating, risk factors, prospective/retrospective assessment, cost caps, and (c) supervise insurance boards in regard to their rating methods. As a form of state power peculiar to societies divided among classes, one that tends to overwhelmingly favour the many capitalists, the capitalist state is paramount to the functioning of lost-time injury rates as a class relation of exchange and distribution of lost labour power. In accordance with a class-structured society, these agencies administer the circuit of metamorphosis of lost labour power, a process that reunites the two classes via the conversion of lost value into money value – i.e., the act of buying the guarantee by the capitalist – and the reconversion of lost value into medical value and wage-replacement value – i.e., the act of delivering compensation benefits to wage labourers. State-owned and state-sponsored insurance boards do not function to solve the problem of mass accidents but to minimize and socialize their costs among the many capitalists.

Here, the historical role of state power is key. As the chronicled response to the social unrest caused by industrial accidents, the high costs of the Liability System and the calls to introduce a costlier Strict Liability System (see Chapter 2), it was the executive branch of the capitalist state – i.e.

government – that successfully overturned the juridical system based on principles of justice to distribute lost labour power. In its replacement, governments around the world established insurance systems to spread lost labour power based on exchange value principles through the informational commodification of lost labour power via lost-time injury rates. The origin of lost-time injury rates can therefore be found in an intervention of political practice, in other words, the dissolution and replacement of a litigation-based mode of compensation with an information-intensive mode of compensation. In line with its profit ethos, the capitalist state, rather than protecting the wellbeing of wage labourers, opted for defending the many capitalists against the high costs of lawsuits by means of abolishing an expensive juridical system. The capitalist class needs the power of the state not only to regulate wages but to adjust compensation benefits and force them into the limits suitable for making a profit. In addition, by deciding on a collective system for socializing compensation payments among firms of the same risk class within a branch of industry, the capitalist state made lost-time injury rates the main input to statistically predict the mass of lost labour power in large aggregates to set social averages as magnitudes of payment compensation. Lost-time injury rates as a social relation of exchange and distribution constitute an example of what Miliband (2009) calls the 'bastard forms of socialisation' the capitalist state engages in to preserve the private character of capitalist firms and their inalienable right to exploit wage labourers. Once this 'bastard form of socialisation' was historically introduced by the executive of many capitalist countries, it was again the capitalist state that was called to the task of implementing and supervising the informational commodification of lost labour power via its administrative body. By means of bureaucracy, the compensation of lost labour power was set apart from a juridical order into an administrative one. Bureaucracy made a juridical problem an administrative matter. It is the state bureaucracy that has the responsibility not only of determining compensable injuries but of supervising the correct application of a set of parameters, procedures and rules related to the correct functioning of lost-time injury rates as a class relation of exchange and distribution.

Drawing from the social totality, a level of generality that brings into focus the social relations of the capitalist mode of production, the category of lost-time injury rates is finally presented as what it is, a class relation belonging to capital and articulated to specific capitalist relations. On the one hand, its being is determined by the existence of specific capitalist relations – e.g., labour power, wage labour, commodity, private property, capitalists – and on the other, its functioning is highly conditioned by other specific capitalist relations – e.g. money, value, exchange value, wages, price, profit, the capitalist state in its many branches. In this regard, the category can be seen as a complex capitalist relation whose existence and functioning encompass the interaction of the other social relations established by capital. The properties received by lost-time injury rates to function as a class relation of exchange and distribution – e.g., labour power, wage labour, commodity, value, exchange value, money, wages – are not attributes of WCS s but of the capitalist mode of production. What passes into lost-time injury rates is not a novel product of WCS s but a set of already established social relations that lead to the materialization of a newborn social relation, namely, the exchange and distribution of lost labour power. In this regard, WCS s' informational process to compensate lost labour power in replacement of a juridical order does not constitute an absolute origin but simply a reorganization of already existing capitalist relations. An information-intensive mode of compensation leaves the existing capitalist relations stable while reorganizing the process of measuring, exchanging and distributing lost labour power.

It is interesting to note that these capitalist relations that coalesce into this newborn social relation tend to disappear in the result of the process itself. The whole circuit of metamorphosis, which includes the commodification of lost labour power via lost-time injury rates and the conversion of lost value into compensation costs and benefits, is characterized by the disappearance of the capitalist relations that merge and enable the process to take place. This leads to the nonrecognition of the aforementioned capitalist relations. However, located out of human consciousness, these capitalist relations still exert pressure over the newborn social relation, making it dependent and contingent on the social totality. Lost-time injury rates, in which specific capitalist relations coalesce and vanish, inherit the motion that the capitalist mode of production conditions. This happens because lost-time injury rates find themselves filled with capitalist relations that condition their movement. Therefore, the relation of lost-time injury rates as an exchanger and distributor of lost labour power can only be sustained by a set of pre-existing capitalist relations that merge into the category. Lost-time injury rates not only presuppose the capitalist character of the mode of production in society but the assimilation of those same social relations that sustain capital in the forming of the underlying basis of what the category actually is. As a class relation of exchange and distribution, lost-time injury rates are a bearer of capitalist relations; however, they are misrecognized as a thing or as a group of inductive indicators. Only on the basis of the capitalist mode of production do lost-time injury rates become a bearer of capitalist relations that lead to the materialization of a newborn relation of exchange and distribution of lost labour power. Summing up, the determinate historical constitution of lost-time injury rates – i.e., as a class relation of exchange and distribution of lost labour power – depends entirely on the recognition of the capitalist mode of production and its social relations as its real subject or origin. This ontological and epistemological rupture, which is made possible by a level of generality that brings into focus capitalist relations and the analysis of the category in terms of the reorganization and realization of those relations, explains why mainstream scholars fail in their attempt to understand the category. Caught in positivist epistemology – i.e., simply correlating lost-time injury rates to multiple factors as fact-finding input – traditional scholars cannot comprehend the movements, conditioning, and contradictions of lost-time injury rates in their functioning as a class relation of exchange and distribution of lost labour power.

2.3   *Lost Labour Power as Multiple Forms of Value*

Under the aegis of WCSs, the value form of lost labour power tends to appear simply as the premium or the money value to be paid by individual capitalists for the lost-labour-power commodity. This misrecognition occurs because the capitalist is confronted by the premium rate, that is, a wage-relation formula that reflects the firm's contribution to the expected lost labour power in an aggregate and the firm's deviation from such aggregate. The capitalist tends to confuse value with the form of existence of value – i.e., the premium rate. However, as Marx (1990) notes, only prices are known in the exchange of commodities, not values. In regard to the lost-labour-power commodity, only its price or the premium is known at the moment of exchange. This feature of commodity exchange obscures the multiple value forms that lost labour power adopts during its transition from the commodity form to its final destination as medical and wage-replacement benefits. Uninterested in elaborating on how the various value forms of lost labour power come into being, mainstream scholars neglect the development of forms of value of lost labour power. By dismissing the many forms of value, the premium rate naturally dissolves all the different value forms and synthesizes them into itself as an essential premise. The premium rate appears therefore as the only form of value of lost labour power. This conceptual oversight does not allow for the recognition that the premium or the money value, which is itself a phenomenal form of lost labour power, constitutes only one form of value-existence of lost labour power among many other value forms. This critique differentiates, distinguishes and restores these value forms as phenomenal forms of the underlying essence of lost labour power, namely, lost value. By formulating the conceptual model of the circuit of metamorphosis of lost labour power, the value form of lost labour power is put at the forefront in order to reveal its capacity to change into multiple phenomenal forms of value. In addition, this model reveals the process of transformation of lost value as a dynamics, in other words, as a movement on the basis of an inner structure that sets limits and imposes pressures to the metamorphosis of lost value into other value forms.

As covered in Chapter 3, the circuit of metamorphosis of lost labour power (C – M – I – MW) brings into light how the underlying value of lost labour power – i.e., lost value – mutates into four different forms of value: money value (M), investment value (I), medical value, and wage-replacement value (MW). These unnatural and artificial value forms are the result of insurance boards' informational commodification of lost labour power, represented by C (see Chapter 4). The movement C – M, which appears as a spontaneous movement, is only possible if lost labour power enters into a process of informational commodification. Through the information-producing operations of recording and processing wage-labour-related injuries, diseases and fatalities, lost labour power is commodified by insurance boards into a guarantee of exchangeability with money. Thus, the impossible relation of C – M can only be sustained by insurance boards' informational commodification of lost labour power and by the presence on the market of this unique commodity. Now, what is peculiar to this circuit is that it has as its principle the transformation of non-equivalents, of lost value into value, which the act C – M clearly expresses. It is the transformation of lost value into money value that makes possible the subsequent forms of value of the circuit of metamorphosis, that is, investment value, medical value and wage-replacement value.

The circuit of metamorphosis of lost labour power and its series of value-form transformations is of the most relevance (see Chapter 3). In the first place, it reveals that the underlying value of lost labour power – i.e., lost value – not only has the ability to mutate into various value forms but is the underlying value of all other value forms. Thus, all the value forms that lost labour power adopts during the circuit of metamorphosis, namely, money value, investment value, medical value and wage-replacement value, constitute a manifestation of lost value. Lost value is the essence of each and every value form of the circuit of metamorphosis. To better understand this phenomenon, it is helpful to look at it through the lens of the dialectical relation of essence/appearance and identity/difference. While the appearance of lost value can be distinctively recognized as money value, investment value, medical value, and wage-replacement value, in essence these value forms are nothing more than the manifestation of lost value. Thus, in terms of their value form, the forms of money value, investment value, medical value, and wage-replacement value are all different; however, in terms of value, they are identical as modes of the existence of lost value. The relation of essence and identity is not only possible because one value form – e.g., money value – becomes another value form – e.g., investment value – but because all these value forms are equal as manifestations of lost value. Money value, investment value, medical value, and wage-replacement value are modes of realization of lost value in the form of its opposite – i.e., value – equal value forms in terms of the conditions imposed by the meta-morphosis of lost labour power established by insurance boards. These man-ifestations or modes of existence of lost value as value forms are specifically determined by insurance boards' informational process of commodifying lost labour power.

In the second place, if we take into consideration that the many value forms appear once insurance boards have performed the first act of metamorphosis, C – M, where lost value in the commodity form (C) is transformed into money value (M), it can be said that the motor of the circuit of metamorphosis is lost value. The whole circuit begins when lost value is crystallized in the commod-ity. The different forms of value thus presuppose the existence of lost value – i.e., lost-time accidents, lost-time diseases and fatalities – and its informational commodification without which lost value cannot be transformed into value. In an inversion of Marx's (1990) general formula for capital, which begins with value in the form of money, the circuit of metamorphosis of lost labour power begins with lost value in the form of the lost-labour-power commodity. Here, it is lost value crystallized in the lost-labour-power commodity, which is the trigger of the whole process. The circuit of metamorphosis of lost labour power constitutes a reorganization of existing capitalist relations rather than the emergence of novel ones. While value and surplus-value are the motors of the circuit of money capital, lost value and the appropriation of value as rent (see Chapter 3) are the motors of the exchange and distribution of lost labour power. While industrial capital comprises the institutional foundation for the existence of value in capitalist societies, financial capital – i.e., insurance boards – constitutes the institutional framework for the existence of lost value. There is no longer any question of a process of production but only of a con-tract – i.e., a guarantee – between insurance boards and individual capitalists and of the mysterious faculty lost labour power possesses to transform itself into money value, investment value, medical value, and wage-replacement value. In the domain of lost labour power, industrial capital is subordinated to financial capital and its fictitious attribute. In this regard, the transformation of lost value in capitalist societies is even more mediated, more fetishized and more alienated than the transformation and valorization of value.

In the third place, we have the factors of contradiction and class struggle. These relations contain the most important insights into these value-form transformations, beyond their plurality as manifestations of lost value. In this regard, the significance of the circuit of metamorphosis as a conceptual model is that it structurally explains oppositions and conflict among capitalists and wage labourers with regard to the transformation and exchange of lost labour power. As a movement in opposite directions and of mutual undermining, the circuit of metamorphosis entails a tension between lost labour power in the form of money value (M) and lost labour power in the form of medical and wage-replacement value (MW). On the one hand, lost labour power in the form of money value pulls capitalists in the direction of decreasing the premium, while, on the other hand, as medical and wage-replacement value, lost labour power pulls wage labourers in the direction of increasing medical and wage-replacement benefits. Lost labour power in the form of money value, represented by the premium rate, stands in opposition to lost labour power in the form of medical and wage-replacement value. This occurs due to the class-division nature of the circuit of metamorphosis. While the total mass of lost value in the form of the commodity value is converted into money value or the premium to be paid by the capitalist class – i.e., compensation costs – the total mass of lost value in the form of medical and wage-replacement value is meant to reconvert injured workers' effective lost value – i.e., compensation benefits. In terms of value formation, compensation costs and compensation benefits are directly reciprocal; higher premium rates translate into larger medical and wage-replacement benefits. However, in terms of class interests, compensation costs and compensation benefits are inversely reciprocal; higher premium rates tend to displease capitalists, while larger medical and wage-replacement benefits tend to please wage labourers. The empiricist epistemology of traditional scholars and their lack of concern for elaborating the many value forms of lost labour power has resulted in the cover-up and suppression of fundamental contradictions.

Due to the multiple value forms that lost labour power adopts in the circuit of metamorphosis, these class contradictions are theoretically difficult to observe and address. Let us have a closer look at this. We have seen that the premium is a phenomenal form of lost value in which the informational determination of value by lost-time injury rates – i.e., lost-time accidents, diseases and fatalities effectively processed by insurance boards – has disappeared. We have also seen that medical/wage-replacement benefits are also a phenomenal form of lost value in which the informational determination of value by lost-time injury rates has also disappeared. Both premiums and medical/wage-replacement benefits are not only phenomenal forms of lost value but forms of the concealment of value, with medical/wage-replacement benefits being the most mediated and alienated form of lost value due to their position at the end of the circuit of metamorphosis. Notwithstanding their difference, the fact that both premiums and medical/wage-replacement benefits are highly mediated forms of concealment of value explains the circuit of metamorphosis' ability to hide this contradiction. In other words, this contradiction is masked by the circuit of metamorphosis' ability to remove from sight the reciprocal value formation between the premium and medical/wage-replacement benefits, where higher premiums translate into larger medical/wage-replacement benefits. The disappearance of the origin is simultaneously a disappearance of the limit, a limit determined by the origin of lost value. It is the total mass of lost value that determines both the boundaries of the premium and medical/wage-replacement benefits, which as already shown positively correlate to each other. Lost through the one-sided concept of the value formation of lost labour power, the premium rate or money value appears as autonomous and disconnected from medical/wage-replacement value. Here we have the mechanism of appearance as the blurriness between the common constitution of two value forms and their perception. This disconnection is reinforced by bourgeois policy makers and state officials, who tend to praise and advance low premiums as in the general interest of society. The people at large are left unaware that the value formation of premiums – i.e., compensation costs – and medical/wage-replacement benefits – i.e., compensation benefits – are both based on lost value, that is, insurance boards' process of commodifying lost labour power through the information-producing operations of recording and processing work injuries. It is this convoluted information-intensive process that effectively conceals the value formation of premiums and medical/wage-replacement benefits and their positive correlation. Thus, the reciprocal connection between them tends to disappear from social consciousness. This blind spot allows state officials to put pressure on reducing premiums as if the value of premiums were a separate entity disconnected from the value of medical/wage-replacement benefits.

For example, in British Columbia, Canada in 2002, under the rule of a Liberal government and an aggressive lobbying effort by capitalists, structural changes were proposed under the fallacious view that the system was unbalanced and unsustainable. The Canadian lawyer Alan Winter recommended entitlement reductions by claiming that "[...] the level of entitlement for workers must be balanced against the costs to employers of funding the system" (Guenther et al., 2009, p.12). However, the level of entitlement – i.e., medical/wage-replacement benefits – is always balanced against the costs of funding the system – i.e., premiums – due to the fact that the value formation of premiums and compensation benefits are directly reciprocal. Premiums go higher because more work injuries, diseases and fatalities are produced by the capitalist class; therefore, more medical and wage-replacement benefits are needed to replace the total mass of newly created lost value. In this respect, Winter's quote is misleading and dishonest. His real goal was to decrease premiums below the effective total mass of lost value produced in a given period, which he accomplished. Among other things, Winter succeeded in the elimination of pensions based on the actual long-term loss of earnings of injured workers, the limit of payable pensions up to age 65 rather than for life, and the reduction of benefit rates from 75% gross income to 90% of net income, resulting in a reduction of benefits by 13% (Guenther et al., 2009). The point here is that Winter's argument hides the fact that the value of the premium is actually the money representation of the rate of compensation, which is nothing but the wage expression of a firm's contribution to and deviation from the total mass of expected lost labour power in an aggregate. The circuit of metamorphosis reveals that the value of the premium – i.e., the money value of the total mass of lost value – is directly proportional to the value of compensation benefits – i.e., the total mass of expected lost value in the form of medical and wage-replacement benefits. In this way, the circuit of metamorphosis, as a revelation, discloses and specifies the limits that multiple value forms of lost labour power take within the whole process.

As shown, the contradiction and conflict of the multiple value forms of lost labour power within the circuit of metamorphosis can only exist in the form of their concealment. The movement and direction of the various value forms of lost labour power are not equally beneficial to the general interest of society. While a reduction of the form of money value – i.e., premiums – and of medical/wage-replacement value is in the interests of capitalists, it is not so for wage labourers. Along the same lines, while an increase of medical/wage-replacement value and of money value is in the interest of wage labourers, it is not so for capitalists. To shed light on this elusive contradiction, I suggest conceptualizing both premiums and medical/wage-replacement benefits as a unity of opposites, with their directly reciprocal value formation remaining connected to their inversely reciprocal intersectional interests. This would help to make sense of compensation costs and compensation benefits as an unbreakable relation in terms of their quantity and their class interests. I have chosen to conceptualize premiums and medical/wage-replacement benefits as a wage for the consumption of lost labour power. Let us review the process through which this wage functions.

In the first stage of the circuit of metamorphosis (C – M), lost labour power is consumed by capital in the form of a guarantee; it exists for capital. Capitalists buy the lost-labour-power commodity from insurance boards at a price, the premium rate, which is nothing but the money expression of the percentage of the wage bill that represents the firms' contribution and deviation from the total mass of expected lost labour power in an aggregate.

Capitalists consume future lost labour power in the form of a guarantee that shields them against disputes in courts and the direct costs of compensating injured workers. In the third stage (I – MW), lost labour power is consumed by wage labourers in the form of medical and wage-replacement benefits; it exists for wage labour. Insurance boards liquidate their invested fund (I) to compensate injured workers by paying their medical expenses and their wage-loss (MW) during the days of disability. Wage labourers consume their own lost value in the form of medical and wage-replacement benefits in order to repair, recover and maintain their labour power during the days of disability. Therefore, while lost labour power appears in the first stage of the circuit as costs for capital, in the third stage it appears as benefits for wage labourers. While capital consumes lost labour power as a guarantee, wage labourers consume lost labour power as medical and wage-replacement benefits. For capital, the consumption of lost labour power is simply an input for the labour process of production. For wage labourers, the consumption of lost labour power is the value replacement of the wear and tear of their own labour power due to wage-labour-related accidents, diseases or death. Although the consumption of lost labour power looks different from the two sides of the capital/wage-labour relation, they are intimately connected. The amount of lost labour power consumed by capital in the form of a guarantee matches the amount of lost labour power consumed by injured workers in the form of medical expenses and wage-replacement benefits. In terms of value, there is an unbreakable unity. Since premiums and benefits are directly reciprocal in terms of value but inversely reciprocal in terms of class interest, they can be properly conceptualized as a wage. Contrary to the traditional wage, which pays for the consumption of labour power within the capitalist labour process, this wage pays for the consumption of lost labour power. However, rather than being paid directly by the capitalist, it is collectively and indirectly paid by insurance boards in the form of medical and wage-replacement benefits. The unity of premiums and benefits, forces that move in opposite and undermining directions, is for both capitalists and wage labourers only a wage. This conceptualization reveals the direct and inverse reciprocity feature among premiums and benefits. While capitalists want to pay the cheapest wage for lost labour power – i.e., the premium rate – workers want to receive the highest wage for their lost labour power in case of an injury – i.e., medical and wage-replacement benefits. In a nutshell, cheap premiums translate into higher profits but meager medical and wage-replacement benefits. Paraphrasing Marx (1990), the accumulation of wealth at one pole is at the same time the accumulation of physical suffering, misery, agony of toil, and mental degradation at the opposite pole.

Lastly, it is important to note that this wage, as a unity of opposites, has the propensity to alternatively undermine the satisfaction of injured workers' physiological and necessary needs or the satisfaction of capitalists' rate of profit (see Azaroff et al., 2004; Brown and Barab, 2007; D'Andrea and Meyer, 2004; Dembe and Boden, 2000; Hellinger, 1998; Lax, 1996; MacEachen et al., 2011, 2012; Mansfield et al., 2012; McInerney, 2010; Mechanic, 2001; Sommers et al., 2001; Wagner et al., 2011; Young, 2010). Depending upon the balance of class forces, this collective wage may alternatively be expanded or contracted to satisfy either capitalists' rate of profit or workers' necessary needs. However, the resolution of this contradiction cannot be permanently achieved since it is rooted within insurance boards' circuit of metamorphosis. Since it is an inner contradiction of the circuit, the resolution takes the form of a partial movement that aims to reduce the friction between the two classes. Periodic changes in premiums and benefits are thus the result of capitalists and wage labourers pressing in opposite directions, a movement that periodically erupts in order to partially reduce the inner contradiction of the circuit of metamorphosis of lost labour power. This contradiction manifests itself in the form of a gap, or what workers' organizations and unions identify as the difference between partial compensation versus full compensation. This gap is the terrain of class struggle. While capitalists try to decrease the collective wage below the total lost value effectively produced by a work injury – i.e., partial compensation – wage labourers press to preserve the wage at the total lost value effectively produced by a work injury – i.e., full compensation. A resolution is periodically achieved through class struggle. Depending upon the balance of class forces, the collective wage that pays for the lost value of labour power may be expanded or contracted to satisfy either capitalists' rate of profit or workers' full necessary needs. Thus, where labour is weak, capitalists and their representatives – i.e., the capitalist state – may choose to minimize compensation benefits via insurance boards. Alternatively, where labour is strong, insurance boards may be forced to provide more compensation. How insurance boards are managed reflects this power dynamic, a fact that can be seen in comparing the level of compensation benefits in different countries and jurisdictions. For example, in Canada the collective wage has always been kept low to the advantage of capitalists by setting a portion and a ceiling upon the amount of wage-replacement benefits a wage labourer can receive (see Barnetson, 2010). It has never been 100% for all wages, and it ranges between 75% and 90% of net earnings in all provinces (see Barnetson, 2010). Benefits such as paid holidays, vacation, overtime, and incentive bonus are not taken into consideration to set the rate of compensation. Also, there are waiting periods (a three-day waiting period in some provinces) that artificially decrease the mass of lost labour power to be transformed into the premium rate, thus decreasing the amount of lost value to be reconverted into medical and wage-replacement benefits. Notwithstanding this fact, compensation benefits in Canada are generally greater than those in the United States, particularly for workers in the southern states, a fact that reflects the relative power of unions in the different jurisdictions.

In conclusion, although the system is designed to convert lost value into money value at the real value of lost labour power, it is precisely class struggle that alternatively disables or enables the conversion of lost value into money value at the real value of lost labour power. However, as we shall see in the section that follows, the variation only takes place between the limits set by a series of procedural and economic-structural dynamics established by WCS s. Going back to Alan Winters' claim, the system is certainly not perfectly balanced, and there is not an exact match between premiums and the necessary needs to be satisfied by compensation benefits; however, it is unbalanced in favor of capital, not labour. Just as the value of labour power has the tendency to adjust to its price (Marx, 1990), the lost value of labour power has the tendency to adjust to the premium rate, which is the price or money value determined by insurance boards' circuit of metamorphosis rather than the actual value of lost labour power.

2.4   *The Lost-Labour-Power Commodity Is Not the Bearer of Lost Value*
As already explained, the multiple value forms that lost labour power takes on through its transformation along the circuit of metamorphosis, from commodity value (C) to the ultimate form medical/wage-replacement value (MW), constitute manifestations of lost value. Lost value manifests itself throughout the circuit of metamorphosis as commodity value, money value, investment value, medical value and wage-replacement value. However, this does not mean the lost-labour-power commodity is a bearer of lost value. Viewed as the holder of the total mass of lost value produced in capitalist societies, the lost-labour-power commodity appears as a homogeneous mass composed of innumerable individual units of human suffering in the form of working days lost, fatality rates, permanent impairment rates and the loss of earnings rate. The commodity asserts itself as the embodiment of the *de facto* total mass of lost value produced during the capitalist labour process. However, this is just an appearance. This critique debunks the semblance of the injury-driven determination of the magnitude of value of the commodity. The commodity is not a bearer of lost value due to wage-labour-related accidents, diseases and fatalities but a value form that sprouts from a series of procedural mechanics, economic-structural dynamics and power relations established by WCS s. While as a substance the

commodity is certainly an injury-driven formation, namely, lost labour power, as a magnitude of value the commodity is the outcome of procedurally, structurally and class-hidden social relations. The value of the commodity as a quantity, be it in the form of the group rate, the experience rate, the rate of compensation or the premium, is conditioned by the aforementioned hidden social relations. The commodity finds its quantitative value in the intersection of these hidden social relations (see Figure 2). Thus, as a magnitude, the commodity never escapes being quantitatively conditioned by the dynamics imposed by the circuit of metamorphosis of lost labour power which forces its value into the limits of profit.

As described in detail in Chapter 5, these procedurally, structurally and class-hidden social relations preclude the commodity from effectively embodying the total mass of lost value produced during the capitalist labour process. The reporting procedure, the rate-setting mechanics, the level of underemployment, the business cycle, the underreporting practices, and the early-return-to-work programs, among other social relations, set limits and exert pressure on the total amount of lost value to be crystallized in the commodity. It is important to note that these hidden social relations do not determine the magnitude of the value of the commodity in any direct, accurate or error-free manner. On the contrary, the commodity's value fluctuates due to the direction, magnitude and combination of these social relations, which in different mixtures together increase, decrease or maintain the commodity's value. For example, it is possible, given more aggressive rate-setting mechanics, for the value of the commodity to drop even though there is an increase in the number of working days

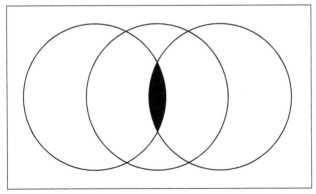

Procedurally hidden   Class-hidden   Structurally hidden
social relations   social relations   social relations

FIGURE 2   The commodity's value

lost, an increase in the number of reported injury claims and a decrease in the number of injury claim rejections. This occurs because the magnitude of more aggressive rate-setting mechanics exceeds the magnitude of the other social relations combined together. However, it is possible that under the same scenario for the value of the commodity to grow if the magnitude of the increase in the number of working days lost, the number of reported injury claims and the decrease in the number of injury claim rejections together exceed more aggressive rate-setting mechanics. Also, it is possible for the value of the commodity to remain the same if the magnitude of more aggressive rate-setting mechanics and the magnitude of the other social relations balance each other. The same happens with the relative value of the commodity or the experience premium. For example, a variation in the movement of underreporting injury claims and appealing injury claims, their increase or diminution, causes the relative value – i.e., the experience premium – to move in an opposite direction only if it is accompanied by a movement in total value – i.e., the base premium – in the same upward direction at a magnitude that exceeds the total lost value of underreporting claims and appealing claims or in the same downward direction at a magnitude that falls behind the total lost value of underreporting claims and appealing claims. As explained in Chapter 5, this happens because the magnitude of the relative value varies with the extent to which it deviates from the total value. The impact of underreporting claims and appealing claims on the experience premium always depends on the movement of the base premium. When capitalists engage in class-hidden social relations – e.g., appealing injury claims, managed care, early-return-to-work practices – to decrease the experience premium they are always gambling against the procedurally and structurally hidden social relations that condition the base premium. All these social relations do not determine the value of the commodity in a sequential manner but rather in a broken fashion, forcefully conditioning the commodity's value by imposing limits and exerting pressures in a systemic way. Here we have structural causality rather than transitive causality. The value of the commodity, as a magnitude that sprouts from a series of social relations and their scattered combination, acquires its size through fractured and opposing movements rather than a successive, fluid, and in-sequence chain-like motion. It is not therefore a simple result of multiple social relations but the relationship between their connections, interdependence and articulation; it is not a sum of sequential movements but a complex movement of its own. As such, it can be clearly seen that rather than an injury-driven phenomenal form, the value-magnitude of the commodity is a manifestation of the aforementioned hidden social relations. Therefore, it is impossible for the commodity to be a bearer of lost value since its quantity is not determined by wage-labour-related accidents, diseases and fatalities but by the random articulation of a series of social relations established by WCS s, which acquire an autonomous movement of their own.

Is the lost-labour-power commodity exchanged at its value? The answer is unequivocally no. Let us remember that although insurance boards consume value – i.e., wage labour employed by insurance boards – to produce the commodity, the value consumed by insurance boards does not get objectified into the commodity (see Chapter 4). The commodity is mainly composed of lost value. Thus, the commodity is exchanged at its lost value or exchange value, namely, the rate of compensation or the wage expression of a firm's contribution to and deviation from the total mass of expected lost labour power in an aggregate. Then, is the lost-labour-power commodity exchanged at its lost value? This question is far more complex. The answer is yes and no at the same time. From the vantage point of the amount of lost value crystallized in the commodity, it can certainly be said that it is exchanged at its lost value. As described in Chapter 4, insurance boards' information apparatuses are designed to effectively construct a commodity capable of transforming lost value into value at equivalent proportions. Based on a set of coded instructions, the commodity converts lost value into value in a manner that assures corresponding equivalences. These corresponding equivalences are key to balancing compensation costs and compensation benefits within the circuit of metamorphosis of lost labour power. The commodity is therefore forcefully exchanged at its lost value due to insurance boards' need to convert lost value into money value – i.e., premiums – and at a later stage to reconvert money value into medical and wage-replacement benefits. In other words, the money value that capitalists pay for the commodity corresponds to the amount of lost value embodied in the commodity. The commodity is therefore exchanged at its lost value. However, from the vantage point of the amount of lost value effectively produced by work accidents, illnesses and fatalities, the account is quite different. From this side, the commodity is never exchanged at its lost value. This occurs because the commodity never embodies the total mass of lost value produced in society. The abovementioned procedurally, structurally and class-hidden social relations hinder the commodity to effectively crystallize the total mass of lost value due to wage-labour-related injuries. It is not only that nonwage losses do not enter insurance boards' calculations for compensation – e.g., out-of-pocket payments, loss of quality of life – as argued by Guzman et al. (2013) but that entitled medical and wage losses never get compensated due to reporting barriers, waiting periods, a biomedical model of causation, compensation ceilings, compensation exclusions, cost-shifting, business cycles, precarious-work contracts, stringent deeming processes, underreporting claims, appealing claims, managed care, early-return-to-work programs, and so forth. Real or *de facto* lost value never gets reconverted into the form of medical and wage-replacement benefits because it never gets fully embodied in the commodity. The capitalist class is substantially favoured by a system that exchanges a guarantee against lost labour power at its lost value but below the real lost value produced by a work injury. Full compensation under wcs s is simply unattainable, a mirage. By producing a commodity that is not sold at its real lost value, insurance boards depreciate the value of lost labour power in the interest of capital but at the expense of wage labour. From the vantage point of capital, the merit of insurance boards is to perform an information-intensive process to commodify lost labour power at its lost value, that is, at the lost value effectively embodied in the commodity, and at the same time below its lost value, in other words, below the real lost value produced by a work injury. This is performed by insurance boards in a most secretive way: by indirectly controlling the crystallization of lost value into the commodity. The mystery of the contradictory like/unlike exchange of lost value is unveiled. Although the commodity is exchanged at its lost value, wage labourers will never be fully compensated. Just as the traditional wage that pays for the consumption of labour power will never amount to the value effectively produced by wage labour, this commodity or collective wage that pays for the consumption of lost labour power will never amount to the lost value effectively produced during the capitalist labouring process. By design, wcs s underallocate medical and wage-replacement resources.

The exchange of lost labour power in capitalist societies is not set at the point where lost value is fully exchanged in the form of medical and wage-replacement value but rather where the realization of profit imposes this. Compensation benefits are limited by capital accumulation, not by the necessary needs of injured workers. This constitutes the subtle manner in which profit enters onto the scene, by the back door of insurance boards' informational-commodification process. Under the aegis of wcs s, exploitation in capitalist societies is no longer exclusively about the extraction of surplus value, that is, unpaid labour, but also about the extraction of surplus lost value, in other words, unpaid lost labour. wcs s ensure the systematic and permanent robbery of wage labourers in the form of unpaid lost labour or the nonpayment of medical and wage-replacement benefits. An information-intensive mode of compensation not only yields a commodity whose underlying substance is lost value but surplus lost value or unpaid lost labour. This specific mode of exploitation, the extraction of unpaid lost labour in capitalist societies, is immanent to every information-intensive mode of compensation. Similar to profit, interest, and rent that are modes of appropriation of surplus value (Marx, 1990), the premium rate is a mode of appropriation of surplus lost value. The premium is essentially a form of concealment of surplus lost value in which the quantitative determination of value – i.e., the money value of the premium – by *de facto* lost value has disappeared. The concept of surplus lost value, which this examination discovers, expresses the essence of an information-intensive mode of compensation or the unity of its material and social relations. Therefore, not only is an information-intensive mode of compensation incapable of attending to justice as recognition, as Holdren (2020) correctly points out, but to distributive justice – i.e., the fair allocation of resources.

Lastly, it is important to note that it is not the personal aim of the capitalist but the tendencies specific to capital and WCS s, namely, the structural law of an information-intensive mode of compensation based on the commodification of lost labour power, that, through the phenomenon of profit maximization are internalized as motives by the many capitalists. Since the capitalist is confronted by the commodity as a means of production or an externality, that is, a cost of running companies, his behaviour towards the value of the commodity is in tune with profit motives. What he does or does not do is conditioned by economic gain. Here, I am not passing moral judgement on the capitalist himself for engaging in class-hidden social relations – e.g., underreporting injury claims, appealing injury claims, managed care, early return to work – to decrease the value of the commodity. I am plainly revealing how the social totality indirectly conditions the value of the commodity through the internalization of profit on the part of the capitalist as an inducement. As far as the capitalist is capital personified, as Marx (1990) cleverly puts it, his motivating force is not the full supply of medical and wage-replacement benefits but the partial price of the lost-labour-power commodity – i.e., the premium. Here, Marx's (1990) contradiction between the commodity's exchange value and use value is the inner mechanism through which class-hidden relations are put into motion to minimize the value of the commodity. Firms aim to maximize the use value of the commodity and to minimize its exchange value, the rate of compensation or the premium rate; they try hard to cheapen the commodity by any means. It is the unstoppable thirst for unpaid lost value that chiefly drives injury claims down. Now, it is important to note that mainstream scholars, neoclassical economists, insurance boards and capitalists tend to romanticize this economic logic (experience of author). Drawing from economic rationality and a positivist epistemology (see Teleky, 1948), they argue that the introduction of differential premiums based on individual performance – i.e., experience premium – induce employers to improve workers' safety. The assumption is that the experience premium actively encourages firms to

enforce preventive measures to reduce their contribution; however, this situation never actually happens. Capitalists do not engage in the improvement
of working conditions, maintenance of machinery, provision of safety training and the delivering of safety personnel equipment. As argued, capitalists
tend to underreport injury claims, misreport injury claims and appeal injury
claims, among other cost saving strategies, to decrease the commodity's value.
It is much cheaper for capitalists to engage in class-hidden social relations to
cheapen the price of the commodity than to invest in optimal prevention measures. Why? It is due to the economic logic of commodifying lost labour power
as an externality. Therefore, from this vantage point, we can conclude that the
lost-labour-power commodity, rather than a bearer of lost value, is a bearer
of a set of social relations that insurance boards' act of exchange establishes,
whose articulation reflects, on the one hand, the contradiction between use
value and exchange value, and on the other hand, the personification of capital in its never-ending quest of maximizing profit.

2.5   *Lost-Time Injury Rates Do Not Provide Accurate Information*

What capitalist societies under the guidance of wcs s know about workplace
health is a function of insurance boards' information-producing operations
of recording and processing work injuries to commodify lost labour power.
Health knowledge at work is thus a synthesis focused on lost-time injury rates
as a proxy for work accidents, diseases and fatalities. Lost-time injury rates
constitute the substratum of truth, the foundation of health at work knowledge. Under this semblance, insurance boards' management, state officials,
bourgeois policy makers and mainstream scholars feel tempted to draw com-
parisons and conclusions among countries or jurisdictions based on lost-
time injury rates (experience of author).[1] However, lost-time injury rates are
not truth itself but only a representation of truth. They are mere signals of
what happens in the workplace in terms of health at work. The question that
matters is whether lost-time injury rates act as an accurate representation of
wage-labour-related accidents, diseases and fatalities. Do lost-time injury rates
reflect health at work? This critique refutes the capacity of lost-time injury
rates to deliver accurate health information. It questions the taken-for-granted
idea that insurance boards' lost-time injury rates communicate risk levels and
enable optimal preventive responses. Here, I not only dispute that lost-time

---

1   In 2018, the business school of Pontificia Universidad Católica de Chile invited me to partic-
     ipate in an all-encompassing study to assess Chilean insurance boards' performance against
     their international peers based on lost-time injury rates. After expounding my theoretical
     concerns, I declined.

injury rates contain all the relevant information needed to make sense of health at work but that an information-intensive mode of compensation, one that commodifies lost labour power as an insurance guarantee for capital, is structurally doomed to deliver work-injury misinformation. Lost-time injury rates comprise an exemplary case of the failure of markets to deliver accurate information. Let us analyze this informational dilemma from the standpoint of Friedrich Hayek, one of the key theoreticians of market-price signals as a system of information.

Hayek claims that market-price mechanisms contain all the information needed to make good decisions (see Mirowski and Nik-Khah, 2017). Under Hayek's view, the signals that prices constitute provide knowledge from scattered cases on which people have no direct access. "[...] it enables us to make effective use of information about thousands of facts of which nobody can have full knowledge" (Hayek, 1978, p. 6). As an intensive-information processor, the market is conceptualized as an "ordering mechanism" (Hayek, 1978, p. 2), one that concentrates widely dispersed knowledge of particular instances via the signals of prices. As signals, prices allow individuals to adapt to facts they are unaware of, thus providing society with a means of "coping with ignorance" (Hayek, 1978, p. 3). By stressing the function of knowledge, Hayek reframes the economic problem as an informational one. He claims, "[...] the economic problem of society is thus not merely a problem of how to allocate "given" resources [...] to put it briefly, it is a problem of the utilization of knowledge not given to anyone in its totality" (Hayek, 1945, p. 519–520). In addition, Hayek (1945) defines an efficient economic system as one that best utilizes knowledge initially scattered across society. Thus, by celebrating the decentralized way that markets build knowledge, that is, via concentrating scattered information of particular instances on the basis of price signals, Hayek (1945) dismisses central planning or any form of centralized authority to guide the economy. He affirms, "[...] in a system where the knowledge of the relevant facts is dispersed among many people, prices can act to coordinate the separate actions of different people" (Hayek, 1945, p. 526). In defense of a market economy, Hayek (1945) adds that the price system, as a system of telecommunications, "[...] fulfils less perfectly as prices grow more rigid" (p. 526).

In regard to health knowledge, we can certainly follow Hayek's theory and conceptualize insurance boards as an information processor. Insurance boards do perform the task of gathering, recording and processing widely dispersed information on work injuries to commodify lost labour power and allocate lost labor power in the form of compensation costs and compensation benefits among capitalists and wage labourers, respectively. Based on evidence provided by particular instances via reported injury claims, insurance boards

engage in the recording moment, the processing moment, and the programming moment in order to produce a commodity capable of converting lost
value into money value. This informational commodification process not only
results in the lost-labour-power commodity but in a commodity exchangeable
at an exchange value and a price – i.e., the premium rate – that reflects the contribution to and deviation from the total mass of lost labour power in different
aggregates. By virtue of insurance boards' exclusive control over the informational commodification of lost labour power, the riskiness of every workplace
or the risk signals emitted by every workplace in the form of work injuries,
diseases and fatalities are converted into price signals in order to monetize,
exchange, convert and distribute lost labour power in the form of compensation costs and compensation benefits. Therefore, it can be seen that insurance
boards concentrate widely dispersed risk signals emitted by individual firms in
the form of price signals, thus providing decentralized knowledge from scattered cases about health at work, which people have no direct access to.

Now, should we concede to Hayek's (1978) assertion that we should start
with the most comprehensive information we can obtain – i.e., price signals,
statistical figures, aggregates and averages – to make sense of workplace health
and its facts? The answer is no. I claim that premiums are not only incapable
of conveying all relevant information about work injuries but even incapable
of accurately conveying the number of injuries and their severity in a given
period – i.e., the risk level – thus disabling the possibility to adjust the repertoire of preventive measures to improve workers' safety. Let us delve into the
matter more closely.

The main question to be answered is whether the money form of the commodity – i.e., the premium – reflects the real lost value of work injuries to be
compensated, thus triggering compelling safety actions or, in the words of
Hayek, whether price signals provide all the information needed to assure
the provision of safety resources and bring about optimal prevention strategies. Let us examine this question from Hayek's own viewpoint. Drawing from
Hayek, the price charged for the lost-labour-power commodity, the premium
rate, provides a signal on whether to increase or decrease the quantity of safety
resources supplied. Let us remember that the price of the commodity confronts individual capitalists as the money value of the wage bill that represents
the firm's contribution to the total mass of expected lost labour power in an
aggregate – i.e., the base premium – and its deviation – i.e., the experience
premium. The growth of the premium rate, that is, the sum of the base and the
experience premium, results in a potentially larger amount of lost value to be
reconverted into the form of medical and wage-replacement benefits. On the
contrary, a fall of the premium rate results in a potentially smaller amount of

lost value to be reconverted into the form of medical and wage-replacement benefits. The amount of lost value to be reconverted is always potential rather than effective since insurance boards adjust premiums at the beginning of a period based on past lost-time injury rates. Now, what exactly does the probability of a larger or smaller amount of lost value to be reconverted into medical and wage-replacement benefits communicate? It simply communicates risk. A growth or fall of the premium rate communicates the level of risk of a workplace. While a higher premium rate conveys a greater risk of wage-labour-related accidents, diseases or fatalities, a lower premium conveys a lesser risk of wage-labour-related accidents, diseases or fatalities. Paraphrasing Hayek, as signals, premiums allow firms to adapt to workplace risks they are not aware of, thus enabling capitalist societies to cope with ignorance.

How do capitalists cope with workplace risks? They do so mainly via primary prevention or those measures that come before the onset of work injuries such as administrative control, engineering control and the use of personal protective equipment. These preventive measures are meant to physically remove hazards, replace hazards, isolate people from hazards, change the way people work and provide protection equipment against hazards. Therefore, based on Hayek, it can be inferred that the information signaled by premiums – i.e., risk level – exerts the essential function of coordinating primary prevention in terms of what, how, when and to what extent to carry out preventive measures. Does it actually work in this way? Do premiums communicate risk levels to coordinate the provision of safety resources? Regrettably, they do not. What actually happens is just the opposite. Premiums tend to provide misinformation about risk levels. To understand this communication failure, it is necessary to recapitulate to the value formation of the commodity.

As already covered in the previous subsection, the value of the commodity and its money value form or price – i.e., the premium rate – does not directly sprout from injury-driven events but from a series of social relations and their scattered combination. As a complex movement of its own, the value of the commodity and its premium form reflect the fractured and opposing movements of procedurally, structurally and class-hidden social relations. The magnitude of the premium rate is conditioned in a disorderly manner by working days lost, underreporting practices, deeming injury claims, appealing claims, rate-setting mechanics, the level of underemployment, the business cycle, and early-return-to-work programs, among other social relations that altogether tend to place a limit on the amount of lost value crystallized in the commodity. Therefore, just as the value magnitude of the commodity does not reflect the *de facto* lost value of a work injury, its price form or the premium rate does not reflect it either. The commodity is not sold at a price whose magnitude reflects work injuries but at a price whose magnitude reflects a complex movement of a set of social relations. Understanding or doing economic accounting on the premium rate is unthinkable without penetrating the movements, connections, articulation and interdependence of the procedurally, structurally and class-hidden social relations that condition its magnitude. In addition, it must be noted that there are no in-sequence or chain-like movements between aggregates or averages that allow us to isolate the injury-driven portion from the general movement of the aforementioned social relations in order to single out the injury-driven manifestation of the premium rate. The details of the general movement are hidden behind the stability of aggregates and the premium rate itself, which as a magnitude is nothing but the money manifestation of large statistical aggregates. As the money value of aggregates and averages, the premium rate can neither show the inner details of this general movement nor their composition. Therefore, the premium rate cannot be relied upon as a proxy of risk levels because it is the embodiment of disorganized complexity and the structural inability to be set aside from it. As a signal of risk, namely, the *de facto* lost value of a work injury, the premium rate is inconceivable. A growth or fall of the premium rate cannot communicate greater or lesser risk of work injuries, respectively. Along the same lines, the premium rate cannot make individual firms adjust or change their preventive plans in the direction made necessary by factual changes in workplace accidents. In sum, the premium can neither give firms information about the highest or lowest cost at which they can compensate the wearing out of labour power or at which they can efficiently protect wage labourers against accidents, diseases or fatalities. Thus, with regard to the premium formation of the lost-labour-power commodity, Hayek's presumption that firms can coordinate their provision of preventive resources based on the information conveyed by market-price mechanisms is proven simply wrong.

Now, what about the information conveyed by lost-time injury rates? Do lost-time injury rates accurately depict lost-time accidents, diseases and fatalities? Do they represent what they are intended to represent? Do lost-time injury rates, as an aggregate of risk information, effectively articulate unknowable things in order to make good decisions? We already know that lost-time injury rates are not inductive indicators or a medium of measurement (see the first subsection of this chapter). Notwithstanding the fact that lost-time injury rates do not exist to integrate and disseminate health information so much as they serve to allocate compensation costs and benefits, the question that remains to be answered is whether they accurately represent work injuries. This question can be answered by examining the relationship between lost-time injury rates and the premium formation of the commodity. In this regard, if we realize that the premium rate is the money form of the rate of compensation, which at the same time is nothing but the resulting processing of lost-time injury rates – e.g., working days lost, the disease rate, the permanent impairment rate, loss of earnings – we cannot but accept the truth that if the premium rate does not reflect the *de facto* lost value of work injuries, then lost-time injury rates do not either. The premium rate, as the money expression of the rate of compensation, is the outcome of insurance boards' informational process of reporting, recording, processing and programming lost-time injury rates to commodify lost labour power. The fact that the premium rate does not reflect *de facto* lost value is specifically because of the aforementioned procedurally, structurally and class-hidden social relations that disrupt the successive stages that lost-time injury rates undergo within the commodification process to become the premium. For example, misreporting and underreporting practices tend to decrease the premium rate because they target the reporting moment of the commodification process where the filing of injury claims takes place. Appealing claims, early-return-to-work programs and managed care practices tend to cheapen the premium because they target the recording moment where lost value comes into being as a material object. Vocational rehabilitation interventions decrease the premium via targeting the processing moment or the set of operational rules that transform lost-time injury information into rates. These disruptions distort the number of working days lost, the disease rate, the permanent impairment rate and the loss of earnings rate, among others, thus depreciating the premium rate. The premium rate is a reflection of lost-time-injury-rate distortions as much as the lost-time injury rates misshape the premium rate itself. In other words, the premium rate is as corrupted as lost-time injury rates; both mirror each other in their level of corruption.

This highly distorted informational commodification process leads to the misrepresentation of work injuries. Lost-time injury rates, as a group of signs resulting from insurance boards' informational process to commodify lost labour power at its lost value but at a premium below the *de facto* lost value, leads to the underrepresentation of work injuries. A rosy picture of health at work, namely, an insufficient and inaccurate depiction of work accidents, diseases and fatalities, is constructed, exhibited and maintained by lost-time injury rates. This rosy picture is a direct result of a set of out-of-sight social relations that hinder the reporting, recording, processing and programming of lost-time injury rates, thus derailing the value and the premium formation of the commodity. The fact that lost-time injury rates might misrepresent work injuries is not exceptional but conventional. Lost-time injury rates underrepresent work injuries because these distortions are internally ingrained within insurance boards' informational process as a series of social structures, economic dynamics, mechanisms and power relations. Thus, the relation between the transformation of lost value into value to pay for compensation benefits and the appropriation of unpaid lost value by capitalists explains the underrepresentation of work injuries in capitalist societies. This manipulation cannot be interpreted as the personal aim of individual capitalists but as the unfolding of the structural law of an information-intensive mode of compensation based on the commodification of lost labour power via lost-time injury information. As a result, lost-time injury rates cannot account for what takes place at the workplace or be employed to identify workplace hazards, prop up awareness, provide advice on health risks, or respond to hazards successfully in order to protect wage labourers. The use of lost-time injury rates for preventive purposes is an act of the bastardization of the lost-labour-power commodity. Lost-time injury rates embody the unfeasibility of understanding health at work. They do not contain all the information needed to make good health and safety decisions, allow firms to make effective use of information about work injuries, coordinate the provision of health and safety resources, or allow society to cope with ignorance about health at work. Insurance boards' informational commodification process offers a stark case in point of how lost-time injury rates and price signals do not convey information to cope with ignorance but, on the contrary, provide misinformation that leads to capitulation under ignorance. I call this failure the informational contradiction of an information-intensive mode of compensation, where success in recording and processing injury information to allocate compensation payments and benefits stands in opposition to the indispensable information needed to coordinate the provision of preventive resources.

2.6   *Lost-Time Injury Rates as a Structural Epistemological Ideology*

This critique demonstrates that the establishment of an information-intensive mode of compensation that commodifies lost labour power results both in the underallocation of medical and wage-replacement resources and the under-representation of health at work. WCSs' information-intensive process fails wage labourers on both fronts. On the one side, it impedes full compensation and the satisfaction of wage labourers' necessary needs, and on the other it fails to protect wage labourers against work injuries by producing misinformation, resulting in the misallocation of optimal safety measures. Regardless of the centrality played by the economic dimension of WCSs' informational apparatuses, which has occupied the majority of this academic effort, it is important to examine further the ideological nature of lost-time injury rates. This is so because injury information occupies a central place in maintaining wage labourers' health and safety in capitalist societies. In this regard, it is relevant to note that the establishment of WCSs and their information-producing operations to commodify lost labour power not only mask a set of social relations that lock the allocation of medical and wage-replacement resources below workers' necessary needs but a series of ideas that advance the interests of capital at the expense of wage labourers.

As an information-intensive mode of compensation, WCSs comprise the epitome of Marx's base/superstructure metaphor. Paraphrasing Marx, this mode of compensation of material life conditions the social, political and intellectual life of workplace health. It is not the health consciousness of wage labourers that conditions their being but WCSs' activity of processing widely dispersed information on work injuries to commodify and distribute lost labour power in the form of compensation costs and benefits. The underrepresentation of work injuries and rosy picture of workplace health and safety is an illusion produced by WCSs' daily information-producing operations. Here, there is no crude economic determination, only strong conditioning. WCSs' informational commodification process sets limits and imposes pressures on lost-time injury rates as accurate signals of workplace accidents, diseases and fatalities. As an underrepresentation of work injuries, lost-time injury rates are, above all, structural phenomena. This falsification does not arise directly from a conscious ruling class that uses distortion as a way to defend their class interests. Although in some cases capitalists do hold/alter crucial injury information – e.g., underreporting and misreporting practices – there is no willingness on the part of employers to consciously falsify information. These practices are the embodiment of the economic law of an information-intensive mode of compensation that commodifies lost labour power as a means of production, and capitalists' aim to pay for this externality at its cheapest price. As a movement conditioned by economic gain, lost-time injury rates as a distortion arise from the material structure of society, namely, WCSs' informational commodification of lost labour power. The lost-labour-power commodity automatically supplies the underrepresentation of work injuries via its routine material logic of the everyday. Thus, combating the misrepresentation of work injuries cannot be done through ideas, accurate concepts or verifiable explanations since this distortion is anchored in the material contradictions – e.g., use value/exchange value – immanent to the commodity form that lost labour power assumes under WCSs. Amending this falsification would require a change of the material conditions themselves, in this case, the abolition of WCSs and their information-intensive process of commodifying lost labour power as a means of production to allocate compensation payments and benefits in class societies.

As a result of this distortion, we are confronted with an epistemological ideology (see Eagleton, 2007). Rather than a political ideology that attends legitimate conflicting ideas, this epistemological ideology expresses itself as false consciousness. This is not a Gramscian (1971) or Leninist (1992) positive ideological formation, one that promotes particular sectional interests in the face of oppositional interests, but a negative ideological formation, one that falsifies truth. In a subversion of reality, the ideological form of lost-time injury rates renders an epistemically false notion of work injuries. Lost-time injury rates do not correspond to the number and severity of work injuries, to workers' factual impairment, or to their real loss of earnings. They are always a depreciated representation of work injuries, be it in terms of the injury rate, the working days lost, the impairment rate or any other measure. This ideology is morally unacceptable because it gives birth to a massive fiction: that the workplace is healthier and safer than it actually is. It promotes the idea of a safe labour process. Now, the falseness of this ideology is not located at the level of its underlying substance or quality – i.e., lost value – but of its concealed value-formation or magnitude. As already explained, while lost-time injury rates' underlying substance is an injury-driven formation, namely, lost value, lost-time injury rates' magnitude is not an injury-driven formation, namely, the total mass of lost value. Lost-time injury rates are an ideology because their magnitude never corresponds to the total mass of lost value produced during the capitalist labouring process but to procedurally, structurally and class-hidden social relations that hinder the embodiment of the total mass of lost value. Lost-time injury rates render the epistemically quantitative deception of a less hazardous workplace. As it is true at one level – i.e., its underlying substance – but false at another – i.e., its magnitude – lost-time injury rates' distortion is not easy to grasp. In their cryptic form, lost-time injury rates play a major role in presenting work injuries in a deceptive way, particularly by the act of suppressing, excluding and concealing the contested nature of the quantitative value-formation process that sprouts from a series of hidden social relations and their scattered combination.

Along with their epistemological nature, lost-time injury rates make reference to power relations that serve to sustain class relations of domination. As the embodiment of class power, ideologies tend to perform a series of strategic functions such as rationalizing, legitimating and naturalizing that advance the sectional interests of some at the expense of others (Eagleton, 2007). Ideologies, whether in their Marxist or Gramscian tradition, are precisely such because they do not advance complementary interests but sectional ones (Eagleton, 2007). In addition, from an orthodox Marxist perspective, but certainly not from a Gramscian or Leninist one, ideologies tend to advance the sectional interests of the ruling class. In the case of lost-time injury rates, it can be seen that they perform a series of strategic functions for capital. It is not wage labourers but capitalists' interests that are mainly served. In the first place, by reducing accidents, diseases and fatalities to units of the same kind, numbers and rates, lost-time injury rates naturalize work injuries. The quantitative abstraction of work injuries to working days lost, impairment rates, injury rates, fatality rates, and the loss of earning rates, among others, present work injuries as a statement of facts, as common sense, as to what Barthes (1957) calls a myth. Work accidents, diseases and fatalities are naturalized and presented as part of the labouring process or as ordinary events that cannot be prevented but only reduced in frequency and intensity. Following Barthes's (1957) analysis, lost-time injury rates freeze history by decoupling work injuries from their particular origin, time and place, converting them into a phenomenon that is natural and inevitable. Historically, lost-time injury rates conceal the conflict between the forces of production and the relations of production during the Industrial Revolution that manifested in the form of horrendous mass accidents. Juridically, they conceal the establishment of liability acts and their abolition due to an avalanche of costly litigation. Morally, they mask the fact that employers were increasingly found guilty and at fault for industrial accidents. Economically, they sweep under the rug the fact that the strict liability system was putting at stake the expansion of profit and the survival of capitalism. And politically, lost-time injury rates establish the decision to compensate work injuries rather than prevent them from happening. In sum, by obscuring the political economic history of workplace accidents, lost-time injury rates present work injuries as self-evident and natural phenomena that cannot be prevented from occurring. The naturalization of labour accidents, which serves the interests of those who own and control the means of production and the capitalist state that promotes their interests, effectively halts, contains and limits the investigation of work accidents. In this regard, it is interesting to note that the Chilean Government Commission Report on the 33 miners trapped 700 meters underground stated as their leading conclusion that accidents will happen no matter what (see Comisión Asesora Presidencial para la Seguridad en el Trabajo, 2010). The perception of accidents as normal events resulting from the modern labour process is commonplace among governments. As Moses (2018) notes, it was in part their 'unpreventable' nature that historically made work injuries something to be determined probabilistically without the laying of blame. Naturalizing work injuries is critical for the capitalist class; and lost-time injury rates, as a quantitative abstraction of accidents, diseases and fatalities, play an important role in concealing their preventable nature. The dominant practice of quantitatively measuring work injuries as a set of regularities at the expense of qualitatively distinguishing them from one another converts them as a natural feature of the labouring process.

As an ideology, lost-time injury rates not only naturalize work injuries but rationalize them. This does not mean that lost-time injury rates provide a rational exposition, that is, a logical explanation for the occurrence of work injuries. They do not. Their numeric nature prevents them from answering why work accidents, diseases and fatalities happen. What lost-time injury rates do is put forth an economic rationality, namely, the logical proposition of compensating work injuries rather than establishing their causes. The idea that work accidents are not preventable is concomitant with the notion of compensating them. In the form of pecuniary damages, lost-time injury rates calculate human worth in money terms, thus lessening human dignity. The values of a finger, an arm, a leg, disfigurement or a deep psychological scar become simple knowable quantities defined by the market. This economic proposition is accompanied by the process of reification and homogeniza-tion, that is, the equating of accidents, diseases and fatalities as lost-time injury rates in order to create economic equivalences. Lost-time injury rates reify, homogenize and situate work injuries in relation to rates rather than distinctive types of accidents, diseases and fatalities. Falls, cuts, strains and burns are represented as the same quantitative units – e.g., working days lost, permanent impairment rates, the loss of earnings rates – to convert them into money value. By reducing work injuries to homogenized abstractions, the quality and uniqueness of a work injury is removed. Reified and homogenized in terms of lost-time injury rates, accidents, diseases and fatalities are noth-ing but a quantity to be exchanged rather than a quality to be investigated. Based on economic rationality, lost-time injury rates put expository and moral rationalities in the background. Rather than bringing injury informa-tion into being for a moral judgement, like the previous liability system did, or for preventive reasoning to increase workplace health and safety, lost-time injury information comes into being for exchange imperatives. Governed by the power of economic abstraction and the principle of exchange value, lost-time injury rates abdicate the goal of discovering work injury causes in favour of exchanging and compensating lost labour power in the form of medical and wage-replacement benefits. The rationale of wage labourers' physical exposure to work risks is not only displaced from center stage but obliterated. Thus, as an ideology, lost-time injury rates rationalize work injuries as a mat-ter of economic exchange particularly in terms of fairness or the economic justice of compensating wage labourers for their *de facto* lost value, which, as already seen, never takes place. Lost-time injury rates involve the victory of economic rationality over expository, social, ethical or historical rationalities. They are nothing but the imposition of an exchange rationality by and for the capitalist class.

Lost-time injury rates' economic rationality or the proposition that work injuries are to be compensated rather than prevented acquires a universal aspiration. Their production, distribution and promotion universalize the belief that compensating injuries is the logical, ethical and acceptable way of managing workplace accidents. Injury information for exchange rather than for use value – i.e., measuring the existence and degree of health for optimal preventive responses – appears as both advantageous for capitalists and wage labourers. Is it, however, truly beneficial for both classes? Of course, it is not. As described in Chapter 2, WCS s' information-intensive process emerges not only when the conflict between the forces of production and the relations of production manifest in the form of horrendous mass accidents but when productivity – i.e., the technical and social process of extracting surplus value – has been effectively insulated from legislation by the capitalist state. Lost-time injury rates are the outcome of drifting towards damage compensation rather than introducing legislation to halt, limit or inspect the forces of production – e.g., machinery, technology, and equipment. Lost-time injury rates stand in opposition to safety laws, tax reform, collective bargaining and preventive activities proposed by socialists, progressive intellectuals and unions (see Eghigian, 2000). Damage compensation was a desirable solution because it costs less than focusing on prevention – e.g., installing preventive devices was expensive and could hinder productivity. As Mazzola (cited in Moses, 2018) notes, premiums could be raised on a regular basis, making insurance a prudent mechanism. As an indivisible unity, lost-time injury rates and damage compensation constitute the manifestation of sectional interests, the establishment of capitalists' interests as broadly and universally acceptable. Medical and wage-replacement benefits cease to appear as what they really are, sectional interests, and assume the aura of the common interest of society. Confused by this ideology, wage labourers (experience of author) and mainstream scholars (Azaroff et al., 2004; Guzman et al., 2013; Tompa et al., 2012a; Tompa et al., 2016) tend to demand full compensation rather than the abolition of a system to compensate lost labour power. Capitalists succeed in universalizing their aim by keeping it from appearing as in their own sectional interest. Through the universalization of injury compensation, lost-time injury rates secure from wage labourers their consent to an abstract authority, namely, the mental prison of exchange value. In its power as a mode of abstract domination, lost-time injury rates subject society to judge workplace health on the basis of quantitative exchange criteria.

3   Coda: The Solidification between Oppressor and Oppressed

It is appropriate to end this critique with reference to social class not only because it occupies a central place in WCSS' economic and ideological processes of the exchange of lost labour power but because it is essential to passing from a litigation-based mode of compensation to an information-intensive mode of compensation. As described in Chapter 2, lost-time injury rates emerge where, when and to the extent that class contradictions in the form of mass accidents cannot be reconciled or their reconciliation via the traditional juridical system is no longer satisfactory to the ruling class. This critique reveals that an information-intensive mode of compensation is not only a by-product of society at a certain stage of development, namely, the second industrial phase of the capitalist mode of production, but of a society that has become entangled in unappeasable class antagonisms. In this regard, it can be said that lost-time injury rates dialectically embody both the irreconcilability and the reconciliation of class contradictions. On the one hand, lost-time injury rates historically emerge due to irreconcilable class antagonisms displayed in the form of mass accidents, and on the other hand as a way to reconcile class conflict via the allocation of medical and wage-replacement benefits.

Arising in the midst of the conflict between the forces of production and the relations of production that historically manifested as mass accidents, lost-time injury rates emerge to hold class struggle in check through the exchange, distribution and compensation of lost labour power. Rather than the expression of a social-justice reform approach, lost-time injury rates are the personification and reification of an instrumental-reform approach: a reform that aims at social stability. Similar to the bourgeois state, which exists to organize the working class for the maintenance of the capitalist mode of production (Engels, 1978; Lenin, 1992), an information-intensive mode of compensation exists to replace the value of the necessary means of repair, recovery and maintenance of labour power – i.e., productive consumption – in order to keep labour power in reserve and thereby the perpetuation of capitalist relations of production. The preservation of the working class at their barest level of repair, recovery and maintenance, that is, the wage labourer as a natural subject in conditions that facilitate exploitation, leads to the need to falsify reality to hold class contradictions in check. An information-intensive mode of compensation needs to be conceived as being about giving wage labourers what they really need rather than about operating regardless of their real needs for the benefit of the capitalist class. False consciousness is deeply rooted in this mode of compensation. Such a system cannot operate in class societies unless work injuries are naturalized, economically rationalized, universalized and underrepresented. In this regard, what an information-intensive mode of compensation on the whole does is to structurally prevent social change. By design, this mode of compensation prevents the rise of wage labourers. Let us look at this closely.

Historically, the superstructural transformation – i.e., the replacement of a litigation-based mode of compensation by an information-intensive mode of compensation – put forth by the conflict between the revolutionized forces of production and wage labourers did not erode the economic base of capitalist societies. On the contrary, this historical superstructural change added support to the capitalist mode of production by reinforcing the key existing relations of production – i.e., capitalists and wage labourers. This information-intensive mode of compensation resulted in the solidification of the capitalist/wage-labour bond, that is, a stronger bond between oppressor and oppressed. In this regard, mainstream scholars are often heard legitimizing WCSs based on the rationalization that without stable and reliable forms of compensation, injured workers would be far worse off. This is certainly true. However, they do not take into account that the abolition of the present mode of compensation would require the establishment of new social relations. Similar to American anti-abolitionists who opposed the end of slavery under the rationalization that once liberated African Americans would not be able to find jobs to survive, mainstream scholars rationalize WCSs based on the maintenance of the existing relations of compensation. In addition, they do not recognize that compensating lost labour power needs in the first place the existence of labour power as a disposable social relation, that is, as a huge mass of wage labourers. As detailed in Chapter 2, an information-intensive mode of compensation emerges only when the sale, purchase, consumption and massive destruction of labour power has been socially met, namely, in capitalist societies in their second industrial phase.

From a level of generality that brings into focus the division of society into classes, an information-intensive mode of compensation represents the joint effort of the capitalist state and its controllers to further integrate wage labourers. It constitutes the halting of an epoch of social revolution and the perpetuation of the capitalist/wage-labourer dyad – i.e., those who own the means of production and those who only own their labour-power. By smoothing class contradictions via medical and wage-replacement benefits at a value below the real lost value of work injuries, an information-intensive mode of compensation secures disposable labour power at an average that is convenient for capital and overcomes the inherent class conflict of capital. Therefore, an information-intensive mode of compensation is the historical manifestation of the conquering of the working class. It involves the victory of damage compensation over risk prevention, of instrumental rationality over social justice, of exchange over measurement, of profit over injury, of value over lost value, of capital over life.

References

Althusser, L. (2015). The object of capital. In L. Althusser (Ed.), *Reading capital: The complete edition* (pp. 215–355). New York: Verso.

Allende, S. (1939). *La realidad médico-social chilena.* Santiago: Ministerio de Salubridad, Previsión y Asistencia Social.

Azaroff, L. S., Lax, M. B., Levenstein, C., and Wegman, D.H. (2004). Wounding the messenger: The new economy makes occupational health indicators too good to be true. *International Journal of Health Services, 34*(2), 271–303.

Balka, E., and Freilich, J. (2008). Evaluating nurses injury rates: Challenges associated with information technology and indicator content and design. *Policy and Practice in Health and Safety, 6*(2), 83–99.

Balka, E., Messing, K., and Armstrong, P. (2006). Indicators for all: Including occupational health in indicators for a sustainable healthcare system. *Policy and Practice in Health and Safety, 4*(1), 46–61.

Barnetson, B. (2010). *Political economy of workplace injury in Canada.* Edmonton, AB: AU Press.

Barthes, R. (1957). *Mythologies.* New York: Hill and Wang.

Baumol, W. J. (1974). The transformation of values: What Marx "really" meant (an interpretation). *Journal of Economic Literature, 12*(1), 51–62.

Bernays, E. (2005). *Propaganda.* Brooklyn, NY: Ig Publishing.

Bhaskar, R. (1979). *The possibility of naturalism: A philosophical critique of the contemporary human sciences.* London: Routledge.

Bhaskar, R. (1986). *Scientific realism and human emancipation.* London: Verso.

Bird, F., and Loftus, R. (1976). *Loss control management.* Georgia: Institute Press.

Bitran Asociados. (2011). *Análisis de la situación de las enfermedades laborales en Chile y sus repercusiones en el sistema ISAPRE.* Santiago: Chile.

Bolaño, C. (2015). *The culture industry, information and capitalism.* New York: Palgrave Macmillan.

Broadway, M. J., and Stull, D. D. (2008). I'll do whatever you want, but it hurts: Worker safety and community health in modern meatpacking. *Labor: Studies in Working – Class History of the Americas, 5*(2), 27–37.

Brooker, A. S., Frank, J. W., and Tarasuk, V.S. (1997). Back pain claim rates and the business cycle. *Social Science & Medicine, 45*(3), 429–439.

Brown, G. D., and Barab J. (2007). Cooking the books. *Behavior-based safety at the San Francisco Bay Bridge. New Solutions, 17*(4), 311–324.

Bukharin, N. (1971). Theory and practice from the standpoint of dialectical materialism. In N. Bukharin (Ed.), *Science at the cross roads* (pp. 11–33). London: Frank Cass.

Burkett, P. (1999). *Marx and nature: A red and green perspective.* New York: St. Martin's Press.

Cantril, H. (2005). *The invasion from Mars: A study in the psychology of panic.* New York, NY: Routledge.

Campioleti, M., Hyatt, D., and Thomason, T. (2006). Experience rating, work injuries and benefit costs: Some new evidence. *Industrial Relations, 61*(1), 118–145.

Castells, M. (1996) *The rise of the network society.* Oxford: Blackwell Publishing.

Clayton, A. (2002). *The prevention of occupational injuries and illness: The role of economic incentives.* Unpublished manuscript, Australian National University, Canberra.

Comte, A. (1999). *Discurso sobre el espíritu positivo.* Madrid: Editorial Biblioteca Nueva.

Comisión Asesora Presidencial para la Seguridad en el Trabajo. (2010). *Informe final* Santiago: Superintendencia de Seguridad Social.

Conway, H., and Svenson, J. (1998). Occupational injury and illness rates, 1992–96; why they fell. *Monthly Labour Review, 121*, 36–58.

Cox, R., and Lippel, K. (2008). Falling through the legal cracks: The pitfalls of using workers compensation data as indicators of work-related injuries and illnesses. *Policy and* Practice in Health and Safety, 6(2), 9–30.

D'Andrea, D. C., and Meyer, J. D. (2004). Workers' compensation reform. *Clinics in Occupational and Environmental Medicine, 4*(2), 259–271.

Davies, R., Jones, P., and Nunez, I. (2009). The impact of the business cycle on occupational injuries in the UK. *Social Science & Medicine, 69*, 178–182.

Dawson, H. W. (1912, June 22). Social insurance in Germany, 1883–1911: Its history, operation, results and a comparison with the national insurance act, 1911. *The Athenaeum,* p. 702.

Dembe, A. E., and Boden, L. I. (2000). Moral hazard: a question of morality? *New Solutions 2000, 10*(3), 257–259.

Dew, K., and Taupo, T. (2009). The moral regulation of the workplace: presenteeism and public health. *Sociology of Health & Illness, 31*(7), 994–1010.

Dümmer, W. (1997). Occupational health and workman's compensation in Chile. *Applied Occupational and Environmental Hygiene, 12*(12), 805–812.

Eagleton, T. (2007). *Ideology: An introduction.* London: Verso.

Eghigian, G. (2000). *Making security social: Disability, insurance, and the birth of the social entitlement state in Germany.* Ann Arbor: The University of Michigan Press.

Emmett, E. A. (2002). Occupational contact dermatitis I: Incidence and return to work pressures. *American Journal Contact Dermatitis, 13*(1), 30–34.

Engels, F. (1845). *The conditions of the working class in England.* London: Penguin.

Engels, F. (1978). The origin of the family, private property, and the state. In R. Tucker (Ed.), *The Marx-Engels reader* (2nd Ed.) (pp. 734–759). New York: W. W. Norton & Company.

Ewald, F. (1991). Insurance and risk. In G. Burchell et al., (Eds.), *The Foucault effect* (pp. 197–210). Chicago: The University of Chicago Press.

Finkelstein, R. (2018). Productive labour in the information sector. *Canadian Journal of Communication, 43*(4), 567–582.

Fleetwood, S. (2001). What kind of theory is Marx's labour theory of value? A critical realist inquiry. *Capital & Class, 73*, 41–77.

Fletcher, M. (2001). Safety awareness cutting comp claims. *Business Insurance, 35*(18), 6–7.

Foley, D. (1982). The value of money, the value of labor power and the Marxian transformation Problem. *Review of Radical Political Economics, 14*(2), 37–47.

Foley, D. (1998). Recent Developments in the labor theory of value. *Review of Radical Political Economics, 32*(1), 1–39.

Foley, D. (2013). Rethinking financial capitalism and the 'information' economy. *Review of Radical Political Economics, 45*(3), 257–268.

Foster, J. (2000). *Marx's ecology: Materialism and nature.* New York: Monthly Review Press.

Foster, J., and Burkett, P. (2008). Classical marxism and the second law of thermodynamics. *Organization & Environment, 21*(1), 3–37.

Fortin, B., and Lanoie, P. (1992). Substitution between unemployment insurance and workers' compensation: an analysis applied to the risk of workplace accidents. *Journal of Public Economics, 49*(3), 287–312.

Fortin, B., Lanoie, P., and Laporte, C. (1996). Unemployment insurance and the duration of workplace accidents. *Canadian Journal of Economics, 29*(1), 17–24.

Fuchs, C. (2011). *Foundations of critical media and information studies.* New York, NY: Routledge.

Garnham, N. (1990). *Capitalism and communication: Global culture and the economics of information.* London: Sage Publications.

Garnham, N. (2014). The political economy of communication revisited. In J. Wasko, G. Murdock and H. Sousa (Eds.), *The handbook of political economy of communications* (pp. 41–61). Oxford: John Wiley.

Galizzi, M., Miesmaa, P., Punnett, L., Slatin, C., and Phase in Healthcare Research Team. (2010). Injured workers' underreporting in the health care industry: An analysis using quantitative, qualitative, and observational data. *Industrial Relations, 49*(1), 22–43.

Geller, G. (1996). The truth about safety incentives. *Professional Safety, 41*(10), 34–29.

Gerstenberger, H. (1985). The poor and the respectable worker: On the introduction of social insurance in Germany. *Labour History, 48*, 69–85.

Gramsci, A. (1971). *Selections from the prison notebooks.* New York: International Publishers.

Greenwood, M., and Woods, H. M. (1919). *The incidence of industrial accidents upon individuals with special reference to multiple accidents.* Industrial Fatigue Research Board, Report 4, London: Her Majesty's Stationery Office.

Guback, T. (1969). *The international film industry: Western Europe and America since 1945.* Bloomington, IN: Indiana University Press.

Guenther, S., Patterson J., and O'Leary, S. (2009). *Insult to injury: Changes to the BC workers' compensation system (2002–2008).* Report to the BC Federation of Labour. British Columbia: Canada.

Guinnane, T., and Streb, J. (2015). Incentives that (could have) saved lives: Government regulation of accident insurance associations in Germany, 1884–1914. *The Journal of Economic History, 75*(4), 1196–1227.

Guzman, J., Ibrahimova, A., Tompa, E., Koehoorn, M., and Alamgir, H. (2013). Nonwage losses associated with occupational injury among health care workers. *American College of Occupational and Environmental Medicine, 55*(8), 910–916.

Hart, S. M. (2010). Self-regulation, corporate social responsibility, and the business case: Do they work in achieving workplace equality and safety? *Journal of Business Ethics, 92*(4), 585–600.

Hartwig, R. P., Kahley, W. J., Restrepo T. E., and Retterath, R. C. (1997). Workers' compensation and economic cycles: a longitudinal approach. *Proceedings of the Casualty Actuarial Society, 84*, 660–700.

Harvey, D. (1990). *The condition of postmodernity.* Oxford: Blackwell.

Harvey, D. (2002). The art of rent: Globalization, monopoly and the commodification of culture. *Socialist Register, 38*, 93–110.

Harvey, D. (2005). *A brief history of neoliberalism.* New York: Oxford University Press.

Harvey, D. (2010). *A companion to Marx's capital.* New York: Verso.

Hayek, F. (1945). The Use of Knowledge in Society. *American Economic Review, 35*, 519–30.

Hayek, F. (1978). Coping with ignorance. *Imprimis*, 7, 1–6.

Hegel, G. W. F. (1977). *Phenomenology of spirit.* Oxford: Clarendon Press.

Heinrich, H. W. (1950). *Industrial accident prevention: A scientific approach* (3rd Ed.). New York: McGraw-Hill.

Herman, E., and Chomsky, N. (2002). *Manufacturing consent: The political economy of the mass media.* New York: Pantheon.

Hill, J. M. M., and Trist, E. L. (1953). A consideration of industrial accidents as a means of withdrawal from the work situation'. *Human Relations, 6*(4), 357–380.

Hellinger, F. J. (1998). The effect of managed care on quality: A review of recent evidence. *Archives of Internal Medicine, 158*(8), 833–841.

Hobbs, C. W. (1939). *Workmen's compensation insurance, including employers liability insurance.* New York: McGraw-Hill.

Holdren, N. (2020). *Injury impoverished: Workplace accidents, capitalism, and law in the progressive era.* Cambridge: Cambridge University Press.

Horkheimer, M., and Adorno, T. W. (2006). *La dialéctica de la ilustración. Fragmentos filosóficos.* Madrid: Editorial Trotta.

Hyatt, D., and Kralj, B. (1995). The impact of workers' compensation experience rating on employer appeals activity. *Industrial Relations, 34*(1), 95–106.

Ison, T. G. (1986). The therapeutic significance of compensation structures. *Canadian Bar Review, 64*(4), 605–637.

Ison, T. G. (1993). Changes to the accident compensation system: An international perspective. *Victoria University of Wellington Law Review, 23*(3), 25–43.

Ison, T. G. (2009). Administrative law – The operational realities. *Canadian Journal of Administrative Law & Practice, 22*(3), 315–337.

Jenks, W. A. (1965). *Austria under the iron ring, 1879–1893.* Charlottesville: University Press of Virginia.

Katz, E., and Lazarsfeld, P. F. (2006). *Personal influence: The part played by people in the flow of mass communications.* New York, NY: Routledge.

Kleeberg, J. M. (2003). From strict liability to workers' compensation: The prussian railroad law, the German Liability Act, and the introduction of Bismarck's accident insurance in Germany, 1838–1884. *Journal of International Law and Politics, 36,* 53–132.

Klein, N. (2007). *The shock doctrine: The rise of disaster capitalism.* New York: Metropolitan Books.

Koning, P. (2009). Experience rating and the inflow into disability insurance. *De Economist, 157*(3), 315–335.

Kossoris, M. D. (1938). Industrial injuries and the business cycle. *Monthly Labour Review, 46*(3), 579–594.

Kralj, B. (1994). Employer responses to workers' compensation insurance experience rating. *Industrial Relations, 49*(1), 41–61.

LaDou, J. (2006). Occupational and environmental medicine in the United States: A proposal to abolish workers' compensation and reestablish the public health model. *International Journal of Occupational & Environmental Health, 12*(2), 154–168.

Laswell, H. (2013). *Propaganda technique in the world war.* Connecticut: Martino Fine Books.

Lax, M. B. (1996). Occupational disease: Addressing the problem of under-diagnosis. *New Solutions, 6*(3), 81–92.

Lebowitz, M. (1986). Too many blindspots on the media. *Studies in Political Economy, 21*(1), 165–173.

Lebowitz, M. (2003). *Beyond capital: Marx's political economy of the working class.* New York: Palgrave Macmillan.

Lee, C. (1993). Marx's labour theory of value revisited. *Cambridge Journal of Economics,* *17*(4), 463–478.

Lenin, V. (1992). *The state and revolution.* London: Penguin Classics.

Lippel, K. (1999). Therapeutic and anti-therapeutic consequences of workers' compensation. *International Journal of Law and Psychiatry, 22*(5–6), 521–546.

Lippel, K. (2003). The private policing of injured workers in Canada: Legitimate management practices or human rights violations? *Policy and Practice in Health and Safety, 1*(2), 97–118.

Lippel, K. (2007). Workers describe the effect of the workers' compensation process on their health: A Québec study. *International Journal of Law and Psychiatry, 30*(4–5), 427–443.

Lippmann, W. (2020). *Public opinion.* Lawrence, KS: Digi Reads.

Lukács, G. (1999). *History and class consciousness: Studies in Marxist dialectics.* Massachusetts: The MIT Press.

MacEachen, E. (2000). The mundane administration of worker bodies: From welfarism to neoliberalism. *Health, Risk & Society, 2*(3), 315–327.

MacEachen, E., Kosny, A., Ferrier, S., and Chambers, L. (2011). The "toxic dose" of system problems: Why some injured workers don't return to work as expected. *Journal of Occupational Rehabilitation, 20*(3), 349–366.

MacEachen, E., Kosny, A., Ferrier, S., Lippel, K., Neilson, C., R. L. Franche., and Pugliese, D. (2012). The 'ability' paradigm in vocational rehabilitation: Challenges in an Ontario injured worker retraining program. *Journal of Occupational Rehabilitation, 22,* 105–117.

MacEachen, E., Kosny, A., Ferrier, S., Lippel, K., Neilson, C., Franche, R.L., and Pugliese, D. (2013). The ideal of consumer choice in social services: Challenges with implementation in an Ontario injured worker vocational retraining programme. *Disability and Rehabilitation, 35*(25), 2171–2179.

Machlup, F. (1962). *The production and distribution of knowledge in the United States.* New Jersey: Princeton University Press.

Mandel, E. (1992). Introduction. In K. Marx, *Capital, volume II* (pp. 11–79). London: Penguin Classics.

Mansfield, L., MacEachen, E., Tompa, E., Kalcevich, C., Endicott, M., and Yeung, N. (2012). A critical review of literature on experience rating in workers; compensation systems. *Policy and Practice in Health and Safety, 10*(1), 3–25.

Martin, M. (2001). Comp benefits, costs continue decline in '99. *Occupational Hazards, 63*(8), 23–24.

Marx, K. (1978a). Preface to a contribution to the critique of political economy. In R. Tucker (Ed.), *The Marx-Engels reader* (2nd Ed.) (pp. 3–7). New York: W. W. Norton & Company.

Marx, K. (1978b). The German ideology: Part I. In R. Tucker (Ed.), *The Marx-Engels reader* (2nd Ed.) (pp. 146–200). New York: W. W. Norton & Company.

Marx, K. (1978d). Contribution to the critique of Hegel's philosophy of right. In R. Tucker (Ed.), *The Marx-Engels reader* (2nd Ed.) (pp. 16–25). New York: W. W. Norton & Company.

Marx, K. (1990). *Capital: A critique of political economy, volume I*. London: Penguin Classics.

Marx, K. (1991). *Capital: A critique of political economy, volume III*. London: Penguin Classics.

Marx, K. (1992). *Capital: A critique of political economy, volume II*. London: Penguin Classics.

Marx, K. (1993). *Grundrisse: Foundations of the critique of political economy*. London: Penguin Classics.

Matthews, L. R., Hanley, F., Lewis, V., and Howe, C. (2015) Rehabilitation of compensable workplace injuries: Effective payment models for quality vocational rehabilitation outcomes in a changing social landscape. *Disability and Rehabilitation, 37*(6), 548–552.

McInerney, M. (2010). Privatizing public services and strategic behavior: The impact of incentives to reduce workers' compensation claim duration. *Journal of Public Economics, 94*(9–10), 777–789.

McNally, D. (1993). *Against the market: Political economy, market socialism and the Marxist critique*. London: Verso.

Mechanic, D. (2001). The managed care backlash: Perceptions and rhetoric in health care policy and the potential for health care reform. *Milbank Quarterly, 79*(1), 35–54.

Meehan, E. (2012). Gendering the commodity audience: Critical media research, feminism, and political economy. In M. Durham and D. Kellner (Eds.), *Media and cultural studies: Key works* (2nd Ed.) (pp. 242–249). West Sussex, UK: Wiley-Blackwell.

Meiksins, E. W. (2002). *The origin of capitalism: A longer view*. London: Verso.

Meredith, R. (1913). *Province of Ontario final report on laws relating to the liability of employers*. WorkSafe BC. Retrieved from http://www.worksafebc.com/Publications /reports/historical_ reports/meredith_report/default.asp.

Miliband, R. (2009). *The state in capitalist society*. Wales: The Merlin Press.

Mills, C. W. (1961). *The sociological imagination*. New York: Grove Press.

Mirowski, P., and Nik-Khah, E. (2017). *The knowledge we have lost in information: The history of information in modern economics*. New York: Oxford University Press.

Moore, I.C., and Tompa, E. (2011). Understanding changes over time in workers' compensation claim rates using time series analytic techniques. *Occupational and Environmental Medicine, 68*(11), 837–841.

Mosco, V. (2005). *The digital sublime: Myth, power and cyberspace*. Cambridge: The MIT Press.

Mosco, V. (2009). *The political economy of communication*. London: Sage.

Mosco, V. (2014). *To the cloud: Big data in a turbulent world*. Boulder: Paradigm Publishers.

Moses, J. (2018). *The first modern risk: Workplace accidents and the origins of European social states*. Cambridge: Cambridge University Press.

Moya, E. (1999). Introducción. In A. Comte, *Discurso sobre el espíritu positivo* (pp. 15–46). Madrid: Editorial Biblioteca Nueva.

Murdock, G., and Golding, P. (1973). For a political economy of mass communications. In R. Miliband and J. Saville (Eds.), *The socialist register* (pp. 205–234). London: The Merlin Press.

Murray, J. E., and Nilsson, L. (2007). Accident risk compensation in late imperial Austria: Wage differentials and social insurance. *Explorations in Economic History*, *44*, 568–587.

Navarro, V. (1980). Work, ideology, and science: The case of medicine. *International Journal of Health Services*, *10*(4), 523–550.

Navarro, V. (1982). The labour process and health: A historical materialist interpretation. *International Journal of Health Services*, *12*(1), 5–29.

Ollman, B. (2003). *Dance of the dialectic: Steps in Marx's method*. Urbana: University of Illinois Press.

Orwell, G. (2008). *Animal farm*. London: Penguin Books.

Panitch, L. (2009). Foreword. In R. Miliband, *The state in capitalist society* (ix-xxvii). Wales: The Merlin Press.

Polanyi, K. (2001). *The great transformation: The political and economic origins of our time*. Boston: Beacon Press.

Pendakur, M. (1990). *Canadian dreams & American control: The political economy of the Canadian film industry*. Detroit, MI: Wayne State University Press.

Pendakur, M. (2003). *Indian popular cinema: Industry, ideology, and consciousness*. Cresskill, NJ: Hampton Press.

Pransky, G., Snyder, T., Dembe, A., and Himmelstein, J. (1999) Under-reporting of work-related disorders in the workplace: A case study and review of the literature. *Ergonomics, 42*(1), 171–182.

Purse, K. (1998). Workers' compensation, employment security and the return to work process. *Economic and Labor Relations Review, 9*(2), 246–261.

Ranciere, J. (2015). Critique and Science in Capital. In L. Althusser (Ed.), *Reading capital: The complete edition* (pp. 100–169). New York: Verso.

Reasons, C., Ross, L., and Paterson, C. (1981). *Assault on the worker: Occupational health and safety in Canada*. Toronto: Butterworths.

Rogers, E. (2003). *Diffusion of innovations*. New York: Free Press.

Robinson, J. C. (1988). The rising long-term trend in occupational injury rates. *American Journal of Public Health, 78*(3), 276–281.

Robinson, R., and Paquette, S. (2013). Vocational rehabilitation process and work life. *Physical Medicine and Rehabilitation Clinics of North America, 24*(3), 521–538.

Ruser, J. (1999). The changing composition of lost-workday injuries. *Monthly Labor Review/ U.S. Department of Labor, Bureau of Labor Statistics, 122,* 11–17.

Schiller, D. (2007). *How to think about information.* Illinois: University of Illinois Press.

Schiller, H. (1973). *The mind managers.* Boston: Beacon Press.

Schiller, H. (1976). *Communication and cultural domination.* White Plains, NY: International Arts and Sciences Press.

Schiller, H. (1989). *Culture, inc.* New York: Oxford University Press.

Sears, J. M., Wickizer, T. M., and Schulman, B. A. (2014a). Improving vocational rehabilitation services for injured workers in Washington State. *Evaluation & Program Planning, 44,* 26–35.

Sears, J.M., Wickizer, T.M., and Schulman, B. A. (2014b). Injured workers' assessment of vocational rehabilitation services before and after retraining. *Journal of Occupational Rehabilitation, 24,* 458–468.

Shannon, H. S., and Lowe, G. S. (2002). How many injured workers do not file claims for workers' compensation benefits? *American Journal of Industrial Medicine, 42,* 467–473.

Shuford, H., and Wolf, W. (2006, August). *An analysis affecting changes in manufacturing incidence rates.* NCCI Research Brief. Boca Raton, FL.

Smythe, D. (1957). *The structure and policy of electronic communications.* Urbana, IL: University of Illinois Press.

Smythe, D. (1977). Communications: Blindspot of western Marxism. *Canadian Journal of Political and Social Theory 1*(3), 1–27.

Sommers, L. S., Hacker, T. W., Schneider, D. M., Pugno, P. A., and Garrett, J. B. (2001). A descriptive study of managed-care hassles in 26 practices. *Western Journal of Medicine, 174*(3), 175–179.

Starr, P., and Immergut, E. (1987) Health care and the boundaries of politics. In C. Maier (Ed.), *Changing boundaries of the political* (pp. 221–54). Cambridge: Cambridge University Press.

Strunin, L., and Boden, L. I. (2004). The workers' compensation system: Worker friend or foe? *American Journal of Industrial Medicine, 45*(4), 338–345.

Superintendencia de Seguridad Social (2017). *Informe anual estadísticas de seguridad social 2016.* Retrieved from: http://www.suseso.cl.

Sweezy, P. (2004). Capitalism and the environment. *Monthly Review, 56*(5), 86–93.

Teleky, L. (1948) *History of factory and mine hygiene.* New York: Science History.

Thomason, T. (2005). Economic incentives and workplace safety. In K. Roberts, J. Burton, and M. Bodah (Eds.), *Workplace injuries and diseases: Prevention and compensation essays in honor of Terry Thomason.* Michigan: W. E. Upjohn Institute for Employment Research.

Thomason, T., and Pozzebon, S. (2002). Determinants of firm workplace health and safety and claims management practices. *Industrial & Labour Relations Review*, 55(2), 286–307.

Tompa, E. (2012). Experience rating in workers' compensation: Guest editor editorial. *Policy and Practice in Health and Safety. Special Issue*, 10(1), 1–2.

Tompa, E., Cullen, K., and McLeod, C. (2012b). Update on a systematic literature review on the effectiveness of experience rating. *Policy and Practice in Health and Safety*, 10(2), 47–65.

Tompa, E., Dolinschi, R., and de Oliveira, C. (2006) Practice and potential of economic evaluation of workplace-based interventions for occupational health and safety. *Journal Occupational Rehabilitation*, 16, 375–400.

Tompa, E., Hogg-Johnson, S., Amick, B., Wang, Y., Shen, E., Mustard, C., and Robson, L. (2012a). Financial incentives in workers' compensation: An analysis of the experience rating in Ontario. *Policy and Practice in Health and Safety*, 10(1), 117–137.

Tompa, E., Hogg-Johnson, S., Amick, B., Wang, Y., Shen, E., Mustard, C., Robson, L., and Saunders, R. (2013). Financial incentives of experience rating in Workers' Compensation: New evidence from a program change in Ontario Canada. *Journal of Occupational and Environmental Medicine*, 55(3), 292–304.

Tompa, E., McLeod, C., and Mustard, C. (2016). A comparative analysis of the financial incentives of two distinct experience rating programs. *Journal of Occupational and Environmental Medicine*, 58(7), 718–727.

Ussif, A. (2004). An international analysis of workplace injuries. *Monthly Labor Review*, 127(3), 41–51.

Wagner, S. L., Wessel, J.M., and Harder, H.G. (2011) Workers' perspectives on vocational rehabilitation services. *Rehabilitation Counseling Bulletin*, 55(1) 46–61.

Waitzkin, H. (1981). The social origins of illness: A neglected history. *International Journal of Health Services*, 11(1), 77–103.

Walker, G. W. (2010). A safety counterculture challenge to a 'safety climate'. *Safety Science*, 48(3), 333–341.

Webster, F. (1995). *Theories of the information society*. New York, NY: Routledge.

Weiler, P. (1983). *Protecting the worker from disability*. Toronto: Government of Ontario.

Young, A. E. (2010). Return to work following disabling occupational injury-facilitators of employment continuation. *Scandinavian Journal of Work, Environment & Health*, 36(6), 473–483.

York, R., and Clark, B. (2006). Marxism, positivism, and scientific sociology: Social gravity and historicity. *The Sociological Quarterly*, 47(3), 425–450.

Zoller, H. (2003). Health on the line: Identity and disciplinary control in employee occupational health and safety discourse. *Journal of Applied Communication Research*, 13(2), 118–139.

Index

CPSIA information can be obtained
at www.ICGtesting.com
Printed in the USA
JSHW062352230323
39374JS00004BA/20